Across the
Dark Islands

Floyd Radike, Fort Benning, Georgia, after the ceremony
commissioning him as an officer on July 23, 1941.

Across the Dark Islands

THE WAR IN THE PACIFIC

Floyd W. Radike

PRESIDIO
PRESS

BALLANTINE BOOKS • NEW YORK

Text design by Joseph Rutt
Frontispiece photograph courtesy of Mildred Radike
Maps by Phil Schwartzberg, Meridian Mapping, Minneapolis

Manufactured in the United States of America

First Edition: September 2003

10   9   8   7   6   5   4   3   2   1

To Lydia Julianne Radike
My war bride and lifelong companion

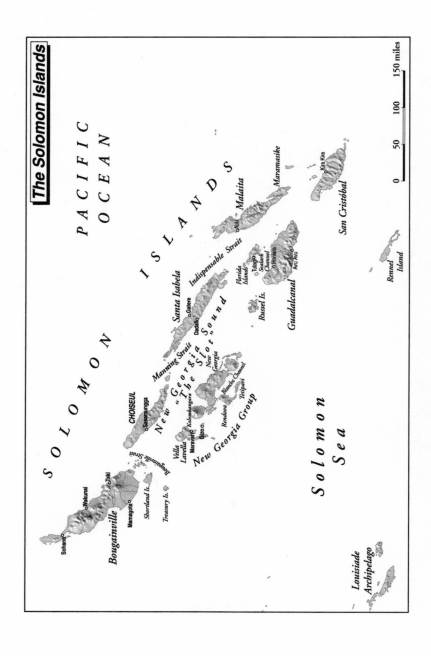

The Solomon Islands

Contents

The Fork in the Road

Once more unto the breach, dear friends, once more.

We stood at the rail looking out in the darkness of Nandi Bay. There was no moon, but the light that flows back from the sky even on the darkest nights showed the ships of the convoy, like great sleeping cats resting on the smooth, unruffled waters.

Off to the east we could see the occasional flicker of light from the native huts on the shore. "Every ship in the bay is blacked out," Obie said. "You'd think the natives would be told to keep their lights under cover."

I had been thinking about something else, and only picked up some reference to "natives" in Obie's remark.

"What about natives?" I asked. Obie pointed out into the darkness.

"If there's an enemy submarine out there, he can tell there are ships in the bay by the way those lights are blacked out as he moves across the entrance."

"That sounds a little far-fetched," I retorted. That destroyer screen we saw out there at sunset would keep them too far out for that kind of look-see. Besides, I'm sure the Japanese know we're here. They seem to know everything that goes in or out of Pearl.

"And," I added as a clincher, "those two calls to general quarters we had on the way here were for real, according to the navy guys we eat with."

We could hear the motor of an approaching navy launch. Looking over the side, we could see a blacked-out flashlight being swung back and forth as its owner looked for the gangplank. He evidently found it because we heard a loud thud, the sound of voices from the launch, and the crisp bark from the deck officer to "look sharp."

Several men debarked and ramped up the gangway, including the owner of the flashlight. We moved closer to see who was coming aboard. It was too dark to see the faces clearly, but one arrival had the cotton uniform of an army officer, while the other, surprisingly, was wearing shorts, kneesocks, and a large cap.

"British," Obie whispered.

"Or colonial," I replied.

"What?" Obie questioned.

"Colonial—Aussie or New Zealander," I answered. We moved back to our former position. There was a lot of activity on the ship. Men passed us and clattered down the iron ladders. Others clattered up the ladders and moved in the opposite direction. Strangely, these travelers were silent. Usually you could pick up a conversation as they moved along slowly in the dark. By the time they had passed out of earshot, you knew what the topic of their conversation was.

"Something must be up," Obie said.

"You mean, because nobody's talkin'?"

"That's right," Obie continued. "I haven't heard so much silence since that sub scare off the Horn Islands."

We each settled back into our thoughts. I began reviewing the events of the past week.

The departure from Pearl had been an "event." It took place on the first anniversary of the "sneak attack." There were ceremonies all over the place, bands playing, "Taps" being sounded on a half-sunk battleship, and overflights of navy fighters. But our interest was elsewhere, the harbor being full of troopships, cargo carriers, tankers, and destroyers.

Before noon, we had upped anchor and joined the long line going through the submarine nets at the harbor entrance.

Several hours out we picked up some "big stuff," a cruiser, a carrier, and a battleship. We were positioned midway in the convoy, and this gave us a seat on the fifty-yard line: in every direction we saw the evidence of resurgent military and naval power. It was comforting to see this much hardware, after the horror stories we'd heard on Oahu of the poor shape we were supposed to be in.

The next several days were uneventful. Our quarters below-decks were the navy version of the Black Hole of Calcutta: the bunks were stacked five high, the top bunk had eighteen inches of vertical space—and you knew that every guy you saw with a bruise on his forehead slept in a top bunk.

The bottom bunk was six inches off the deck, which ensured your being stepped on or kicked by someone blundering along in the light from a single bulb. It was hot, humid, and without any possibility of fresh air, and it stank of all the unwashed, perspiring, and seasick inmates of this bedlam.

Despite all the nagging shortcomings of heat, crummy chow, crowding, and smell, the men soon settled into a routine. The American soldier is the most adaptable of men. Within a few hours, no matter how crude the environment, he will have mastered his surroundings and be prepared to go on for days with his pattern of accommodation.

The day was divided into three parts—breakfast, lunch, and dinner. Each meal called for an hour in the steam room the navy facetiously called a "mess." After each meal some time was passed on deck reveling in the fresh air and sunshine, then it was below-decks for sack time until the next "Now hear this . . ." announced the next punishing ritual in the steam room.

Such activities, desperate and meaningless as they were, could lead to a parallel condition of thought known as "coming apart at the seams." But this was forestalled by the glue, the adhesive if you will, that bound everyone together, gave them social cohesion and purpose—the rumor.

We didn't know where we were going, the vast majority of us, that is. And that meant that positive information had to be supplanted by pulling together chance remarks, the appearance of strangers, the slowdown in mail, and the propaganda blandishments of Tokyo Rose.

It is hard for anyone outside the service to understand the power and pervasiveness of the rumor. Office gossip, back-fence conversation, the ritual coffee clique, the informal channel of communication—none of these civilian counterparts, no matter how frequently used, or how freighted with purported significance, can hold a taper to the military rumor.

It is the nature of service life that you never know what will happen next. The ostensible purpose of keeping the troops in the dark is to prevent the enemy from finding out what is in the works. But nature abhors a vacuum, we are told, and in the void created by his masters the soldier creates his own scenario. No intelligence service is more rigorous in examining every happening for a clue to the future, because a good rumor must always begin with, "A guy over at —— who works for G—— said." The blanks can be filled in with any reasonable place or name that seems to enhance the validity of the rumor.

For one to be called in to see a field-grade officer, to be engaged in an eyeball-to-eyeball conversation with a ship's first mate, to meet a bustling lieutenant coming out of the communications shack— any of these will prompt our friends to inquire, "What's the latest rumor?"

Rumors are highly contagious, like the bubonic plague. A rumor passed on by a third-class deckhand will make its way to the forward lookout in twenty minutes.

It is seldom that rumors forecast anything bad. They usually point to a pleasant way out of the present fix. And in a certain sense it is well that they do. Such happy expectations give a lift of morale, and counter the heavy foreboding of combat, disaster, and death that we know in our heart of hearts is just around the corner. It is too gruesome to continually contemplate the Beast—the specter of violent and crushing injury or fatality, particularly when it is certain that that's what the future holds. So we pick up our little clues, hints, and indications, and dress them up with what legitimacy we can muster and hurry off to spread the good word.

After leaving Pearl Harbor the convoy headed south, as close as we could tell, without a compass. After three or four days, we began to wonder when we would get some definite word as to our destination. We knew we were not combat-loaded, and we had heard (no rumor) that our artillery, tanks, and jungle gear would be waiting for us.

These factors led to certain alternatives. First, we would not be going directly into combat, but to a staging area. Second, such a staging area could be New Caledonia, New Zealand, Australia, the Hebrides, Samoa, or Fiji. To a boatload of soldiers from places like Ames, Peoria, Bismarck, or Waco, the islands of the Pacific had the ring of adventure, palm trees, tropic nights, and primitive peoples loosely controlled by the "colonials."

When we passed the Horn Islands (the mate told us that was their name)—seeing a volcanic cove covered with lush vegetation and wearing white clouds for a cap—we knew we were going to Fiji or would pass close to these British islands. Any of our concern was allayed a few hours later when the ship's captain got on the horn and told us we would dock at Suva that day.

There is nothing quite like approaching a Pacific island in a ship. First, mountaintops and the ever-present cloud caps are seen, then the whole mountain, and finally the spreading plains and valleys in vibrant green to contrast with the blue sea and sky. The odor, or aroma, of the tropical vegetation reaches miles out to sea and gives an added incentive to be ashore where the solid ground, the lush green growth, and the tropical miasma contrast with the never-ceasing roll of the ships, the smell of burning fuel oil, and the stark gray of the ship's paint.

We docked at Suva to find a town out of Somerset Maugham with white buildings, palm-lined streets, and a military band that played "The Star-spangled Banner" like a Bach chorale. We were impressed with that playing and cheered loud and long at its conclusion.

To our surprise the word was passed that we were going ashore. We quickly donned our battle gear and weapons and clattered down the gangway onto the wooden dock. We were quickly formed into companies and marched off past the warehouses and the custom-house, and up the main street past the government house to a point about a mile from the docks. Here we were halted and stared back at the populace that was staring at us. There were whites, Indians, Chinese, and Fijians. These latter were magnificent specimens with chocolate-brown skin and great heads of black hair, and wearing skirts, usually white, that were cut into a jagged pattern at the bottom. Almost everybody spoke English with an accent that would have been at home in Piccadilly as easily as Suva.

After a short rest, we returned to the ship with the universal conclusion that Fiji was not to be our staging area. Shortly before dark we left the docks and proceeded to Nandi Bay, where we anchored in the dark under full blackout conditions.

This was now the second night spent at Nandi, and we were again completely at sea as to our mission. It was obvious we weren't going to stage in the Fijis or we would have off-loaded at Suva. We had been convinced that we were needed somewhere in the Pacific where the Japanese were still largely in control, and we were the most available combat-ready division. Why then this delay? Why this waste of valuable time a year after the war had started, with no signs that we were making any inroads against the enemy in New Guinea or the Solomon Islands?

But this was to be the last night for rumors, conjectures, and secrecy.

The public address system crackled and a voice blared out, "All officers to the wardroom. On the double." The message was re-

peated again without modification. A further crackle as the system was turned off. Then silence.

I looked at Obie.

"Let's go," he said, "maybe this is the word."

We moved forward to the wardroom door, pushed through the blackout curtains and into the smoky brightness of the wardroom. The tables and chairs were turned to face one end of the room where an easel with a covered map board was the main exhibit.

The brass were already seated at the front tables and each company commander herded his junior officers to a place where they could sit together. Everyone seemed in a gay mood, with considerable yelling and joking between groups.

In a few minutes the wardroom was packed and standing room only was available. At this point a door behind the easel opened, someone yelled "Attention!" and two men entered. One of them was the regiment executive officer (XO) and the other a British officer, the one we had observed coming aboard earlier.

By rights, our battalion commander should have been commanding officer (CO) of troops, but some brain wanted to avoid losing all the vaunted talent of the regiment's headquarters to a single torpedo. The result was that the XO and some minor staff officers were assigned to our ship.

The XO motioned us to sit down and waited for absolute quiet. He was a tall, thin, distinguished-looking cuss with sleek black hair, parted in the middle and showing a touch of gray. He had a reputation for being quiet but capable—a perfect foil for his flamboyant and posturing superior.

He appeared to be enjoying this moment enormously. I had seen that expression before on the faces of those who, all along the path from Louisiana to Suva, finally revealed the identity of our destination.

"Gentlemen," he said, "the division was initially ordered to proceed to Australia. We were to join General MacArthur's command and engage in operations in New Guinea."

He paused, looked down at the floor, and smoothed out a wrinkle in the rug.

"A situation has emerged that has forced the cancellation of that mission. A large ship, carrying the major portion of a division, has gone aground on a reef west of Fiji. That division's mission has now been given to us, and our purpose tonight is to give you as much information as we can, knowing that we do not have the orders, directives, intelligence, and maps that we need."

He moved to the easel and grasped the bottom of the canvas that covered the map board.

"Gentlemen," he said quietly, "this is our objective." He lifted the canvas and exposed a map of a large, long, crooked island.

"We are going to Guadalcanal," he said.

PART

——

1

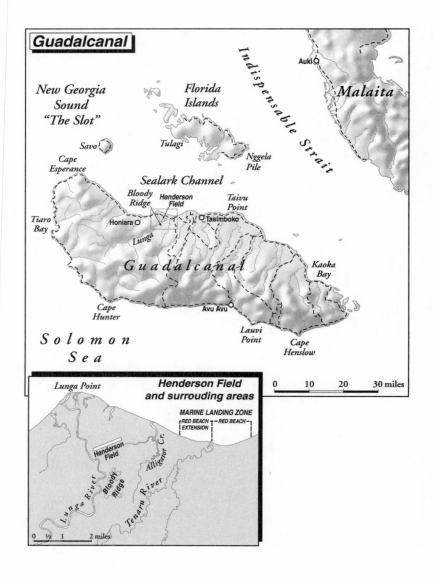

Guadalcanal

New Georgia
Sound
"The Slot"

Florida
Islands

Indispensable Strait

Auki

Malaita

Savo

Tulagi

Cape
Esperance

Nggela
Pile

Sealark Channel

Bloody
Ridge

Henderson
Field

Taivu
Point

Tiaro
Bay

Honiara

Tasimboko

Lunga

Guadalcanal

Kaoka
Bay

Cape
Hunter

Avu Avu

Lauvi
Point

Cape
Henslow

*Solomon
Sea*

Lunga Point

Henderson Field
and surrouding areas

0   10   20   30 miles

MARINE LANDING ZONE

RED BEACH ┬ RED BEACH
EXTENSION

Henderson
Field

Alligator Cr.

Lunga River

Bloody
Ridge

Tenaru River

0   ½   1   2 miles

CHAPTER ONE

Background

Guadalcanal. We knew as much about the island as we did about the dark side of the moon. Most of what we knew came from the flow of war correspondent stories that appeared daily—stories emphasizing the bravery of the marines, the maniacal courage of the Japanese, and the hot, dark, mysterious, disease-filled jungle.

The best impression I could call up was of something dark—dark and sinister and shapeless. This was a place where the form and outline of battle was lost in the free flow and violence of the jungle encounter; a place where the enemy was never there, but here.

The announcement of our destination created a stunned silence, followed almost immediately by an uproar of conversation. Our captain leaned toward us and said, "This will give us a chance to get at those slant-eyed monkeys quicker. We ought to be able to clear the island in a few weeks, I'll bet that. . . ."

But he was interrupted by the XO who figured that there had been enough chatter.

"I attended a meeting this afternoon on the command ship, and there is little or no written information available for distribution here. After all, when we left Pearl we were heading for Australia to join General MacArthur's forces."

That remark brought a few whistles and considerable shuffling around. After all, we knew a little about the country "down under"—the swagger of its fighting men, the lovely girls, the kangaroo and wallaby, the walkabout, and the rambunctious history of a people who had tackled a tough continent similar to our own and conquered it.

But that was not to be.

The XO continued. "One of our regiments is already going ashore there [Guadalcanal]. As soon as the navy can turn its convoy protection around and send it back for us, we'll be on our way."

He paused, looked down, and once again smoothed the rug with the toe of his shiny low-quarter shoe.

"What information do we have? You know there is a marine division there along with some army regiments that have been sent in. The fighting in the early days was very bitter, and the marines kicked the hell out of the Japs whenever they used their banzai tactics.

"But," he said, "the Japs have been reinforced. There have been a lot of naval battles in the Solomons and the navy has been closed-mouthed about the results. Which means we didn't win.

"The marines are still game, but tired, sick, and their strength is down. The army units are beginning to look the same way. So it looks like it's going to be up to us—to this division—to complete the job."

He pointed at the red line that marked U.S.-held territory on Guadalcanal. It started at the sea, twisted inland, and finally emerged at the coast farther west.

"That's what we control now. I'm not saying the enemy controls the rest of the island, because he doesn't. But you will soon find out that what's in the perimeter is what's yours. There's a meaning to perimeter there that you never read in a field manual. You'll find out a lot more about it when we get there."

He was right. Perimeter was going to be a way of life.

"We will have to fight with what we are carrying on these

ships. Most of our combat gear and heavy equipment is on the docks in Brisbane. We'll have to depend on the army and marine units on the island for support. And that," he paused and looked at us, scanning the room from side to side, "is not a hell of a lot."

He lit up a cigar and puffed a few times, creating a small cloud in front of the map. He motioned to the British officer he had brought with him.

"This is Captain McGregor. He is the deputy resident commissioner for the Solomon Islands. He has been at his post for a little more than four years, and he was at Tulagi when the Japs came. He escaped to one of the other islands and has been an advisor to the marines since the early days in August.

"He will try to give you some ideas of what may be ahead."

The captain stood up, saluted smartly, stood "at ease" and smiled at us.

If there was a stereotype of a British officer, McGregor was the complete and perfect example. He was tall, and well set up with a fitted, starched uniform. His hair was much longer than U.S. officers wore. His mustache was copious but in good repair.

"Well, chaps," he started with the same accent we had heard in Suva, "let me give you a short geography and history lesson.

"The Solomons are a chain of volcanic islands that stretch from southeast to northwest between the equator and ten degrees south. They are hot, covered with rain forest and jungle, and infested with tropical diseases, the worst of which is malaria.

"Before the war, a number of companies had opened up plantations on the coast for the growing of coconuts, and the preparation of copra. As you know copra is processed for coconut oil, which is an ingredient of many of the soaps you Yanks use.

"Other than the plantation owners and government personnel, there were a number of missionaries in the various islands."

He turned and looked at the map and directed his words to it rather than to us.

"It was an out-of-the-way place—these islands—of no great importance to the Crown, of minor importance economically, of no importance politically."

He turned back to us.

"That is, until the Japanese came. Now they seem suddenly to have become one of the strategic prizes of the war."

Somebody raised a hand.

"Why has the fighting stayed in such a small area?" a voice queried.

"A good question," McGregor replied.

"There is little flat land in these islands. The Jap was quick to notice that the small plain where Henderson Field is located now would be ideal for an airfield. The war up to this point has involved seizing the airfield and protecting it from the enemy.

"And as I understand it, pushing the Jap farther up the coast, and away from Henderson, will be your mission."

Another hand was raised and another question.

"What about the natives?"

"Most of them are short, dark, and not very good-looking," he said with a twinkle in his eye. Laughter.

"They have been under pressure by the enemy to cooperate with them, but most have gone to bush and are loyal to the Allies."

At this point the XO intervened.

"In the next few days we'll try to get you as much information as we can. Captain McGregor will be sailing with us, and you'll have lots of opportunities to talk to him."

Somebody hollered, "Attention!" We stood. The XO and the British captain disappeared behind the map.

Somebody hollered, "Dismissed!" We shuffled out of the smoky brightness of the wardroom into the warm, humid darkness.

THE ROLL CALL

Up to this point in the narrative we have identified only the time and place of an action that was to change all of our lives, for better or worse.

Only a few of the players have been identified who were to play out an epic drama of heroism, cowardice, brilliance, and stupidity in an environment and against a foe unique in our military history.

We shall concern ourselves with the regiment, my regiment. Numbering 3,000 men, it is small enough to have allowed for interaction between many of its members. It is large enough to have engaged in a variety of actions and to have exhibited all the positive and negative aspects of a military organization subjected to the rigors of war in the Pacific.

Of all the groups to which men belong—family, church, lodge, friends at work—none is more difficult to describe in terms of how men relate to each other than the military. A man joins a unit, and almost immediately he establishes a relationship with one or two others. In a day or so he will be on speaking terms with his superiors and his peers. The relationship with subordinates, if any, is handled in a more gingerly manner. The object is to give the best possible impression to those you command, and this usually involves finding out as much as you can about them while maintaining an appropriate social distance.

A man in uniform is no different from any other man. Some make quick friendships with a few, others with many. Some make no friends and remain aloof from intimate conversation or group activities.

In the regiment we divided into two natural groupings, the "state" group and the "outsiders." The regiment had been part of a National Guard division in the States; but after Pearl Harbor, the regiment had been sent to the Pacific and found itself part of a Regular Army division on Oahu. The field-grade officers, from the regiment commander to the majors in battalions, were from the "state" group, as were most of the company commanders. Most of the junior officers, lieutenants like myself, were fresh from the various service schools in the United States. We had little in common with each other, coming from everywhere in the "forty-eight," except our common heritage of having attended the infantry or artillery school.

We had joined the regiment in September, had some weeks to train our platoons, some more weeks to load up our supplies and equipment, and then set sail in December. To be in a National Guard regiment in an active army division was to be second best. The "professionals," or West Pointers, who dominated all the other division units, could hardly be enthusiastic about having a third of their ground-pounders represented by a force that they held in polite low esteem.

Now that we were going into combat we would be watched like hawks, subject to intense scrutiny by generals and staff officers, examined in a strong light like that of a jeweler looking at a diamond and prepared to find a flaw.

For the professionals, war was their cup of tea; it is what they were there for, their raison d'être. It was the main chance, the golden opportunity to test their mettle and move into the stream of quick promotions that accompanies combat.

I had been a National Guardsman before the war and had left my regiment in California to attend infantry school. I should have felt at home joining another Guard unit, but such was not the case. I was as much of an outsider in the regiment as the regiment was in the division. I had hopes that all this would change, but I knew if it did that it would be a long time in the future.

The most immediate point of reference for an infantryman is the company, the workhorse of the army. When the front line is defined on a map at battalion or corps headquarters, what is shown is the positions of the rifle companies. Nothing is in front of them but the enemy; everything is in back of them. This is a tough place to be. Most of the deaths and injuries in the army are sustained by the rifle companies.

A company is commanded by a captain. Ours was a smooth, gregarious thirty-five-year-old lawyer named Roger Evans. He wore glasses, which I thought unusual for a rifle company commander; in fact I never saw him without them, even in the shower. The first time I met him we discussed how things were back in the States, and then he rushed off to a meeting or party with his close friends. He was always rushing off, spending little or no time with his officers or his command. He was a master of decentralizing authority: in fact, he was so to the point that no one went to him for decisions.

I learned that he thoroughly enjoyed himself in the islands. The war was exciting, travel was stimulating, and a coterie of friends was available that he had known personally and professionally in his hometown. He was an inveterate partygoer and party giver: Oahu had countless settings for a good time, and Evans knew them all.

He was a good, intelligent man. He was not an infantry commander. He must have resisted transfer to an assignment more in keeping with his legal background and social status. Maybe he had stayed in the infantry because he was fearless, or because he totally missed the point that he had the most dangerous command assignment in the army.

The second most important man in the company is the first sergeant, who is the link between the officers and enlisted men. He is usually respected but disliked by those in both groups, who are afraid of him. Our "topkick" was 1st Sgt. Frank Begley. He was a year older than the captain, red of face, brawny, and loud when he had to be.

He had been a die maker in civilian life and belonged to the Guard as a hobby. He was great at fixing trucks, iceboxes, and screen doors. When he got excited he held his hands partly open as if looking for a hammer or wrench to pick up.

He was the first man you saw in the morning and the last you saw at night. He snored horribly and as a result had a tent to himself. He was given to short sermons at the reveille formation, embracing such subjects as sloppy tents, reports from the military police (MPs), and failure to read the duty roster.

On board ship he had lost his power and authority: the mess hall and latrines were under the control of the navy; there were no formations, no sermons. The men obeyed only the loudspeaker. In the few days since we had sailed he started to look very old and tired.

The company had three lieutenants besides me. Clint O'Berry, the executive officer and second in command, was a pleasant, Irish farm boy with a big grin that seemed permanently affixed to his face. He had an "Aw, shucks" manner of speaking and tried to handle trouble as if it were nothing to be excited about. He had come from the States with the regiment and had connections with most of the brass. Obie, as everyone called him, was well liked by both the officers and men, and because the captain spent so much time up the line, Obie pretty well ran the company. Mark Bemish was a New Yorker; he had a reserve commission based on the Reserve Officer Training Corps (ROTC, or "Rotsie") and had been called up in 1940. He'd engaged in a lot of squirreling around trying to avoid an overseas assignment, volunteering for a lot of staff jobs at various posts, but was consistently turned down because his orders were coded for overseas duty. When he landed in Oahu, he launched another campaign in the island command, but his pattern of failure continued. He was moved inexorably to the last place he wanted to go in the army—in an infantry company leading an infantry platoon.

Mark, furthermore, was a graduate of Columbia University and considered himself an intellectual. He was always anxious to explore the heights and depths of some topic, and often said he would rather have a good conversation than eat. We were prone to doubt that statement when we saw the agility with which he handled a knife and fork.

Wayne Matlock (Matt, to most of us) had been a reserve officer with a commission in the MPs. He had been a cop in one of the Midwestern cities, but when the war broke out he volunteered for active duty in the MPs. Naturally, the processors of assignment whose reasoning was known only to God and higher headquarters assigned him to the infantry. He had twisted and turned to get back into his proper branch, but to no avail. Matt looked like a fullback with a broad pair of shoulders, well-muscled arms, and a thick neck. If he had been a short-tempered or aggressive fellow, he would have been a holy terror. But the opposite was true. He was quiet, considerate of others, and with a wry sense of humor. He was a natural to teach calisthenics and unarmed combat, and the men respected his concern for their physical shape and well-being.

One other member of the company deserves introduction, my platoon sergeant, "Pop" Benson. He was the oldest man in the platoon (and two years senior to me). He was of moderate height and thin, with a hawk-like nose that protruded from the prow of an otherwise nondescript face.

Pop was "Old Guard." He had come through the ranks slowly and learned his lessons well: he knew his men; there wasn't a trick he hadn't seen before, and he had three ways to counter each one. Unlike most platoon sergeants, he didn't take himself too seriously and he had a lively sense of humor. We accepted each other on sight (probably because I was "Old Guard," too). He did his best to help me get to know the men.

It is time now to move higher up and observe the brass of battalion and regiment headquarters. We won't meet them all—that will happen in due time—but we'll notice those who were to have an impact on the events just ahead.

"Lieutenant Colonel Welby Graber, commanding officer, 1st Battalion" was the imposing title on the door the first time I knocked and entered. I was unimpressed at the outset. He had a sallow complexion and an undistinguished, if not homely, face. He usually chomped on a cigar, which I assume he felt gave him an air of toughness and determination. He didn't appear to be in good shape, and it was evident that the high living he had engaged in after the regiment had come to Oahu had taken its toll.

He had been a grocer in the States, and the Guard was both his hobby and his passion. It was inconceivable to me how someone with his lack of wit and bearing had moved up to a silver maple leaf. Inconceivable that is, until I found out he was the regiment colonel's son-in-law. By sticking close to his father-in-law he had gained a series of "safe" assignments, and his raters had one eye on the father-in-law when they listed him as an "excellent" officer.

And now at last there was a war, and a chance for Welby to make it big. When the regiment was sent overseas, some of the officers felt to be too old for combat were given stateside assignments, and his father-in-law proudly gave him a battalion and pinned one of his own silver leaves on the new lieutenant colonel's collar.

One other officer at the battalion level should be listed at this point, the S-3, the battalion operations officer, Maj. Harley Sample. His many enemies often called him "Simple," and it was a deserved corruption of his name: he was a nitpicker for the wrong reasons. He loved to criticize and make snide remarks that showed, ostensibly, his ability to spot the rotten apple in the barrel.

Harley was also "Old Guard." He had studiously followed in Graber's footsteps, and now they were both field-grade officers going into combat. Sample would relish the combat activity to come, not because he was courageous, but because he wanted so desperately to exercise power in moving men around—something his civilian occupation of bookkeeper in a department store had never offered him.

Harley's outstanding characteristic was his dental work, his front teeth protruding like a beaver's and giving him a hideous, sardonic smile. He was an ugly man in appearance and disposition. We deserved better, but circumstance had given this small-minded man an opportunity to sidle into a position of responsibility, and we were stuck with him.

This partial roll call concludes with the most interesting character of them all, Col. Herman Popper, the regiment commander. From his appearance and his love of the military, Popper was in the wrong army. He was a Prussian, a *junker*. He wore his hair cropped close to the skull; sported a narrow, Hitler-like, gray mustache; wore immaculate uniforms; and often stood with hands on hips, surveying his domain.

Popper had been a prosperous lawyer, but the Guard was always his first love. He had impressed his Regular Army counterparts when the regiment came to Oahu, and carried out his responsibilities with snap and enthusiasm.

He felt that a regiment commander was a person of great authority and responsibility, which caused him to adopt a rather imperial attitude that was reflected in his words and posture. He believed in social distance: the lower the rank, the greater the distance. He invariably called an enlisted man "son," and a junior officer "young man."

The first time I ate in his mess I was struck by the silence. When I asked Obie about it I was shushed. Toward the end of the meal everyone was looking at the colonel. When he finally carefully crossed his knife and fork on his plate, everybody began talking while he lit up a Perfecto. I was impressed, but not favorably.

Popper had talked to me once—the day I joined the regiment. He was glad I was Old Guard and assigned me to a rifle company. He indeed was in the wrong army, and one war too late.

The convoy left Nandi before dawn and headed northwest to the Solomon Islands. The troopships were strung out on the sea in a single file, with destroyers and a single cruiser some distance away on the flanks. There was a high haze over the ocean, which gave the sea a gray cast. There was little or no breeze, and the Pacific was as smooth as a pool table. Looking up the line of heavily laden ships, they seemed like great brown cats hunkered down on a gray blanket. It was probably the last serene and peaceful scene we would see in a long time.

Since no one knew anything about the Solomons, we chased around the ship, joining every knot of men to see whether anyone knew anything. (We were going into one of the least-known areas of the world.) Even the navy men professed ignorance of the chain of islands that we'd set a course for. We tried to remember some of the early articles that had appeared in newspapers and magazines after the U.S. Marines' landing in August 1942. What we could recall was a collective stereotype of every South Sea island the movies or *National Geographic* had ever portrayed. We settled on the following description. It was hot, rainy, with palm trees, dark-skinned natives, and a mountainous interior. It was unhealthy, with all the tropical diseases known to man. We were unsure about snakes, alligators or crocodiles, spiders, or other venomous insects.

The word was passed for everyone to check out his equipment and clean rifles and other weapons. Since there was no room for such activity in the crowded quarters belowdecks, everyone erupted from below with cleaning rods, oilcans, and bales of patches. The aisles, stairways, and hatch covers were soon tightly occupied with freely perspiring soldiers busily pumping rods up and down in rifle barrels. Field-stripping a weapon was hazardous because in the press of so many bodies, a bolt or follower could easily slip away and clatter to the deck.

As this activity proceeded, we noticed that there was less and less conversation and that the usual ebullience of the men was being replaced by expressions of concern or deep thought. We were less than two days sailing from our entry into combat.

What was developing was that sense of trepidation that would occupy our waking hours and make our nights disordered with fitful sleep. It was beginning to occur to all of us, quicker to some than others, that after two years of training, maneuvers, exercises, movements, and preparation, now at last we would put it to use. We were to know the meaning of war—a word that has chilled and excited the hearts of millions through the centuries. We were to be faced with the ultimate price of war—swift, sudden, unexpected death. Each man hoped that he would not pay that price. But, he might have to, and that galling prospect would bedevil him until V-J day.

And what of the Japanese? They were almost as unknown a quantity as the Solomons. What we knew about them was another collective stereotype. We knew the women went mincing around like Madame Butterfly, and that their emperor was nearsighted and rode a white horse. We had seen newsreels of their savagery in China and their bravado at Singapore. We had seen them yelling "banzai," or something, at the tunnel into Corregidor. We knew the officers carried swords and often beheaded prisoners with this weapon. We had seen the pictures of their dead piled up outside the marines' defensive positions on Guadalcanal. And we knew their snipers were invisible and were everywhere.

As a whole, we were going into a battle where we knew little or nothing about the land, and had only a smattering of knowledge about the enemy. Because we had not expected this assignment we had no maps, no aerial photos, no intelligence reports, and none of the voluminous background studies the army usually provided to troops preparing for combat. In particular we knew almost nothing of the enemy soldiers we would encounter.

No experience in travel is as compelling as approaching an island from the sea. My first experience with this fascinating phenomenon had occurred as we neared the Hawaiian Islands three months earlier. The first indication that land was near was the aroma that engulfed us—a mixture of fruit, wood, and grass, undefinable but unmistakable. Then we noticed weeds, leaves, and branches in the water, and the appearance of land birds. Finally, on the horizon was a burden of clouds with a blue base that, as we came near, turned to brilliant or dark green, depending on sunshine or shadow. With each passing mile the island rose higher, until at last the white ribbon of rolling surf told us that the full glory of Oahu was revealed.

The approach to Guadalcanal had less beauty and attraction. When the light of dawn came, a large part of the island was visible. There was a haze aloft that blurred our vision, and the heavy clouds that hung over the land gave it a gloomy and foreboding appearance. Perhaps it was our apprehension about the future that influenced our perception. But as we drew nearer and the cloud cover thinned in the hot morning sun, we could see the great mountainous spine of Guadalcanal and the dark and light patches on the foothills and desecrated plains that spread out from the spine to the northern beaches.

We were sailing up the waters between parallel chains of islands. San Cristobal had appeared and been passed on the port side, and now we moved between Guadalcanal on the left and Malaita on the right. Ahead, a small island, midway between the former islands, was Florida Island with a tiny inlet on its south coast— Tulagi, the residence of the British commissioner.

The public address system had been blaring out orders since dawn. The scene belowdecks was a military version of bedlam. Packs were being rolled, bags were packed with everything we didn't want to carry. Men were clattering up and down the ladders adding to the din.

We all heard the engines stop: all action ceased and there was an eerie silence. No one moved or spoke. Then we heard the anchor chain clanking over the side and knew this trip was over.

When it was my turn to bring the platoon up on deck, I was surprised at how close to the island we had come. The impressions we had formed from a distance were confirmed now that we were anchored less than a mile off the shore. All of the ingredients for a tropical paradise were there: palm trees, beaches, hills, and mountains. But it lacked the sunny, green brilliance of Oahu. This was a dark island.

December 30, 1942, 1000 hours—I got my men down the nets and into the landing craft that squirmed around in a gentle swell. Then we cast off, the motors were revved up, and in a few minutes our craft lurched to a full stop and the front ramp slammed down.

We were fifty yards from the beach. I stepped off the ramp into waist-deep water, and a heavy undertow knocked my feet out from under me so that I was sitting on the bottom. I floundered to my feet and led my platoon to the beach. My equipment and I were soaked. I was on Guadalcanal.

CHAPTER TWO

Settling In

There was a magnificent scramble getting all the troops together because the Higgins boats' pilots had their own ideas of where to land. Our men were scattered up and down the beach, and it took a lot of calling and yelling to get them all corralled.

After some time, I had gathered my platoon and was directed to proceed along the coast road to the west. Everyone was surprised to see well-constructed roads on the island. But when we remembered that the masses of swaying palm trees were part of the many coconut plantations that lined the coast, the sight of good roads on what was supposed to be a primitive land was not so baffling.

It felt good to be stretching our legs again and getting away from the stinking, overcrowded ship that had brought us to the Solomons. But the pleasure of getting some exercise was quickly countered by what we were to endure for the next year—the insufferable heat.

Most of us had spent time in the sweltering pine-barren camps of the South, and in the tropical sunshine of Oahu, with the expectation that we would be well-conditioned for the climate in the Solomons. We found that that was a faulty assumption as we experienced the sweat pouring down our necks and foreheads. As I looked around the platoon I found that every man's fatigue jacket was soaked. In fact all of them looked the way I did during my initial landing.

After a half-mile march we turned south on another good road until we spotted First Sergeant Begley, who motioned us off the road and indicated our bivouac area. The evenly spaced coconut palms made it easy to assign areas to squads and platoons: the platoon got an aisle between rows that were ten trees long, and each squad got three trees.

The earth (or rather sand) was covered with a thin grass ideal to bunk down on, and in less than a minute after our arrival the men had removed their helmets, packs, cartridge belts, and jackets to cool off. The palms furnished a little shade from the sun, and the breeze blowing in from the sea was most welcome.

My enjoyment of surcease from heat was cut short as I saw the perspiring stocky figure of the topkick heading in my direction. Seeing that he had my attention, he motioned toward the road and called out: "Captain Evans wants all officers out on the road." Then he turned and headed in that direction himself. Even at a distance it was obvious that First Sergeant Begley was exhausted. His uniform was black with sweat and he kept wiping his neck with a bandana. His face was contorted with fatigue, and he was in considerable pain. I remember thinking as I donned my gear that he wouldn't last long in this climate.

The captain was sitting on the edge of the road as we gathered around. His glasses were steamed and his usually immaculate uniform was sodden; he appeared to be a carbon copy of the topkick. He motioned for us to sit down.

"This heat is really somethin'," he commented.

"But our cargo is coming in down at the beach. We have to find it, put it in a company pile, and guard it until a regimental dump is established."

He paused for a long draw on his canteen. Knowing how much he liked a cocktail in a frosted glass, I could guess what he wished he had. He looked at me.

"Take half of your men and report to the XO down at the beach. He'll tell you what to do. We'll send somebody down to relieve you in a few hours."

He stood up wearily.

"I don't have to tell you that the enemy can be anywhere. Don't let your men wander away from this bivouac area. Particularly keep an eye out toward the south. Japanese were seen in this area two days ago."

He made a gesture that meant the meeting was over. I asked, "Should we take rifles with us?"

He looked at me through his steamed glasses and nodded. "Always." I shared my information with Pop, gathered up two grumbling squads, and headed for the beach.

Chaos is the best description for the condition on the beach. Piles of bags, stacks of footlockers, and assorted boxes were everywhere, including the water. Lighters were coming in continuously. As the ramps crashed down, teams of men rushed in and carried off the cargo, depositing it on the first available square yard of unoccupied beach. Then the ramps clanked up, the motors roared, and the lighters backed out for another load.

The XO was a man besieged. The heat, the confusion, and the babel of voices had unnerved him. The slick, competent officer who had briefed us at Nandi had given way to a sweating, irritable tyrant who roared and gesticulated out of sheer, towering frustration.

When I finally got a word in he recited his litany for the thousandth time: "Find your cargo any way you can. Establish a company supply point back in the trees. Keep a guard on your stuff."

I saluted and returned to the squads, and motioned for the men to gather around.

"Spread out and see if you can find anything with the company markings. If you have any luck bring it to the base of that tree." I pointed to a tall palm that had its fronds shot off. "We'll make a company dump there."

After a few minutes, some men from the first squad found a

pile of our bags and started hauling them in. An hour passed before the second squad had some luck and brought in a collection of foot-lockers. They also brought back an interesting bit of news from the navy beach master. The sling holding a large number of our lockers had broken while they were being lowered over the side, and a lot of personal property was lying on the bottom of Indispensable Strait.

When the group that was to relieve us arrived (late), we had ac-quired a number of bags, lockers, and boxes. I told Bemish what the procedure was, gathered up my tired troops, and trudged back to the bivouac.

HEAT AND WATER

Even though it was late in the afternoon, the heat and humidity were intense. During the march back we began to experience a con-dition that would be in effect as long as we stayed in the Solomons: exuding water in the form of perspiration at a fantastic rate. Our canteens had been emptied long ago and since we had no five-gallon cans or Lister bags, replenishment was a problem.

When we arrived at the bivouac we heard that a detail had been sent for water but had not returned. Our condition was a paradox. Our bodies were saturated with sweat, but our mouths, tongues, and throats were as dry as dirt.

I remembered our training at the infantry school where, after a particularly grueling afternoon in the hot Georgia sun, we would line up in front of the barracks, take out our canteens, and pour the water out. Woe unto him that didn't have most of his water to dump on the red clay. He was unmercifully criticized for not prac-ticing water conservation.

There was only one problem with such training: it wouldn't work on Guadalcanal. The loss of water to exertion, heat, and hu-midity had to be replaced or you passed out. Yelling at the men who had their canteens out was silly in the Solomons. The solution was to carry more water (two canteens) and set up a system for water supply and resupply on a level not before contemplated.

We never solved this problem completely.

It was almost 1800 hours before a jeep pulled up to our area with ten five-gallon cans of water. Of course there was a big rush to fill canteens, and I noticed a lot of water was spilled because we had no simple device to funnel the liquid into the small opening of the canteen. I made a mental note to not let that kind of water wastage occur in the future.

I sat down and leaned against a palm to eat a can of corned beef hash and some crackers. It was hard to swallow with my throat being as dry as it was—and I couldn't afford to wash each mouthful down with a swig of water.

The hash was filling, and the army dietitians claimed it was nutritious, but it didn't keep me from thinking about some great meals I had eaten at home: roast chicken with dressing, mashed potatoes, gravy, stewed tomatoes, apple pie. You had to put such gentle visions out of thought because they hurt too much to contemplate.

As I examined the empty hash can it occurred to me that I had better check on the three essentials before dark: a garbage pit, a slit trench for a latrine, and the guard posts.

I got up and walked over to Pop Benson.

"How're ya doing, Pop?" I said.

He looked up with his thin face, the hawk-like nose, and an air of incredible fatigue.

"Nobody said it would be like this."

"I guess the first day in this climate is the worst," I offered, hopefully.

"I sure hope so, Lieutenant, I sure hope so."

"Let's go find the old man and see what arrangements he wants."

Benson got up, put on his helmet and fatigue jacket, slung on his

M1, and started after me. He looked like a scarecrow with his wrinkled uniform and skinny body. His head was too small for a helmet, and his canvas leggings were too large for his pipe-straw legs. But he was a good soldier. I was glad he was my platoon sergeant.

Captain Evans was sitting in his T-shirt with his legs folded in like a Buddha.

"What's the poop?" I asked, hunkering down next to him.

"Not much," he said wearily. "I guess we'll stay here till we get some orders. Nobody knows what they want us to do yet. We haven't found most of our equipment yet, and the beach master doesn't have any answers."

"What about guards, latrines, and trash pits?" I asked.

"We'll keep two men on the road, and one man in each platoon on the alert. That ought to be good enough for tonight. No reports today of any Nips in the area."

"Latrines and trash pits?"

"See First Sergeant Begley. He has a detail working on that problem."

I started to give him a salute as I got up to leave. Then I remembered the rules for officers here: no salutes, no insignia of rank, no use of title in address.

I told Benson to find First Sergeant Begley, get the poop, and tell the men.

"Where are you going?" he asked.

"I'm going to take a look around before it gets dark. I want to get some feel for where we are."

"OK, Lieutenant."

"Don't call me lieutenant," I said raising my finger in schoolteacher fashion.

"Yes, . . ." he said, almost saying "sir."

I got out to the road and turned south.

The battalion had moved in entirely, each company being allocated two aisles of palms. I walked past C and D Companies and waved to their guards, who were standing just inside the line of trees.

I checked my M1 to see whether it was loaded, and set the safety. I was now about a quarter of a mile from the bivouac. I could no longer hear the voices of men or the clank of water cans. The wind had died down and the rustling of palm fronds had ceased. The silence was complete. I tried to imagine the enemy being nearby and what he might be thinking of this soldier wandering down a plantation road as the darkness closed in.

This area had been a scene of battle. You could see that in the bullet marks on the palms. But it had been a quiet sector for a couple of weeks while the war moved west into the coastal hills and south into the mountains.

I stopped and listened, for what I do not know. If I'd heard anything, I would have been terrified. But there was nothing.

It was almost dark. I felt a chill, a reaction to my foolishness in making this unnecessary foray into the dark and the unknown. I retreated to the bivouac, looking over my shoulder frequently. The chill remained.

I spotted our company guards and left the road. I asked one of them, "What's the sign?"

"Babe Ruth."

"What's the countersign?"

"Yankee."

"Thanks," I said. "Keep your eyes open."

I stumbled around until I found Sergeant Benson. He had spread out his shelter half and was horizontal, smoking a cigarette.

"Where's the latrine?" I asked.

"Next to the third tree in that direction. There's some bung fodder there but you better take your own shovel."

I took the shovel from my pack and worked my way through many recumbent bodies to the latrine. Upon completion of my sanitary actions, I returned to Benson, checking the men on the way. They were in good humor but dog-tired. A few wanted to know what was up, and I had little to offer them. That was a situation I would find myself in more often than not.

I spread out my shelter half next to Benson's, made a pillow of my pack, and lay down. It was not sensibly cooler even though the sun was down and the stars were becoming visible. Benson and I engaged in small talk, and after a while I assumed he fell asleep because he stopped talking.

I must have dozed off, too, because I awoke with a start to find that a strong wind was blowing in from the sea. The stars were gone, obscured by low clouds. The wind increased in intensity, the palm fronds thrashing wildly overhead. Some rain started, first a few drops, then a substantial driving rain.

Benson and I put on our ponchos and helmets while the water cascaded down our necks.

We heard a loud yell from the C Company area. Some hooded flashlights were turned on, and someone yelled for the medics. Benson dug out his flashlight and stood up.

"I'll go over and see what happened."

He disappeared into the dark while the rainstorm raged, and returned in less than a minute.

"One of their men is dead, his head was crushed by a falling coconut."

"Pop, tell all the squad leaders to have their men put on their helmets and sit on the windward side of the palms."

Benson moved off into the darkness. His hooded light bobbed and blinked as he moved through the platoon.

The dark island had claimed its first victim.

The following day we continued looking for our baggage. We never did figure out why it had been spread out all over the beach; after all, it had been loaded according to a plan that was supposed to ensure its being kept together in the debarkation area. The only trouble was that the sailors unloading the hatches and the skippers operating the landing craft hadn't heard of the plan. The era of efficient debarkation or landing plans had not come.

Around noontime Captain Evans was called to headquarters. We suspected that some decision had been made for our deployment. Knowing that the troops we were going to relieve were tired, sick, and reduced in numbers, it was surprising that we had spent so much time lying around on the beach.

Evans returned at about 1300 hours. He called for the officers and noncoms (noncommissioned officers) and had us sit around him in a circle. He was obviously delighted that something was going to happen, and showed it.

"Well, we're moving up. We are going to relieve the regiment on Bloody Ridge. We'll move out of here in about a half hour."

"What about the barracks bags and the ammo?"

"The bags will be left behind. They'll be put in the battalion dump. Whatever you want to take out of them, do it fast.

"As for ammo, each man gets a bandoleer to take along. And be sure to fill your canteens."

We hustled back to get the men informed and gather our gear. There was a minimum of conversation in contrast to the usual uproar that accompanied a move. The men moved quickly and silently. Many of them puzzled over what to put in their packs and what to leave behind. Food supplies that had been carefully hoarded now saw the light of day: cookies and candy were passed around, a can of pineapple was opened.

The topkick's whistle blasted through the groves, and we hurried to the road. By the time I got the platoon lined up, the head of the column had moved out.

We followed a road that paralleled the beach. The storm of the night before had littered the ground with palm fronds, and they crackled as we humped over them.

It seemed hotter than ever before. The sky was cloudless, and the full effect of the tropical sun and galling humidity had us sweating like pigs.

We crossed an engineer bridge over a river that was obviously swollen from the previous night's rain. We left the road and started

up a trail that had its ups and downs. We struggled through the ups
and slipped on the downs. Our march had slowed to a snail's pace,
the men panting loudly and showing the signs of extreme fatigue.
It occurred to me that I had not expected this. These were rested
troops, in good physical condition, well trained, and supposedly
equal to the task. Yet after a march of less than two hours, most of
them were near exhaustion.

We broke out of the forest trail we had been following to a
grassy ridge where a halt was called. Many men collapsed on the
ground, not bothering to remove their packs while they rubbed the
sweat out of their eyes and gasped for breath.

There was a good breeze on the ridge—not a cool breeze, but
one that evaporated the sweat and had a slight cooling effect. I
walked forward to see the captain. He was seated with his head between his legs.

"Ain't this a bitch?" he said.

"Hotter than Georgia," I replied.

When he looked up, I saw how tired he was. His "go get 'em"
expression had faded. His glasses were steamed and slightly askew
on his nose.

"How're the men back there?" he asked.

"Pretty tired—but they'll pick up during this break." It was
obvious he didn't want to spare the breath to talk.

I returned to the platoon. The Russian was drinking from
his canteen. I wanted to yell at him, but then remembered how
that used to irritate me during the hot marches at Fort Benning, in
Georgia. The Russian spotted me looking at him and put his canteen away.

We were beginning to find out how precious water was. And
we would learn more later.

We heard the word being passed "off and on." Men lumbered
to their feet as if heavy with sleep. The break had helped a little.

As we proceeded along the ridge we got high enough to see the
sea and the islands to the north. We could also see Henderson Field,

the reason we were all on Guadalcanal. As we watched, we saw a plane take off and climb into the clear air and blue sky high over the island. I wished I had joined the air force.

The ridge was trending south, and we were marching away from the sea. As we continued forward we could see marks of battle, bullet holes in trees, C-ration cans, helmets, foxholes, and barbed wire.

The column came to a halt; the captain came back to my platoon.

"Put your men in this position. Start over there by that big tree and spread over to where we are standing. Bemish will start his platoon area from here to the south. OK?"

I nodded. Then it occurred to me as Evans was walking away that I had a question.

"Hey, Captain, where the hell are we?"

He looked over his shoulder without stopping. "This is Bloody Ridge," said he.

BLOODY RIDGE

The name had instant recognition. The press had been full of the prolonged defense the U.S. Marines had sustained against Japanese banzai attacks. And now we were on the same ground.

It didn't look very impressive. The ridge was only a few yards wide at the top, and running north and south. To the west was the Lunga River, actually a tropical stream about twenty yards wide. The marines had anchored one end of their line on the ridge and the other end on the river.

The enemy had attacked from the south, and tried for three nights to dislodge the marines. The attack was renewed with vigor each night, causing the marines to fall back twice. But the third position held, and the attacking force broke off the engagement, hauled out most of its dead, and left the ridge in U.S. hands.

What was so important about this nondescript hump stuck in a rain forest? The north end of the ridge overlooked Henderson Field. Enemy weapons or observers on the north ridge could have raised havoc with our planes using the field and could have threatened the perimeter protecting it.

The only evidence of the battle that had been fought was the barbed wire that had been placed at the base of the ridge. Some of the foxholes were still visible, but the heavy rains had obliterated most of them. It was getting dark and we started to dig in. I designated positions for two-man foxholes on both sides of the ridge. After about an hour we were set for the night—and it was dark.

Captain Evans came along the path on the top of the ridge.

"Are all of your men set for the night?" he asked.

"They're all set, but I don't know what to tell them to expect."

"I don't know," Evans replied. "Graber doesn't know either."

"You'd think they'd give us some reason for being here. They sure were in a hell of a hurry to get us here before nightfall."

"I know. Just keep a sharp eye out." He shuffled away in the dark.

I hunkered down next to Pop in a hole a little too small for both of us. "What's the scoop?" he whispered.

"Nobody knows nothin'."

"Think there are any Nips around?"

"Could be, but most of the sounds of firing today seemed to be a long way west of here."

"The men want to know what to do," he said after a long pause.

"Tell them not to get trigger-happy, and stay in their holes."

Pop groaned as he heaved himself out.

"Be careful," I cautioned. He disappeared down the ridge.

I made some preparations for the night. I put my pack at the end of the rectangular hole, where my head would be (the pack would substitute for a pillow). I put my cartridge belt on the parapet we'd formed with the mud we dug out of the hole. I placed my M1 next to the cartridge belt. I lay down in the hole and tested to see whether the rifle was exactly where I could reach it without fumbling around in the dark. I stuck my trench knife in the mud just above where my head would be.

Pop came looming out of the dark, and almost fell in the hole. I reached up and grabbed his outstretched hand and guided him in. It was really dark now.

I nudged him. "How was it?"

He leaned close. "They're all bedded down. Smitty is upset because we don't know what to expect. I told him to set up a 'two on–two off' schedule with his men to be awake."

There was a long pause.

"They'll be all right," he said.

I patted him on the shoulder. "Get some sleep; I'll take the first watch."

He spent some time arranging his gear and scrunched down to sleep. In a few minutes I could hear his deep breathing. He was asleep.

The system we used at night had been suggested by some of the "old hands" we had met during the unloading operation. They gave us the following pointers:

- Two men in a foxhole, head to foot. (One man gets scared all by himself; and if he falls asleep there is a gap in your defense.)

- Each man stays awake for two hours, while his partner sleeps. (Almost everybody had a watch, but luminous dials were a washout—a flashlight was used under a shelter half to see the time. After each such observation you were night-blind for ten minutes.)

- No one gets out of the hole at night. If nature calls, you do it in a helmet. (Getting the helmet clean after dawn was a difficult and nauseating task.)

- Shoot at anything that moves in the dark—that you can see. (That rule made getting out of your hole suicidal.)

I had just started my second watch. It was after midnight. I heard some muffled conversation down the ridge, and the unmistakable sound of an M1's operating handle being drawn back and released was followed immediately by a shot.

Benson scrambled to sit upright.

"What happened?"

"Somebody fired a shot. I don't think it was in our platoon area."

We strained to see something in the dark. We heard the crack of a grenade being ignited, and could trace the trail of sparks as it arced down into the ravine below the ridge. There was a deafening explosion.

I could hear the guys in our platoon talking.

"Quiet down and stay put," I hissed into the darkness.

About five minutes later, another shot was fired, followed in quick succession by a half-dozen more. The sound appeared to be farther away than the grenade's. All thought of sleep had vanished. Pop and I must have looked like two owls peering into the dark. It seemed an eternity before we saw the first blush of dawn (in the forest, only the sky directly above you is visible).

After another eternity we could make out the forms of our men crouching in their holes.

"I think it's safe to get up now." I stood up.

Benson scratched around in his pack and handed me a can of meat and beans. I opened the can and walked down the ridge. Matlock was sitting on the edge of his hole munching on a D-bar.

"What was all the ruckus last night?" I asked.

He got up, motioned for me to follow, and scrambled down the side of the ridge to the barbed wire. A dead pig lay at the edge of the wire.

We had drawn first blood on Bloody Ridge.

The rest of the morning was passed by improving our foxholes, getting rid of the bumps in the bottom that no amount of twisting and turning could accommodate.

I walked over to Evans's foxhole. He was talking to Matlock

and the topkick. Evans looked up wearily, the red eyes and the dark circles under them indicating that he hadn't sleep well either.

"What's the scoop?" I asked.

"Nothing so far. I'm surprised the battalion CO hasn't called a meeting. But then he may not know anything either."

"Is the enemy supposed to be in this area? There was a lot of shooting last night, but all we've got to show for it is a dead pig."

"No," Evans replied. "I haven't been given any intelligence information, and I'm pretty sure that dummy of an S-2 isn't trying to get any. In fact I don't have any idea what our mission is here. When Simple brought me up here yesterday he showed me the flanks of this position, and took off like a scalded cat."

"Probably didn't want to miss anything back at headquarters," Matlock grumbled.

I tramped back to my position. Most of the men were sacked out in the hot sun, trying to make up for the sleep they'd lost the night before.

It was a bother to me that we didn't know what the hell was going on. The last in-depth briefing we'd had was aboard ship. Since then we had moved around two or three times without any indication that we were playing a part in a war.

We could hear sounds of gunfire, artillery, and an occasional bomb in the distance, but we didn't know who was winning, what our next assignment was, or—more important—when we were going to get a hot meal. This sort of thing is called the fog of war. You may know for sure what is going to happen in the next ten minutes, but beyond that the fog takes over. And that's where the rumor comes in. Actually, the rumor is a way of exploring different possibilities when you don't have any information on which to base them. But a vacuum of information is intolerable, especially to soldiers, especially in combat. So the rumor will keep us occupied when our superiors withhold information or don't have any. Knowing the nature of the battalion staff, we wouldn't get any poop until the last possible moment. The battalion staff felt a sense of power in keeping things to themselves that everybody wanted to know. If you wasted your time moseying over to battalion, the standard answer was "when we get something official, we'll call a meeting." This was bull and they knew it. The switchboard was constantly tied up with calls to higher headquarters.

By the staff's definition all this chitchat was not "official" and, while they shared with each other, it was not considered important for the line units to be in on it.

But there was one exception to this rule. The "hometown" Guard buddies of the CO had special access to the throne that the rest of us didn't. (Of course, all such tidbits were issued with the admonition to "keep it under your hat.")

The CO was unaware of the caste system he had fostered with his communication channel to the "hometown" boys. He was effectively dividing his command into two parts: the part that had left the home state and come to Oahu after Pearl Harbor and the "fillers." He did not know that everyone in the battalion knew of this division into sheep and goats. Only Graber himself didn't know it. It was a tribute to his level of intelligence that he thought he was concealing something that everyone else in the battalion knew.

In the afternoon the sun turned the island into an oven. With nothing to do, and the oppressive heat and the lack of sleep the night before, I found a tree down the ridge that offered some shade and sat down to get some sleep. In the distance, I could hear the bang and thud of artillery and the corn-popping sound of rifle and machine gun fire. But it was a long way off and I nodded off and slept.

Someone grabbed my shoulder. I looked up to see Benson's sweaty face in the oversize helmet.

"Come on, the captain's here," he said, scrambling back up the ridge.

I followed him quickly and found Evans with the other officers gathered in a huddle. They were looking at a pencil sketch.

"Here's where we are." He put a forefinger on Bloody Ridge.

"We're going over here." The forefinger indicated a hill mass a considerable distance to the east.

"There's a convoy of jeeps down at the bottom of the ridge. This company will load up first. We're going in to hold the flank of the regiment on the Galloping Horse—that's what they call this mass of hills." Again he pointed to the map feature. "They have been fighting up there for a couple of days against heavy enemy resistance."

He folded up the map and stuck it in his hip pocket. He pushed his helmet back on his head, smiled at us, and clapped his hands together.

"This is it. Get your men together. Tell everybody to stay on his toes. There's no telling what we'll run into getting over there."

He looked at me.

"Load up your platoon first," he said.

"Thanks," I said. "Thanks a lot."

The line of jeeps at the bottom of the ridge was a beautiful sight. This would be the first time we'd ridden in a vehicle since leaving Hawaii.

Evans got into the first jeep with a young, sweating lieutenant who presumably was our guide. In less than a minute the company was loaded, the drivers were revving their engines, and we were pulling away from Bloody Ridge at a very fast clip indeed.

"This figures," I thought. "After a week of putzing around, we are suddenly speeding into battle."

We broke out into the open and saw the considerable plain that had caused all the trouble. We bounced around the end of Henderson Field and could see the runways, bunkers, revetments, and planes that had been the focus of so much action and bloodshed. Marines, soldiers, sailors, and airmen had all played their part in keeping this two-mile strip of real estate in American hands.

We rattled ahead at high speed, slowing down a little bit to cross the bridge on the Lunga River.

As we bounced around we caught a glimpse of the ocean, and finally came to where the road paralleled the beach. Our drivers were all blowing their horns to get the soldiers, Seabees [popular alternative for the acronym CBs, members of U.S. Navy construction battalions], natives, and other vehicles off the roads. Obviously we had priority.

We continued along the beach for about three miles and came to another river, the Matanikau. We could see the wreckage and destruction that had occurred during the vicious battle in October when the marines had stopped a determined Japanese offensive.

"Here at last is real, genuine battlefield," I thought. We had followed the course of this battle on the radio and in the press, and now we were careening through the place on our way to another battlefield that was very much alive and kicking.

We stayed on the marine trail west of the Matanikau River, going much slower now, with the forest close in on both sides of the one-lane road. We noticed how much louder the sounds of artillery were. We could hear the rushing sound as the projectiles floated overhead on their way to the enemy positions.

Evans's jeep stopped. He gave the rotating-finger signal for assembly. We scrambled out of the jeeps, adjusted our packs, and formed a column. The guide and Evans started up the trail. I looked back at my men, who were hot and covered with dust and grime. The noise of the artillery sounded very loud now, and the heavy, fetid smell of the wet jungle seemed enhanced by the proximity of danger—and death.

We had barely moved a hundred yards up the trail when we were confronted with a most amazing sight. Someone had erected a small, nine-by-nine-foot officer's tent a few feet west of the trail. The front flaps had been tied back, and we could see as we approached that someone was sitting inside the tent.

Evans had stopped to talk to the person in the tent and then moved on. As I came abreast of the tent I found to my utter surprise that it was Colonel Popper.

"Lots of luck," he said. "Give 'em hell." He reached out to shake hands. There was little strength to his shake, and I thanked him for the good wishes and moved on.

I was shocked by his appearance. Popper was the kind that always stood erect, chest out, feet wide apart, arms akimbo, and chin up. The man in this tent seemed shrunken, sick, too small for his uniform.

It was obvious he was ill and crushed by the realization that what he had lived for since 1918, to lead troops in battle again, would never be realized. He had come so far but now, within a few miles of the front, he'd run out of gas.

The trail to the Galloping Horse was rough, muddy, and steep in places, and the temperature seemed to rise every minute. Captain Evans was sweating so hard that his uniform looked like he'd taken a shower in it. He held up his arm for a break.

As I walked up to him he was bent over with his hands on his knees, gasping for breath. When he looked up at me, his face was as red as fire and his glasses were so steamed up that it was doubtful that he could see where he was going.

"Ain't this a bitch," he grunted. I agreed, and we spent the next few minutes breathing hard, saying little.

We started up the trail again, and five minutes later we had to stop again. Some of the men were near the final stages of exhaustion.

Foolishly, we had put many articles in our packs for creature comfort, a carryover from field exercises in the States. Now these articles became an intolerable burden. Blankets, extra shirts, underwear, boxes of cookies, and extra shelter halves, poles, and pins were all discarded. Finally, the most useless of our gear—gas masks—were tossed into the brush along the trail.

At last we reached the top of the nearest hill, where we found a slight breeze and sat down to get our breath. But the rest period was short-lived, and we moved out to the positions in the distance where we saw the troops of the 27th Infantry Regiment.

Evans called me forward and introduced me to a lieutenant. My troops were to replace his on the line. The lieutenant was short on words, but quick on his feet: we almost sprinted to his position about 200 yards away.

"It reaches from where we're standing around this turn in the ridge to that pile of empty ammo cases," he said. "Don't go standing on the ridge. The Japanese are firing at us from the ravine below."

He quickly assembled his platoon from the line of foxholes just below the ridge and headed to the rear. I waved to Sergeant Benson, who brought the platoon up to the position. We gave four foxholes to each squad leader and picked out one for ourselves in the middle of the line.

The lieutenant of the 27th was right about the Japanese firing into our location. The shots all went over our heads, but a man standing on the top of the ridge would be riddled.

A few brave souls decided to crawl up to the crest and return fire, but we put a stop to that. They had no targets, and shooting at sounds was a waste of ammunition that had to be hand-carried over the same incredible trail we had just traversed.

Benson and I sat down in our hole.

"Would you want to share a can of corned beef hash?" he asked.

"Might as well," I replied. "There's nothing else to do."

My mouth was dry, understandable because of the oppressive heat and the sweating that saturated my uniform. But my mouth was dry in a new way: my throat hurt and my tongue felt stuck in the back of my mouth. It suddenly occurred to me that I was reacting to fear. I asked myself whether I was afraid and answered yes.

Fear is an all-encompassing emotion. When it is present, nothing else can enter consciousness. One has to shake himself like a wet dog to throw off the effects of fear temporarily.

I gave myself a jerk—reached for my canteen—and sought to initiate a conversation. I shook the canteen.

"I've got about a half canteen left."

Benson shook his canteen.

"Not much in mine," he said ruefully.

I looked over at the men in the foxholes nearby. Sergeant Dunn, a squad leader, responded to my gesture to come over.

"How're your men fixed for water?" I asked.

"Well, sir, the way they were drinking on the hike up here, probably not much," he responded.

"There's an empty five-gallon can over there, but we saw the guys from the 27th filling their canteens before they left."

"Nice guys," he echoed.

Obviously we had a problem. There were a few hours of hot sun left, and we knew from short experience that the nights would be hot and humid too.

I turned to Benson.

"Send somebody over to company and ask them about water. If they don't have any answer, see if they'll let us go back to battalion."

Benson gave a small groan, as he always did when he got up. In a few seconds a young soldier was trotting down the path to the headquarters. I sent Dunn to see the other squad leaders with the intention of enforcing rigid water discipline until we could get some to issue. A few minutes later the GI we sent to company was back.

Benson relayed the message.

"They want a four-man carrying party to go back and get water."

"What are they going to carry it in?"

"They'll give us some cans down at the water point."

"OK, Pop, but be sure to take only one guy from a hole."

Benson scurried around prying the men out of their holes, making sure they had their M1s and cartridge belts.

An occasional shot from the ravine reminded us the enemy was a hundred yards away. They evidently weren't going to come up the ridge to see us—and we weren't fixin' to go down and see them. At least not yet.

It was getting a little dark as the sun moved behind the tall trees to the west. In a little while it would be time for everyone to get into his hole and set up the position for the night. With this in mind Benson and I decided to make a line check before dark.

We hadn't gone far when Captain Evans and an officer I didn't know arrived.

"I've got a mission for you," Evans said. "Come on over here and I'll show you what I want."

We moved over to the east end of the position. In front of this sector a small path led over to another hilltop about 100 yards away. The ground fell away sharply from the path to a line of trees about twenty yards down.

"Battalion wants us to extend our right flank over to that hill," he said, pointing. "The 27th held it for two days but forgot to tell us it was part of our sector."

The officer with Evans chimed in.

"Sometimes the enemy down in the Matanikau try to get through this area by crossing that path and trying to work their way over to the sea."

"When was the last time they used it?" I asked.

"Last night," the officer said.

Evans was impatient.

"It's getting dark. Take a squad, get over there fast, and dig in."

I went back to get my gear. Benson picked up Sergeant Dunn and his squad and had them waiting at the top of the path.

I told Benson: "Spread out the men to cover that right flank. And make sure nobody does any shooting in the direction of that hill. And see if you can get a sound-powered [SP] phone with a line from your hole to my position over there."

I started down the path with Dunn and his squad strung out behind. We kept a sharp eye down both sides of the knife-edged ridge we were walking on. We could hear shots from the ravine, but they weren't aimed at us.

We found four or five holes on the hill and assigned two men to each hole, using those positions that enabled us to cover the path and the top of our hill with fire.

The holes were too shallow, and we started digging like crazy because the light was fading fast. Dunn and I shared the hole overlooking the path and we had just put the finishing touches on it when Tolliver, a second squad man, arrived with the SP phone and a reel of wire. He hooked up the phone, blew in it for a signal, and handed it to me.

"This is Benson," the phone said.

"I hear you five by five, Pop. Suppose you check with me every two hours."

"OK, out," he said. Pop was never one to waste words. Then some shots rang out, aimed at our position.

Dunn hunkered down in the hole.

"This ought to be an interesting night," he said.

I nodded in agreement while looking back across the barely visible path to my former position.

CHAPTER THREE

Time and Motion

There are two kinds of night.

One kind of night is experienced in a safe environment, in time of peace. The other kind of night is experienced in a hostile environment, in time of war.

Peacetime night causes us few problems: after we turn out the lights we spend much of it sleeping. Those who venture out-of-doors without lights usually know where they're going, whether to go fishing, look at the stars, or make love to a girlfriend. There is seldom any sense of fear, any trepidation, because we seldom experience the awesome effect of total darkness.

Wartime night is a totally different phenomenon. We dread its approach and wait with profound impatience for the first blush of light on the eastern horizon. The moon, stars, and planets come to have real significance as you see them rotate across the sky above you.

Without the moon you can't see your hand in front of your face. In such Stygian darkness your eyes play tricks on you. Forms rise, float wherever you look, and evaporate. There is a considerable amount of disorientation because you have no visible object to anchor your mental vision of the surround.

The greatest burden is the knowledge that somewhere, out there, men are perhaps moving toward your position, or preparing to launch a mortar or artillery shell into your hole. This burden generates a heightened sense of vigilance that must be sustained for hours. Peacetime night never afforded the slightest bit of practice for this task except that, once in a while, one might have had to be on the qui vive for a few minutes. But hours of high tension, escalated periodically by the snap of a twig, the hoarse scream of a bird, or the stupid wiggling of a monitor lizard, push the tension near the snapping point.

Our standard operating procedure (SOP) called for the two men occupying a hole to alternate staying awake for two hours at a time. Of course, I found that I was wide awake when it was my turn to rest. I tried to doze off, but found myself awaking with a start after a few minutes. In a short time (so it seemed) your foxhole buddy would shake you to take your shift.

Some men could sleep during such periods. Whether this ability stemmed from physical or psychological sources I know not. But it was not my lot to be so blessed; I would spend my nights in tense wakefulness.

Dunn was sleeping peacefully. Every now and then he started to snore, an event that caused me to shake his arm. His response was to gasp, grunt, and look around, all of which usually made more noise than the snoring. I didn't know which was worse.

A barely audible whoosh was coming from the SP phone. I untangled it from my pack and whispered, "Yeah."

Benson was reporting in.

"We heard some noise down below the ridge like some guys were moving around. How is it by you?"

I allowed as how we hadn't heard anything.

I heard the snap of a grenade and, looking back to the company position, I could see an arc of sparks as it traveled through the air and down into the ravine. There was a loud bang—it sounded much louder in the phone—indicating it was close to Benson's position.

Before I could ask what was going on another grenade was tossed, accompanied by some rifle fire. Then silence.

"Pop," I whispered.

"Some of the guys are getting edgy," Benson said.

"Call me later. Out."

The noise of the grenades and the rifle fire ensured that everybody for a mile in all directions was awake—including the Japanese.

I looked at the luminous dial on my watch: I had another hour to go . . . and Dunn was starting to snore again.

At first light, while a heavy mist hung over the ravine below, the men began stirring and emerging from their holes. Dunn was giving himself a thorough scratching, starting with his scalp and moving steadily down to his legs.

"I think we better dig a latrine. Quick," he said.

"I agree, and the quicker the better. Last night's coffee has worked it's way through."

Dunn pulled on his boots and shuffled over to the next hole to organize a detail.

One of the continual, irksome, even galling problems of troops in the field is the digging of latrines. With thousands of men in the field obeying the call of nature any time of day or night, there is a requirement for a latrine nearby. If the latrine is not nearby, soldiers on their own will improvise and cause sanitation problems of enormous consequence.

When troops are actively engaged in combat, a small hole scooped out with a helmet, shovel, knife, or fingernails suffices. But as soon as a unit stops, or rests in position, somebody is quickly tagged to start digging.

The hole is usually less than a foot wide (otherwise it is extremely difficult to straddle and maintain one's balance). A foot deep is the minimum, with the soil piled neatly at the end of the hole so it can be shoveled back to cover the proceeds. Using the latrine requires the individual to dispense with the last shreds of self-consciousness: one is seldom concealed from the eyes of others, and no one is polite enough to look the other way. So one drops his pants, bares his behind to the world at large, and does his best to remain unconcerned and blasé.

After a few days the battlefield is covered with hundreds of these tributes to sanitation, and woe to the unsuspecting GI that digs into one in the darkness. Regulations require that signs be placed on old latrines, but no one ever determined who would carry the signs when each infantryman was already loaded down with everything (repeat, everything) he would need to eat, drink, fight with, dig with, and cover with.

DAY

Just after dawn a few of Dunn's men started exploring the rest of the ridge. I could see that they had stopped and were looking at something on the ground. One of the men trotted back.

"There's a dead American soldier over there," he said. Dunn and I grabbed our M1s and headed across the ridge. The dead man was lying on his side as if in sleep. I examined his insignia, which were worn inside the lapel of his jacket. A lieutenant. His body was in the initial stage of decay; his skin had turned gray and a strong odor was developing.

I went back to my hole and hissed into the SP. Benson came on the line.

"Pop, we've got a dead American officer over here. Get the word back, and have them send up a detail for his body."

Pop grunted an OK, and then, "How come the 27th didn't report this?"

"I don't know. When we got here last night, it was bug-out time. They sure weren't going to bring up anything that would delay their departure."

Pop said, "Out." I did too.

The men who had discovered the body came over.

"What's going to happen now?" one of them asked.

"I've sent word back for a recovery team from graves registration. They ought to be here soon. I hope."

"He must have been standing on the ridge when he was shot in the stomach," Dunn said.

There was lot more talk about the dead officer. This was the first casualty we had seen, and we were all trying out words and phrases that seemed appropriate to the occasion. We really didn't know what to say, but a dead soldier was lying there slowly disintegrating and we felt we had to say something.

At a later time, after we had seen the death of scores of our men, there would be little talk. Maybe a few words from the man he was closest to. The rest would remain silent: there were no good words for the situation. We hadn't learned that yet, so the conversation lasted awhile.

About 0700 the 27th launched an attack to the north of us. The artillery slammed into the ravines where the enemy positions were located. Bark, branches, and debris exploded upward as the shells detonated in the treetops. Occasionally one of our dive-bombers planted a huge, lethal egg into the forest. The noise was deafening, and you could see the shock waves spreading out from the point of impact like the ripples moving away from a pebble dropped into a pond.

The activity was hidden from our view, but we could hear the sounds of rifle and machine-gun fire. This was only our second day on the front, but we could tell the difference in the sounds of enemy weapons and our own. It was obvious our troops were expending a lot more small-arms ammo than the enemy. (We were told they were running short of supplies. The small amount of fire coming from the enemy seemed to confirm this.)

During the day the supply system caught up to us. We got three cans of water and two cases of C-rations and six bottles of atabrine (about which more later).

In the late afternoon I talked to Evans about the dead officer. He had received no information about a recovery team.

"Look, boss," I said. "No way we're going to let that young fella lie out there all night."

"I'm not sure we're supposed to bury these guys," Evans replied. "We might get in dutch."

"To hell with the rules. We're going to bury this guy, while he still looks like a soldier," I barked. "Nobody should have to fall apart in the sun and rain because the rear echelon can't get organized."

He shook his head and waved me away.

Dunn was waiting for me.

"What's up?" he said.

"We're going to bury the lieutenant. Get a detail and dig a grave—a deep grave. And stay off the ridge or we'll be burying more than one guy today."

A short-handled entrenching shovel was not designed to dig graves: it was hard to get leverage, and the amount scooped up was disappointingly small. It took better than an hour for four teams of diggers to get the grave deep enough. Lowering the body in was a traumatic experience. Swelling was well advanced, and the odor was overpowering. After a considerable struggle, though, he was arranged in the grave with some dignity.

I went back to my pack to get the tiny Bible I carried. I unzipped the leather covering and found the Ninety-first Psalm.

We stood around the grave, and I read the psalm. We hung our heads and said a little prayer for him, each in his own way. Then we filled up the grave, stuck the barrel of his M1 into the ground, and fastened his dog tags to the rifle's butt.

The night was uneventful except for sporadic rifle fire and grenade tossing by nervous Nellies who always heard something moving around in the dark.

Dunn's men either didn't hear anything, or the fact that I was only ten yards away from the farthest foxhole had something to do with it.

Both Dunn and I had stayed awake until midnight peering down into the draw that the Japanese used as an escape route. This was probably an exercise in futility, since it was doubtful that we could have seen a battalion marching by, so complete was the darkness.

At sunup I wandered over to the company command post (CP) to hear what the future held for us. Evans was sitting on the edge of his hole eating a C-ration. He looked weary and had a three-day growth of beard, as did we all.

Obie was smiling as usual and offered me a bite from his D-bar.

"What's the scoop?" I asked. "How long are we going to sit around on this hump?"

"Don't get excited, comrade," Obie retorted. "Battalion is coming over to give us a mission. We got a call about 0500 from Simple telling us that him and Graber would be over."

He shook his head in disbelief.

"Can you imagine that dummy calling at 0500? I couldn't find the damn phone in my hole, and I figured every Jap for a mile around heard it buzzing."

"What do you figure they want?" I asked.

"God knows—but we don't have long to wait. There they are."

Graber was evidently exhausted from his hike along the ridges, and Sample was breathing hard too. Evans greeted both of them with the old-boy effusiveness, and then we all sat down in a circle while Graber took a long draw on his canteen.

Sample asked why there was so much firing during the night.

"Got any dead bodies to show for it?" he asked typically, always ready to get in a dig.

Nobody answered him, and the topic was dismissed.

Graber unfolded a yard-square sheet of paper with faint blue markings (there were no printed maps of Guadalcanal).

Graber put a thick forefinger on a line of hachures.

"This is where you are now. This solid blue line is the Matanikau River down at the bottom of this ridge. Regiment sent a small patrol down to the river yesterday about a mile from here. They spotted some Japs carrying supplies and figured they were going to Mount Austen. The 27th made the same kind of report three days ago—before they moved outta here."

He took another pull on his canteen and continued, "We want to put in a blocking position on the river to interfere with their supply parties."

Looking at Evans, he reached over and slapped him on the knee.

"You're elected, old buddy. I figure it will take about a platoon to set up positions on both sides of the river. If anybody tries to go through, shoot 'em. If they try to go around you, chase 'em. Probably you ought to keep one squad in reserve to patrol around your position every so often."

Evans grinned.

"You son of a gun, Colonel, sir; I knew you'd give me a good one."

"There's a war going on, Roger," Sample pointed out apropos of nothing.

Graber looked around as if expecting questions. There were none.

He stood up, put his helmet on, and buckled his pistol belt. Sample folded up the chart.

"Keep us informed," Graber said. "If you get too much traffic down there, I'll have A Company put in another block downriver." They moved out.

Evans plunged his hands into his pockets and hunched his shoulders.

"Well," he said, "let's get at it. Here's the plan. Matlock, we'll use your platoon first. If we have to hold the block for a while, we'll exchange platoons every day. Get your guys together and be sure to take rations and water."

He paused as if mulling over a problem.

"I'm going with Matlock and help him select the position."

He looked at Obie.

"Give me a couple of men to lay a sound-powered line as we go down. As soon as Wayne is set, I'll be back."

He sat down and relaced the magnificent hunting boots he wore. They were custom-made by a Washington state bootmaker and must have cost a fortune.

He looked at me.

"I oughta have something better than a pistol if I'm going down into the jungle."

"I have just the thing," I replied and returned to my position. I unfolded my shelter half and took the Browning submachine gun the supply sergeant had given me on the beach. I wiped it clean of dust, checked the magazine for a full load, and snapped it into position. It was an awesome-looking weapon. I had seen dozens of movies where mobsters and G-men shot it out with Brownings. Obviously when I'd had a chance to get my hands on one, my boyhood ambition was realized.

I hustled back to Evans.

He gave me his teeth-gritting grin.

"That's great," he said, "just great. Where the hell did you get it?"

"From the supply sergeant," I admitted.

"Didn't know we had these. Is it loaded?"

"It will be when you pull back on this knob and take the safety off." I pointed out the button next to the trigger.

He assumed the position of a G-man ready to blast his way through a wall of malefactors.

"That oughta scare the hell out of 'em," I commented.

Matlock, with his platoon trailing behind him, approached us.

"All set?" Evans asked, buckling on his pack.

"All ready, sir," said Matlock, looking both grim and ready—a leftover from his police experience.

We walked along the ridge to a place where it appeared a path down to the river had once been in use.

Evans looked around at all of us. He motioned to the men with the wire reels and SP phone.

"Let's keep a sharp eye out," he said as he started down into the heavy growth and forest that began about twenty yards below the crest. There was a lot of slipping and scrambling on the precipitous path. One man completely lost his footing and rolled uncontrolled into the brush below.

In a minute they had all disappeared into the valley of the Matanikau.

I walked back to my outpost on the ridge. Dunn's people gathered around to get the scoop. I explained about the Japanese using the Matanikau for a supply route and how the 1st Platoon was going to mount a blocking position. I also indicated that we would take their place tomorrow.

Dunn asked, "Are the Japs coming down the Matanikau from Mount Austen the ones using this draw to get to the coast?"

"It looks that way," I replied. "And when they run into that cover block, I expect a lot more of them will be coming up to see us." The meeting broke up and we proceeded to burn some pieces of a ration box to heat a canteen cup of coffee.

And then it happened: sounds of battle from the valley.

I can't tell how long it had been since Evans and his crew had scrambled down that slippery path. It seems that critical events have a way of squashing the time before their occurrence.

But there were shots—from Japanese and U.S. rifles, a quick burst from a submachine gun, more assorted shots, and at least three or four grenade explosions, two of which sounded different from the other two, indicating that the grenades had come from both sides.

I double-timed over to Benson's position where he was yelling into the SP phone. He was red in the face, under his whiskers.

"Those goddamn dummies haven't hooked up a phone to this wire."

He lifted the double strand of light wire and followed it to the path where the platoon had descended. In a moment there was a group gathered at the top of the trail: Obie, Bemish, Begley, and most of my platoon.

The firing had stopped a few minutes earlier.

"Looks like they ran into something," Obie said, looking as grim as I had ever seen him. "Maybe we ought to go down and find out if they need help."

I agreed and yelled to Ferrigan to get his squad together, when Benson hollered, "There's somebody coming up."

We could see two men just emerging from the tree line below. They were running, as much as you could run going almost straight up, and they weren't running toward—they were running away.

As they came closer we could see exhaustion, fear, and panic written on their features. They were dirty with mud, and their clothes were torn where they had snagged them on branches.

Half a dozen men clambered down to help them get to the top. Both were privates. One of them was crying and yelling, "Oh, God—Oh, God." The other man appeared stunned. He looked from one face to another as if we were strangers.

Between gasps for air he said, "They were waiting for us. The dirty bastards were waiting." He gasped again and he was offered a canteen. He was kneeling with his hands on the ground in front of him.

"The captain and the lieutenant are dead."

A noise like a subdued moan emerged from the group that I had never heard before. It was the sound of tragedy.

Obie was shocked. His acquaintance with Evans went back to the stateside days. Their military relationship had never overshadowed their friendship. He walked around in a circle, raging, cursing, crying, banging his fist into his hand.

By now a few more men were spotted struggling up the path. Obie ran down to meet them. After a few words with them he disappeared into the jungle below.

Bemish looked white and shaken. He turned to me.

"What the hell should we do? He's the company commander, and he runs off without telling us what to do." He was talking because he wanted to have an outlet for his emotions, but he didn't want to say anything.

"Mark. . . ." I grabbed him by the arm, hard. "Let's be calm—for the men," I hissed into his ear.

I saw Begley wiping his eyes. He too had known Evans for years, often calling him "Roger."

"Get ahold of battalion on the phone, and tell them we're in trouble. Tell them we have a report that Evans and Matlock and some men are dead."

He trudged away, slowly, his shoulders hunched, one hand rubbing the back of his neck.

After a while—again, time had collapsed—the remainder of the platoon appeared. Two injured men were being helped. One had a white bandage around his leg, the other had been hit in the arm near the shoulder. More men poured off the ridge to help the wounded. The aid man made both of them sit down while he examined their bandages and gave them water.

We finally saw what we were dreading. Four men, dragging on arms and legs, were bringing up a dead man, one of Matlock's men.

Next they brought up Matlock, his strong neck covered with blood and his mouth hanging open with spittle dropping out.

Then I saw another group with a body. I could tell from the magnificent boots that it was Evans. He looked as if he was hunkered down in sleep. He still had on his glasses, steamed up as usual. His jacket was covered with blood; evidently he had taken several rounds in the chest.

We laid the bodies side by side and covered them with shelter halves. Everybody was gathered around the wounded men—there were seven who were shot or hit with grenade fragments.

Obie was driving himself to keep busy: he moved from one wounded man to the next, patting them, comforting, consoling.

The entourage from battalion moved into the area—-Graber, Sample, the surgeon, the chaplain, some stretcher bearers, the supply officer. There was a lot of milling around as the surgeon and his aid men put the more seriously wounded on the stretchers. The walking wounded were accompanied by helpers who supported them on each side.

Graber got hold of Obie, who was still charging around, busying himself with details, putting off to the last moment the dread realization that his close friend and captain was lying a few feet away—dead. Graber and Obie sat down a distance away from the four canvas-covered humps.

"Obie, sit down, cool off, and let's try to find out what in the hell happened down there."

Obie looked at him blankly, then looked around, and slowly but inevitably burst into tears.

Bemish and I gathered the NCOs of Matlock's platoon a distance away from Obie and Graber. In the highly charged emotional atmosphere it was hard to get a clear story; everybody wanted to talk at once, and whoever was talking was loudly interrupted.

I finally got burned up and told everybody to shut up. Since I couldn't think of anything else, I said, "We're going to hear you in order of seniority. You, Jameson, you're the platoon sergeant, you start."

In this way, and in spite of occasional blurting out of details by others, we finally pieced together the tragic events of the morning.

As the group had gone down the trail, it became easier to follow and apparently had been used by natives and Japanese recently because grass and ferns in the path had been tramped down. Matlock sent a few scouts to the point position, and Evans and he followed about five yards back.

When they were only a stone's throw from the river, the scouts raised their hands to signal a halt.

Evans and Matlock closed up, and the scouts pointed to an enemy soldier leaning against a tree on the riverbank.

At that point all the pent-up heroism that fired Evans's soul came bubbling up. From watching a lot of movies in which Errol Flynn, John Wayne, or Victor McLaglen had put the enemy to flight, he had a powerful but mistaken stereotype of the gallant leader who plunges into battle for God and country. Before Matlock could restrain him, Evans jumped to his feet, brandished his submachine gun, and yelled, "All right, you slant-eyed bastard, put your hands up."

Those were his last words. The enemy had heard the patrol as it stumbled and crashed through the heavy brush, and had positioned riflemen on both sides of the trail, with the one man on the riverbank as a decoy.

Evans was hit immediately, and in the short time Evans remained standing Matlock rose to pull him down and was hit in the head.

The scouts and the nearest men began a firefight to cover the withdrawal, and two more men were fatally wounded. Some of the men threw grenades in the direction of the enemy fire and this proved more effective than firing their rifles at sounds. The enemy withdrew, or at least they didn't fire anymore.

The platoon sergeant, Jameson, ensured that the wounded and dead were hauled out and kept men in firing positions until this grisly evacuation had been completed.

We walked back to Graber and Obie, who were surrounded by exhausted, frightened men, still all talking at the same time.

"At ease," I yelled, "let's clam up for a minute."

"The colonel can handle his own meeting," Sample said, holding his chin high as if to reinforce his tenuous authority.

I paid no attention to his yelping.

"Colonel, I think we have the full story from the NCOs that were down there."

Graber looked at me and then at Sample. "OK, OK," he said, "let's hear it."

I brought the NCOs into the circle.

"I'm going to tell the colonel what you told Bemish and me. Don't interrupt. If you have some additions or corrections, you'll have a chance to put them in."

I proceeded to outline the actions of the platoon members from the time they left the ridge until they had all returned with their dead and wounded. When I got the part where Evans jumped up and was killed, you could hear a pin drop.

Graber shook his head and pounded his fist into the ground. "Roger, Roger—you dumb, wonderful bastard—why?"

Then realizing that everyone was watching, he roughly brushed a tear away with the back of his hand and said, "Any of you men got anything to add?"

They looked at each other and muttered, "No, sir."

I had one more comment.

"The platoon sergeant and some of his men did a heroic job in keeping losses down and recovering the dead and wounded. I think they should all get medals for this action."

Graber stood up slowly.

"I think so too. Send the paperwork to battalion."

He turned to go.

"You men have done a damn good job in your first fight. I'm proud of you."

Looking at Obie, he said, "I'm going to send the mortar and artillery people up here. We're going to pound the living bejeezus out of that valley."

The stretcher detail for the dead arrived. As the bodies were placed on the stretchers, so limp and lifeless, men turned away and walked back to their positions. As the stretcher with Evans's body moved away, Obie touched the canvas tenderly, his face contorted with grief.

So much had happened. So much tragedy had been packed

into a few short hours. The impact on all of us was profound and shattering.

I looked at my watch. It was only noon. Now we knew what war was all about.

About an hour later two things happened.

First, the artillery and mortars started bombarding the Matanikau Valley below our position.

Graber, Sample, and the artillery and mortar observers stood, each with a foot on the parapet, staring into the destruction below. The artillery searched along the trace of the river creating terrible havoc with the forest canopy, which exploded as the shells plunged earthward. I doubted that this expenditure of scarce ammunition was doing any good, but we were satisfied imagining how discomported the bastards were who had killed our men.

Second, there was a new mission for the company: we were to occupy the ridge north of us. The 27th had moved a distance to the west, and it was our job to control the high ground to their rear.

Obie had himself under control now and he led the company column into the new position. We were all glad to leave the scene of so much tragedy and sorrow.

I was given a portion of the north-south ridge that was totally barren of vegetation but had a series of well-positioned foxholes. I selected a large hole in the center of our platoon area that had a magnificent view of the battlefield. Below our position the ridge sloped down for a quarter mile to a forested area, and with my field glasses I could see our troops milling around on the edge of the tree line. There were occasional shots, and now and then an artillery concentration plunged into the woods beyond. Again the deafening noise of the tree bursts must have scared the hell out of the enemy, but I doubt that they caused many casualties to the experienced enemy, who dug holes into hillsides where they were safe from anything but a direct hit.

The rest of the afternoon was uneventful. And as evening approached all firing ceased, and for the first time in a week I could sleep during my two-hour breaks. Dunn, as usual, shared my hole and, as usual, he snored some but did less of it, a result I attribute to the nudges he received every time he gave a particularly loud snort.

THE GENERAL

At dawn Sergeant Dunn and I cooked a helmetful of meat and beans and washed it down with hot coffee. We had just completed this chore and were cleaning up our quarters when we spotted a long line of men coming up from the rear and evidently headed for the B Company position.

As the column drew near, there was no doubt as to who was leading it—the 25th Division commander. What impressed me was that he had a shave and a clean uniform and I had neither. I was also impressed and made a little uncomfortable by the fact that he seemed to be moving directly to my hole. And he did.

I stood up and restrained an impulse to salute (we didn't salute on the battlefield). He held out his hand, I shook it, and managed to blurt out, "What can I do for you, sir?"

"You can move over, Lieutenant, because I am going to share your position with you. I see you picked out the best observation on this line."

I hustled Dunn and his gear out of the hole and tried to make as much room for the DC as possible. The rest of the column had closed up and it looked like I had half the division headquarters on the reverse slope of the ridge. I identified the G-3, G-4, the artillery commander, and the signal officer. There were wiremen, a switchboard crew, and part of a security platoon, among others.

Before you could say "Jack Robinson" three EE-8 phones were wired up and placed on the back parapet of the hole.

Without appearing too obvious I threw a few glances at the

distinguished warrior I was hosting. He had had a brilliant career in the military, possessed a steel-trap mind and remarkable courage, and he was a fighter. The rumors I had picked up said he would be chief of staff some day. He was a marked man and on the way up—way up.

He had a strong, wide face, a firm jaw, and a nose that curved down like a ski jump. His eyes were expressive, not cold.

We had been receiving some sporadic sniper fire from a wooded area to the southwest, and it seemed to pick up with all the activity going on around my hole.

The general was busy talking to his operations officer and then switched to an EE-8. The person on the other end obviously was the 27th's commander; he did a lot of listening. During this conversation a sniper round snapped pretty close to our position. The general handed the phone to the operations officer and turned to me.

"Get a machine gun," he said.

I moved out of the hole on the double and got a light machine gun from our weapons platoon, and the gunner followed me with two boxes of ammo. The general pointed to the southwest and said, "Set up the gun to cover that wooded knoll over there." I emplaced the gun on the parapet and pressed down hard on the legs to give it a stable base. The gunner handed me a box of ammo with which I loaded the gun.

The general gently pushed me aside and lumbered down behind the gun. I was going to ask him if he knew how to fire such a weapon—and in the nick of time remembered that he had written the gun's manual.

He looked over the sights and let a few bursts fly into the knoll. I followed the tracers that found their target.

"Did you see that, Lieutenant?"

"Yes, sir."

"Well, every time you hear them snap off a round from that knoll, you spray them with bullets. Get enough ammo."

I said, "Yes, sir," even though I didn't know how much we were going to fire. Or how persistent those damn snipers might be about disrupting business in my position.

He looked at his watch. "We've got about five minutes to go," he said to me. He settled himself into a sitting position and got a few minutes' rest.

I didn't know what was going to happen, but no lieutenant in the army ever had a better opportunity to sit next to a masterful leader and soldier while he conducted a battle.

The artillery officer moved up to our hole while looking at his watch. He raised his hand and yelled, "Now!" and all hell broke loose. The whining and whistling projectiles sped over our heads and crashed into the forest below. Every artillery piece on the island must have been firing, for it seemed to be coming from all directions.

The general was watching with his field glasses. He had ordered a classic preparation: first deliver fire on the rear installations and positions; then shift to the middle, supporting areas; finally, pound the hell out of the front line while the infantry moved forward and lift the fires when the front elements were ready to contact the enemy.

All of this called for good chart data, for knowledge of the enemy positions, and for split-second timing with the infantry. We didn't have much of any of those elements, but the gunners were doing the best they could.

After about ten minutes the fires were lifted and we could hear sounds of small-arms fire, mostly from the north end of the line.

The G-3 was on the phone behind the general talking to somebody. He relayed his information to the general, who looked at his chart. It was obvious he was disturbed. "Where is he now?" the general asked.

There was more talk on the phone, some of which got very salty.

The general grabbed the phone. "Look, Mike, the charts we've got don't match the terrain, so sending coordinates is no good.

"Have you got your walkie-talkie?" (Pause)

"OK. Now tie a handkerchief around your left arm and move into that clearing so I can see you. [Pause] All right, I've got you spotted."

Then followed a list of instructions, including a shift of direction in a more southerly direction and a more concentrated effort in one company sector.

Progress reports were slow coming in, and nothing could be seen of the action in the forest. The sounds of mortars (ours and theirs), grenades, and rifle and machine-gun fire indicated that a battle was in progress, but, as they say, "the issue was in doubt."

Again and again, the general and the artillery officer planned and called down concentrations on the flank and in front of our forces. There was also an intense discussion about the Japanese holding up our progress by being dug into the side of the hills.

The general told the G-3, "Use the bombers with HE [high-explosive armament]. When they are on station, have the artillery drop a smoke shell into the area where we want the bombs." Again a flurry of calls on the phone, and the general telling the troop commander to pull back at least 200 yards to a safer position.

When you're waiting for something it takes forever. I thought it was hours before the navy bombers were on station east of us.

The artillery went sailing over our heads again and in a minute a white column emerged from the forest. The bombers swung out in a wide circle, gaining altitude, and then each in turn went into a steep dive, unloosing a 500-pound bomb and strafing the area with machine-gun fire. The bomb explosions shook the earth and sent visible shock waves in all directions.

Five bombers had pounded the target and then returned to Henderson.

Again progress reports were slow, but from what I could hear the enemy was putting up a furious fight.

The general and the artillery officer held an intense conversation, both pointing to the southwest. The AO [artillery officer] said, "I can't hit that from my positions. And using high-angle [fire] without observation is unsafe."

The general stood up and looked at the staff and idle observers lounging on the slope. He spotted Graber and Sample.

"Graber, get an 81mm mortar over here and bring plenty of ammunition."

Graber and Sample raced back to the weapons platoon and returned about five minutes later with a mortar squad and a party of ammo bearers.

"Who's the squad leader?" he yelled, and a panting young trooper galloped up to our hole.

"Now, young man, put that mortar in right there and then you come up here and get ready to conduct fire."

It usually takes a while to emplace an 81mm, but it took much less time this day as colonels, majors, and captains helped dig a pit, pound stakes, uncase ammunition, and install the sights.

The sergeant came back up to the hole. The general and the artillery officer were measuring distances and angles. The artillery officer gave the sergeant a distance, azimuth, and a request for HE. The sergeant was businesslike, unflappable, and capable. He used his SP phone to talk to his gunner.

The general was using his walkie-talkie. He paused and spoke to the sergeant.

"You will fire on my command, and I will give you the necessary corrections. Ready?"

The sergeant nodded.

The general spoke into the walkie-talkie; he pointed at the sergeant. The sergeant said, "Fire!" into his SP. The loud plop of the 81 was even louder since it was less than ten yards away and was aimed right at us.

Now began a rhythm of war, the commander on the ground reporting where the rounds were falling, the general giving corrections, and the sergeant plopping out rounds.

After about twenty minutes of this, the sergeant turned to the general and said, "Sir, we're going to need more ammunition if we continue to fire at this rate."

The artillery officer signaled to the G-4, who cranked his phone, spent about two minutes explaining in a loud voice about heads that would roll if that ammo wasn't rolling forward "now."

In about ten minutes three jeeps and trailers loaded to the gunwales rattled up to the mortar position, discharged their cargo with a lot of high-ranking brass giving a hand, and rattled away. And about forty minutes after the loud orders by the G-4 we spotted a long, long line of Solomon natives trotting along the trail, each carrying a cloverleaf of mortar shells.

The firing of the mortar, occasionally abetted by artillery concentrations, went on for about two hours.

Evidently progress was being made because the general stood up, clenched his fist, and thrust it upward, shouting, "That's great, great—keep pushing." He let out a great sigh and smiled broadly. He called his staff and pointed to the clearing where he had initially talked to the ground commander.

"We're going down there. Give the headquarters our new position and let's get communications down there on the double."

He looked at me and stuck out his hand, which I shook.

"Thanks for your hospitality," he said.

"Thanks for the chance to watch you in action," I returned.

He patted the sergeant on his helmet. "Good job, soldier."

The sergeant grinned. The general trotted down the hill.

CONTINUATION

During the remainder of the day, the artillery continued to whoosh over our heads, sometimes close in, often at a distance and traversing across the front. We had never witnessed a display of firepower like this on Guadalcanal, and I'm sure the Japanese hadn't incurred such devastating concentrations either.

Too often the engagements with the enemy by the marines and army troops were exercises in infantry fighting infantry. Small arms and mortars were used, and only occasionally were tanks given limited missions in consideration of the limiting factors of the terrain.

But now, for the first time, we had an illustration of the coordinated firepower developed by a division with air support. It was awesome, and it is a tribute to the tenacity of the Japanese soldier that he absorbed this overpowering punishment before his position was irrevocably broken and he moved to the northeast.

INTERMEZZO

For the next few days, we moved from position to position anchoring the division left flank and ensuring that any movement to or from the Gifu would be kept away from the 27th.

The Gifu—a heavily fortified Japanese position on the side of Mount Austen—had been the special object of attention of the 35th Infantry Regiment since our landing on the "Canal." The fighting had been ferocious, and the firepower directed onto the Gifu was shattering. But the enemy troops clung to their position and fought back with skill, courage, and the stimulus of knowing they were doomed if they didn't wear out the 35th.

While a matter of no direct concern to the regiment, the distant sounds of rifle and machine gun-fire told us that night or day, the struggle for that useless piece of real estate was chewing up lives on both sides.

One night my platoon occupied an interesting position on one of the numerous streams that flowed out the central mountain spine and had cut a steep valley on its way to the sea. What was most unusual was a number of caves just above the waterline.

We put a squad into each of the larger caves we could find.

Dunn and I selected the largest cave for his men. As we explored the interior of this natural apartment we found that it had been occupied by enemy soldiers, for there were bundles of materials evidently used to carry rice or something edible, judging by the smell.

Very soon it was dark, and everyone had selected a dry place to bed down. Dunn and I took up a position at the entrance to the cave. We could see the water rushing by, the white bubbles and froth standing out against the blackness of the stream.

During the night the scream of macaws often shattered our peace of mind, but there was no sound that caused us to snap off the safeties on our M1s.

OUR ARMY

This is probably a good place to address a subject that has been neglected up to this point—the role of a National Guard regiment in an active army division.

Over the years between the interwar period of 1918 to 1941, there was little consideration for the Guard by the active U.S. Army. Now, let me try to put this into some perspective.

The National Guard is made up of the militias of all the States. And, as we know, a state militia organization is constitutionally under the command of the state's governor. This organization can be called out for riots, floods, tornadoes, aircraft crashes, and calamities, natural or man-made.

Under federal law, the National Guard can be called into federal service by the president for a national emergency or, when Congress agrees, for war.

After World War I each state was allocated a number of units, which was called a troop list. If the state organized these units, the U.S. Army would provide equipment and pay the troops for drills (forty-eight per year) and summer camp (two weeks). The army's primary contact with state militia was through a group of advisors, with officers for larger units and NCOs for smaller units.

I used to observe a Regular Army NCO counting noses when we lined up for roll call. This enabled him to certify the morning report's accuracy. He also helped with the lesson plans for the drills: he had a complete set of regulations and training publications.

Once a year, in the fall or winter, we would put on our best uniforms, polish our shoes and brass, clean our rifles, and straighten out our campaign hats. After a roll call a gimlet-eyed, awesome Regular Army officer would go through the ranks asking us questions to determine our knowledge of basic military subjects.

After this exercise in stress and tension we were then watched while we engaged in such training as extended-order drills, squad formations, and musketry.

At the close of this "annual federal inspection," we would again be lined up while the emissary from the army gave us the good news and bad news. If the unit was "passed," the unit commander and his lieutenants adjourned to the officers' club to assuage their frazzled nerves with bourbon and branch water.

Our equipment was of World War I vintage. In my company each soldier received a woolen shirt, woolen breeches, woolen puttees, brown shoes, a black tie, and a campaign hat. Every piece of the uniform had been worn by others, often many others, whose service had preceded ours.

At camp time we received a canvas bag, two blankets, a pack, a shelter half with five pins and a pole, a mess kit, a canteen, and a first aid pack. The condition of this equipment gave eloquent testimony to its having been used in the Meuse-Argonne actions and the Rhineland occupation.

Each infantryman carried a 1903 Springfield rifle that had seen plenty of service and even more firing. There were a few M1911 .45-caliber pistols for the officers.

That was it.

Each year we repeated the training schedule of the previous year. We enlisted for three years, so the brass would try to get us to "re-up" by dangling a corporal's rank with its two stripes in front of us. The senior sergeants were those who had three terms under their belt. They weren't smarter or more knowledgeable about military activities—just senior.

Every company had a World War I veteran or two to provide it with leadership that had been seasoned in combat. Most of the junior officers were given original appointments. Lawyers and teachers found it easy to get a commission. Few enlisted men crossed the abyss to the officers' row. Only when we were mobilized in 1940 did we promote junior officers from the ranks in any great numbers. It was my observation (not sour grapes) that many of those promoted benefited from favoritism and close personal relations back home.

My company had an authorized peacetime strength of forty officers and men, but we seldom took that many to camp.

When we were mobilized we lost old officers and NCOs in droves; physical examinations eliminated others. When we arrived in Louisiana we had a couple of squads, a lot of boxes filled with World War I equipment, and the prospect of being brought up to strength. The regiment I joined in Hawaii, and which now found itself in Guadalcanal, had a similar history.

In the eyes of the regulars we were amateurs. They were the professionals. Their officers were the product of West Point, Virginia Military Institute, the infantry and artillery schools, and the Command and General Staff College.

Regular NCOs had years of experience, and had come up the hard way. True, they had furnished cadres to form other units and had absorbed thousands of draftees, but the hard core was made up of professionals with pride in their regular status. And now, a regular division found that a third of its combat power was to be provided by National Guard troops.

I have no idea of how the division commander and his staff viewed the Guard elements. They had almost a year to "whip them into shape" if that was required, to replace senile or ignorant leadership, and imbue them with the élan and commitment of the Regular Army soldiers.

What was obvious on Guadalcanal was the relegation of the Guard regiment to second-class status. It was not involved in the reduction of the Gifu; it did not participate in the division or corps operations against the main enemy positions. Up to this point in this narrative, the regiment had covered flanks and rear areas and had sent a few patrols into the boondocks (to confirm intelligence reports that no one was there).

I was not sure that the division commander wasn't right. I didn't know whether we could fight, and the "old boys" who dominated the officer corps were less than admirable. I was disgusted with most of the field-grade officers I'd had contact with. The NCOs, including my own, were a mixed lot, few exhibiting any leadership, courage, or initiative.

At any rate, as the battle raged to break the Japanese forces west of the Matanikau River, and while the Gifu was turning into a slaughterhouse, we continued to operate on the periphery of the war as an orphan or unwanted relative.

There was perhaps another reason for the reticence of higher headquarters to use the National Guard regiment in a significant way.

For the regulars a war is the equivalent of the Olympics for an athlete. All the years of training, miscellaneous assignments, and slow promotions were to bear fruit when the nation was mobilized. A vast expansion of the army takes place, new divisions are organized, corps and army headquarters are created, and training facilities and service schools undergo enormous expansion.

For the Regular Army officer and NCO promotions are available and frequent. In peacetime, it may have taken a second lieutenant ten years to move to captain. In war, a captain can look forward to a colonelcy and, if he is lucky and brilliant, even a general's star may be in his future.

While war is important to the regular, combat is even more important. The more battles and campaigns participated in, the greater the readiness for promotion. But the most important assignment is *command*. The combat commander who does well is on a fast track. Staff officers can enhance their reputations by doing out-standing work, but most, if not all regular staff officers make it known that they are ready for command at a moment's notice.

Guadalcanal would be no exception to this hunger for combat, command, and promotion. After years of duty in the U.S. continental armies, Panama, and Hawaii—after a decade of irritatingly slow promotions in the peacetime establishment—now at last the regulars were in a fighting war, in a theater on which all eyes in the United States were focused. This was where sergeants, lieutenants, and captains were mentioned in news dispatches and the names of generals and admirals were household words.

Seen from this perspective, I can understand why the regular regiments wanted this war for themselves, this tiny war on a remote island, where the Japanese were being beaten and would be totally overcome in weeks, if not days.

Glory is a limited entity. There is never enough to go around. This is no time to take chances on the uncertain capacity and dubious leadership of an amateur organization. (Besides, there will be other battles, other campaigns before the war ends.) Much can be learned by watching professionals prosecute a war.

The regulars wanted every chance they could get to distinguish themselves, and then off to more responsible assignments, to Washington, perhaps to Europe. Making hay had to be done right away—while the war still lasted. To start fast is to have a good chance of winning the race.

CHAPTER FOUR

At the Beaches

In the remaining weeks of January 1942, we continued to protect flanks, furnish reserves, cover avenues of approach, and patrol areas long since abandoned by the enemy.

We had one short engagement with the enemy in the following days: we launched an attack at a hill with the designation 87F. Here the battalion received a considerable amount of small-arms fire and halted. Artillery fires were called down in some volume, and the attack resumed. Since the enemy had withdrawn, we continued the attack to Hill 87, some 3,000 yards on, and captured our objective. After three weeks in the line, this was our first taste of battle against a vanishing enemy. But once again, the exploitation of this advance was given to the 27th Infantry. After a few more days of occupying hills and practicing flanking maneuvers, the 25th Division swung a large left hook while U.S. forces on the right fixed the enemy in position. As a result, the 27th drove to the sea, captured the village of Kokumbona, and drove the defending enemy to the west.

Since its first move to the Matanikau, our battalion had been attached to the 27th Regiment, placed under corps control, and then reverted to the division.

Meanwhile, units of the 27th pursued the enemy up the coast to the Poha River, where they were relieved after an exhausting series of actions. The 25th Division, less our 161st Infantry, was placed in reserve. The two regular regiments had fought well, attained their objectives, and deserved a rest.

On February 1, 1943, we marched north over hills and through jungles to the sea. It is difficult to express our feelings of joy and satisfaction that coming to the beaches excited in us. After weeks of floundering around in jungle, deep, serrated valleys, and grassy, dried-out hilltops, the view of the sea—open, clean, and uncomplicated—was a blessing. The air was fresh, untainted by heavy growth and rotting wood and leaves. A lot of us walked out into the surf chest-deep, and scrubbed off the dirt and mud of the interior.

The regiment was to occupy the coast from the recently captured Kokumbona to the mouth of the Matanikau, a river most of us, army or marines, would rather forget.

Obie gave me a section of beach that Benson and I divided up with our three squads. The beach was covered with white and gray coral in small round cylinders about the size of Tootsie Rolls. Here it took only a few minutes to scrape out a hole about a foot deep: I didn't think we needed deep holes. We weren't expecting an attack—and if we dug down too deep we would hit sea level and have a hole full of water.

The word, which was very fragmentary, said that the enemy might try a massive landing of troops to retake Henderson Field and unravel all the hard fighting that the army and marines had engaged in. If there were such an attack, nobody knew where it would strike, so the positions we occupied were someone's best guess.

Lieutenants, however, are not prone to think in terms of high strategy, and I was satisfied to have a comparatively safe position, a good supply road at my back, and the Pacific for my front yard. Straight north was Florida Island and Tulagi, the former residence of the high commissioner of the Solomon Islands. Off to the north-west loomed the small, cone-shaped Savo Island, the scene of so much disaster for the U.S. Navy.

As usual, I shared quarters with Dunn. We decided to cook a gourmet special. We placed a handful of rice, a canteen of water, and four salt tablets in a helmet. The helmet was placed on a fire just big enough to heat the contents. After the water came to a boil, the rice was softened and we added a can of meat and beans, which when brought to a simmer was ready for serving. We moved the helmet to a small hole in the coral and unlimbered our spoons. We alternated taking spoons of the stew, munching on hardtack, and washing it all down with hot coffee.

After the repast Dunn scrubbed the helmet with sand and sea-water, the first good scrubbing it had received in three weeks.

I sauntered back to the company CP to see Obie. He and Beg-ley were trying to get the morning report up-to-date, a task that is particularly difficult when, for instance, some of your people are at regimental rear, a few with battalion, several in the hospital, or on detached duty at corps. When you add up all the figures, the total should equal your assigned strength. Begley had performed his ad-dition and was one short of his strength. Now he was going through a dirty, rain-spotted unit roster counting names.

Obie had his grin back.

"Nice down here by the sea, ain't it?" I said, hunkering down on my helmet.

"Right-o. It'd be even nicer if we could stay here a few days."

He paused and tinkered with his pipe that seemed to have some obstruction in the bowl. With the obstruction removed, he blew a cloud of blue smoke.

"When are you going to be a captain?" I asked, jokingly.

"Well, let's not rush things here," he said, affecting a hillbilly drawl.

"However," he went on, "I won't turn it down. Besides, a

captain has been made in 3d Battalion, so a precedent has been set."

"And besides, you're one of the good ol' boys from Everett," I said, boring in on my favorite subject.

I got a punch in the arm for that remark, but it was worth it. Two punches, no. But one punch, definitely.

Begley emitted an animal-like noise.

"I've got it," he said, shaking the roster angrily. "We forgot to count Meagan, that guy we sent to regiment for letter detail." Begley put on his helmet and cartridge belt.

"I'll take this to battalion," he said, brandishing the morning report, and moving off.

Obie tapped out his pipe.

"How're your men taking it?" he asked.

"Oh, I guess we got a little of everything. Lots of jungle rot, a case of dysentery, two guys that are getting yellow eyeballs from atabrine, and a lot of dirty necks and fingernails."

Obie thought about that. Then, "How about the noncoms. Are they coming through?"

"They're a mixed bag. Pop is a jewel; he's a steadying influence on everybody, including me. Dunn is a good man, so is Ferrigan. Meeks is a goof-off and a bellyacher. That figures, because he's one of the good ol' boys."

I escaped a second punch by a quick move of the upper body.

"Another thing about Meeks, he's not in good shape. On the march over here he had to drop out of the column. When he finally dragged in he was exhausted."

Obie nodded. "He's older than the rest of your squad leaders. A week ago he asked when he'd get to be a platoon sergeant, and . . . I couldn't give him an answer."

We both nodded in agreement.

I looked up at the sky. The sun was down behind the point to the west. I stood up.

"I better get back to the troops."

"Don't get too loose tonight. There may still be Japs hiding out in this area."

"Thanks. Thanks a lot," I said, heading for my platoon.

Back in my area, I checked the positions of the squads with Benson. They all looked pretty good.

Benson complained that some of the jeeps using the coast road were traveling too fast. I told him to flag down the cowboys, or throw coral at them.

He grinned through his beard. (He looked like John the Baptist with his black whiskers, sharp nose, and skinny neck.) He went back to his hole, and I returned to mine. Maybe we could get a night's sleep in this position. There was a warm breeze from the sea; the leaves rustled in the trees; a slight surf bubbled up to the coral shore and receded with a sound like a man shaving.

Dunn and I sat looking at the sea. Each was involved with his own thoughts; no conversation was necessary. I happened to be thinking about the navy. I hadn't seen a ship since we had moved from the beach area to Bloody Ridge. This was hard to figure. The waters we were looking at were desired by two of the world's great navies, and at least a half-dozen, bone-jarring naval battles had taken place already. The sea floor around Savo Island was so littered with sunken ships of both U.S. and Japanese registry to earn it the sobriquet, "Ironbottom Sound." Hundreds if not thousands of men were entombed in their ships. A tough way to die, but a much quicker, cleaner way than to be shot in the mud and filth of Guadalcanal and to spend hours of agony before bleeding to death, untended and alone.

As I've said, there wasn't a ship in sight anywhere. It was getting very dark now, and I couldn't have seen one if it was only a mile offshore.

Then I thought I saw a small blink of light from the direction of Savo.

Before I could think another thought, I heard the unmistakable whoosh of an artillery shell (except it wasn't artillery) and, after a two-count, an earthshaking thud and an earsplitting explosion.

Everybody was awake and talking.

Another blink.

"Get down," I yelled. Whoosh, thud, bang. This one sounded closer than the last one.

"I wonder if those bastards are ranging in on us," said Dunn in a strained voice.

Two more blinks. Two deafening explosions, just as close as the last one, but farther east. I doubted that the enemy gunners were shooting at us. Our target was five yards wide and a mile long, with men dispersed in holes ten yards apart. The Japanese must have figured there was a headquarters, a supply dump, or artillery position somewhere in the vicinity.

There was a whistle on the SP phone. It was Obie.

"The word has come down to be on full alert. The Japs may be trying for a landing."

"OK, Obie," I said, noticing two more blinks. The sound of the shells was different from the hissing of our artillery shells. The frequency of the whooshing was slower, and lower in tone. There was only one answer—these were very large shells, the kind that are fired by a cruiser or battleship.

For the next half hour the shelling continued. The point of impact moved farther inland and eastward.

"Sounds like they're shooting garbage cans," Dunn said.

We kept straining our eyes to spot any signs of an invasion. Nothing. At midnight I passed the word down the foxhole line to go two (hours) on, two (hours) off.

At dawn there was still no invasion.

*   *   *

For the next few days, we played a dismal game of stop and go. An alert would come down the chain. Then we would wait. Finally we would proceed west on the beach road for a few hundred yards, then we'd stop, and then we'd start again until we'd covered about a mile. Then we'd dig in for the night.

Nobody would tell us what was going on. Occasionally we would hear the sounds of heavy gunfire to the west, and lots of artillery was going overhead very low—an indication that the front was less than a thousand yards away. (We kept in mind the rivers flowing out of the central mountain core that bisected the beach road every mile or two. The enemy strategy was to delay us at some of these rivers where swamp, heavy vegetation, and confusing terrain favored the defender.)

On the night of February 4, 1943, there was a lot of navy action a few miles up the coast. We could see the flashes in the night sky and the rumble and burst of naval gunfire. As usual we dug in on the beach and, except for the naval action, spent a relatively quiet night.

The next day we sat around all day. We heard no sounds of combat to the west, no artillery fire, and only a few planes from Henderson passed overhead.

It began to dawn on me that the war was not being pressed too vigorously, and that Japanese opposition was considerably less than the fanatic defenses and spirited withdrawals we had experienced inland. I could think of a few scenarios.

1. We had killed off most of the Japanese, and were fighting the remnants of the army that had invaded the island.

2. The enemy was conducting a skillful retrograde movement, and we would soon run into a heavily defended position farther west.

3. The Japanese were slowly retreating as they were being taken off by their navy at night.

Whatever the scenario, we had a hell of a lot of troops on the island, but not many of them pushing west.

At any rate, the next morning the atmosphere changed. Obie and I attended a meeting at battalion where we learned the following. The 147th Infantry that had been leading the attack was being relieved. The 161st would take its place and continue the attack. The new regimental commander (from the 27th) had assumed command. Our Colonel Popper, desperately sick from malaria, was on his way back to the States. And the 1st Battalion would be in reserve.

ACTION

I went back to the platoon, gathered the men around, and gave them the word. In ten minutes we had everybody lined up on the road, and after a short wait the column moved out. It felt good to be doing something. I had a hunch that the end of the war lay somewhere in the west, and the quicker we got over there, the better.

Shortly after the march the scenery changed. The signs of battle were everywhere—equipment, weapons, dead bodies, and the stench of blood and decaying flesh. The tired, decimated troops of the 147th Infantry were lounging on the beach. They waved at us; we waved back. They looked like they had "had the course." And they had.

We went on, moving very slowly. Two battalions were on line, with the 3d Battalion on the left tramping over hills and through heavy forest. It seemed that we stopped every five minutes while the lead battalion waited for the 2d Battalion's troops to come up on line. I could sympathize with them, though. The heat was oppressive; the going was rough. Everybody was tired, most were sick, and it only took a couple of hours to use up all your energy scrambling around in the boondocks.

The end result of all this backing and filling was about 800 yards of advance down the beach. Since we had heard only one minor skirmish during the entire day, it was incredible that we would be going so slowly. It was evident the new regimental commander was not going to set any records in the race down the coast. Perhaps it was the old business, a regular officer suspicious of his National Guard command.

The next day we continued at a frustrating pace. Stop and go. Stop and go. We heard a flicker of firing during the afternoon. We stopped for the day at about 1700 hours. We had covered a little more than a mile. I could rationalize our turtle's progress if there had been lots of rifle fire and supporting artillery concentrations. Absent such activities, we should have been galloping down the coast like Stonewall Jackson.

After dark we had a repetition of the naval activity on February 4: flashes in the sky, the sounds of naval gunfire, aircraft buzzing around—some enemy, some ours.

The action lasted a long time. According to Obie there were reports that the Japanese had evacuated a lot of troops on February 4. If that was so, undoubtedly a lot of soldiers were being picked up to escape our clutches. And that meant that somewhere up the island chain from the Solomons to Tokyo we might again encounter the men who had successfully eluded our snail-like progress.

The next morning we again pushed west, slowly and deliberately. About noon we heard some rifle and Browning automatic rifle (BAR) fire up ahead. After about an hour's halt, we pushed on, this time a little more briskly, and reached Doma Cove, a slight indentation in the coast, where we stopped for the night.

The next morning the 2d Battalion men were called in from the unit's flank mission. They were pooped out, and the regiment had failed to supply them with food. We had been waiting a month to get into the war and now we were doing a hesitant slow march up the coast, and the logistic system had broken down in two days. Maybe the regulars were right.

The good news was that the 1st Battalion was to pass through the 3d Battalion and take over the attack—if it could be called an attack.

At 0700 Obie gave me the best news. My platoon was to be in the lead. Another company would be on the flank, but a lot closer in than the 2d Battalion had been. I got the platoon together, explained the mission, gave Dunn's squad the point position, and started off to the west.

JUNCTURE

The 2d Battalion of the 132d Infantry Regiment/25th Division had landed a group farther north. It was moving in our direction. When our people met that unit, to all intents and purposes our war would be over. I was impatient to get started.

Finally Obie gave me the signal to move out. I sent two scouts forward with orders to stay about 100 yards ahead of the column that Dunn and I were leading. Two men were sent to the flank to keep contact with C Company.

We moved down the road briskly and covered a mile in a half hour. There was a good breeze blowing in from the sea, and the sun was behind us. But, once again, the tail started wagging the dog. Obie double-timed up to me to complain about going too fast for the flank company. This really curdled my milk.

"Damn it, Obie, there's nobody in front of us. If we keep dawdling like this, we'll never meet the 132d."

"I know, I know," he said. "But battalion wants us to protect the flank."

"Why don't they exchange flankers every hour?" I protested. "A Company is back there doing nothin'."

I knew Obie agreed with me. I also knew that battalion was always worried about purity of line. So I did the only thing I could do: push ahead eating up the terrain until they stopped me, which was often. We crossed one river and went on. At the second river the scouts signaled for a halt. Dunn and I raced to them, but before we got there they had fired a clip or two.

"There were a couple of Japs over there." They pointed to a wooded spot about 100 yards up the river. "When we shot at them they took off."

"We'll let the flankers worry about them," I said. "Let's go ahead."

During the afternoon we played more games of stop and go, one time halting for over an hour. Obie came up and told us to eat while the flankers were getting their breath. I called the scouts in.

"Remember to keep a sharp eye out for those guys from the 132d. We don't need a shooting match with our own people."

One scout, a hillbilly named Bell, spit a stream of tobacco juice. "You know what I think, sir? I think the Japs are gone. There may be a few slants running around out there that missed the boat."

I nodded.

"I think you're right. If they'd let me, I'd get this platoon to Cape Esperance by dark, but as usual battalion is trying hard not to win the war."

Finally the signal came to move out. We crossed a river called the Tenamba on the postcard sketch of the coast I had been given. Next stop was a village marked as "Tenaro" about a mile away.

The scouts were doing a good job of heeling and toeing down the road, but again after a half mile the word came to halt. I noticed a group of our soldiers that was marching off the road to stay out of my formation. They looked like brass, and one of them—a tall, gaunt, red-bearded character with a fatigue hat (no helmet)—seemed very interested in what was going on, but said nothing to me. Again we moved out; it was 1600 hours.

We had moved briskly for about a mile, when the scouts signaled a halt. Dunn and I double-timed to them. About 200 yards up the coast I could see a spread-out column of soldiers. At that distance it was hard to tell what they were, but the enemy didn't march in the open.

We closed the gap, and at about 100 yards we yelled at each

other. I walked ahead to shake hands with the lieutenant from the 132d Infantry.

"I guess this is it," I said, grinning.

"Damn glad to meet you folks," he said, also grinning.

Suddenly we were surrounded by a mob, army and navy brass, photographers, Graber, Sample, et al. Obie was jubilant. He shook my hand and danced around. When he got quiet he pointed at the guy with the red beard, the red bandana, and the fatigue hat.

"That's the new regimental commander."

I noticed that that guy was shaking hands with the assorted brass and gesticulating with his right hand as if chopping wood.

He didn't say anything to me, although he had paralleled my advance for two hours.

February 9, and I didn't care. It was 1625 hours. The war on Guadalcanal was over officially, and my platoon had been in on the kill.

INTERLUDE

After a half hour of backslapping, picture taking, and congratulations, the brass disappeared, ostensibly to inform the world that the enemy had been stopped, the tide turned, and a beginning made on the long road to Tokyo.

A runner came over to me to tell me that Obie wanted me. I told Benson to gather the platoon together in a shady spot and relax. Obie and Bemish were waiting for me.

"The brass want us to establish a beach defense," he said pointing at the blue-inked chart we used for a map. "The battalion will occupy the beach from the Tenamba to the Aruligo River. We'll have the left flank and occupy about 500 yards of frontage. You," he said pointing at me, "will take the left flank, Bemish in the middle, the other platoon on the right. Battalion is going down there now and they will have road guides out. I'm going there now and I will post some of the headquarters people to mark the platoon flanks. Move out in about ten minutes."

He stood up.

"I want to say again what a hell of a job this outfit did today. We'll have a place in the history books for what we accomplished. I love you guys."

We nodded without speaking. There wasn't much to say.

I went back and gathered up the platoon. I explained what our new mission was. One guy asked who we were defending against, since the Japanese had spent the past week in a persistent and aggressive action to get their troops the hell out of here.

I had to agree that the same thought had occurred to me, but maybe higher headquarters knew something we didn't know. I didn't say it out loud, but I was sure headquarters didn't know a damn thing.

It was getting dark before we had marched back to the Tenamba River, selected squad positions, and dug in for the night. Benson and I shared a hole in the middle of the line. Normally a platoon leader and his sergeant stay apart, on the march, in an attack, or in a defensive position. This avoids the probability of their both being killed or wounded by the same blast or burst of gunfire. However, I felt that there was little danger in this beach position— and we had a lot of talking to do.

We mixed up a batch of Canal stew and spent most of an hour in finishing it off.

Then we crisscrossed the past and present, discussing everything from the time I first met him at the Kaneoke racetrack, through the loss of Captain Evans, to the race up the coast to close the pincers on the enemy. As would be expected, we had a bitching session that covered the following:

- The lack of information on what we were doing, or were supposed to do, from Bloody Ridge to Tenaro.

- The failure of logistics to provide enough water to the troops. Sure it had to be hand-carried, but there were hundreds of guys in the rear areas, including artillerymen and engineers, who could have been utilized.

- The lack of maps or aerial photos.

- No jungle boots or uniforms.

- The lack of hot meals and fruit juices (they were there in the rear).

- The side effects of atabrine (malaria medicine)—yellow eyeballs.

We felt better after this healthy ventilating of our gripes. Some of the men came over from adjacent holes and added a lot more items to our list. It's too bad that we didn't have a secretary to take notes, and mail a letter to Washington. The people there needed to know that fighting in the South Pacific was grossly different from scrabbling around the red hills of Fort Benning.

On the plus side there was the M1 rifle. It was the best thing that had ever happened to an infantryman. No matter how dirty it was, or how much sand had penetrated the mechanism, it always fired. And the .30-caliber slug would go through a tree and kill a man on the other side.

But the rest of our equipment was poorly designed and never intended for a theater of operations where the heat was in the nineties, the humidity was always high, rain fell twice a day, and there was no way to dry out.

Benson and I had a good night's sleep. When the sun came up we washed in the surf, although the salt in the water left you sticky and burning if you had any sores or scratches, of which we had plenty.

After polishing off a breakfast of corned beef hash, hardtack, and coffee, Benson and I strolled over to see Obie. He had a message from battalion indicating that we were to improve beach defenses, do some patrolling, salvage Japanese matériel, recover telephone wire, and dispose of the dead—ours and theirs.

Nobody seemed particularly talkative, so Benson and I returned to our position. We gathered the squad leaders and gave them the information. After some discussion, we decided to do the following:

- Deepen our foxholes and strengthen them with logs and branches if any could be found.

- Send Meeks and six men on a patrol up the Tenamba for a mile, where they were to cross the river and come back on the other side.

- Have Dunn and his people look for Japanese matériel south of our position.

- Not recover telephone wire, since we had none to recover.

And, thank God, we had no dead to dispose of.

For the next few days we repeated this plan. We saw no enemy soldiers, found no matériel, and deepened our holes. By now, they were so deep we could stand up in them and just see over the parapet. We slept on the beach next to our holes to avoid spending a night cramped up.

NEW COMMANDER

On the second day of our occupation the new regimental commander, Colonel Weston, dropped in for an inspection. He still had the fatigue hat, the bandana, and the red beard.

We shook hands, and I explained my mission while he looked at the ground in front of his shoes, his hands stuck into his belt.

"Let's troop the line," he said. We walked to the river to start the tour.

"Have your patrols turned up anything?" he asked.

"No, sir. Not even a sign of a bivouac."

We walked along looking at the holes. He noticed a BAR lying on a shelter half.

"Is this a BAR position?"

"Yes, sir."

He jumped into the hole

"It doesn't have a good field of fire. It should be farther forward."

I said, "Yes, sir." But if I were to move it, the tide would give the men in the position wet feet unless the hole was only one foot deep.

When he had finished his inspection he was met by Graber, to whom he explained his desires.

"Carry on," Weston then said.

Not one cordial word had passed between us. It occurred to me that he wanted to establish a reputation as a hard-boiled, no-nonsense commander. I was not impressed; this first meeting left me with a bad taste in my mouth. I had come to see the regular officers as skilled professionals, particularly after my foxhole sharing with the general. But this guy was taking himself too seriously, or his suspicion of the Guard was so intense that any appearance of cordiality would, according to his bias, be seen as weakness.

COMMAND INCIDENT

While we were spending time improving a beach position that we abandoned after three days, an event unfolded that soon had notoriety throughout the division, and was debated with great heat but less light.

Somebody at some level of authority decided to determine

whether any enemy forces were in the area of Visale, a Catholic mission station.

The regimental commander, feeling that the rear-echelon boys had had it easy for the previous month, reached into the S-4 section for an officer to carry out this mission. The lucky individual was a prematurely gray captain, an old boy who found the stream of promotion hard to get into.

At any rate he was provided a few native guides, a couple of mules that the marines had left behind, and six soldiers. His course was indicated on a map—a course that would take him through some heavy country before reaching the coast.

He set off with good heart, which didn't last long. The terrain was rugged. The "guides," who spoke only the most basic English, actually a local pidgin, did a lot of pointing and smiling but were obviously frequently confused.

The progress was extremely slow. The mules were difficult to control and often lost their footing and required the services of the entire patrol to set them upright.

After two days they arrived at a high bluff overlooking the sea. The guides pointed to the village far below and with great shaking of heads intoned, "V'sale, V'sale."

A few hours were spent reconnoitering for a trail down to the beach, but without success. The captain and his men observed the village until the sun went down without spotting any sign of life.

All night long, one or the other members of the patrol watched the village for lights or fires, of which there were none. At dawn the captain held a powwow. Everyone agreed there was no sign of life at Visale and that nothing further would be gained by staying longer.

And so the long trip back was carried out with even greater difficulty than the move to Visale. The captain was showing extreme fatigue and exhaustion; on the second day, the patrol stopped every thirty minutes to let him recover enough stamina to last to the next break. His uniform was covered with sweat, his face was red, and he blinked excessively because of the perspiration running into his eyes.

At last, after an agonizing eternity of fatigue the captain entered the headquarters area. All members of the party were exhausted by the heat and the strain they had undergone. The captain sought a chair where he could pour a canteen of water over his head, and then he sagged forward with his head almost between his knees.

A few minutes later he was requested to report to Colonel Weston. He buttoned his shirt, combed his hair, put on his helmet, and went to his meeting.

The colonel had a very severe look on his face.

"How is it that you didn't report to me when you returned?"

Without waiting for an answer he then said, "I would like to hear your report now."

The captain recited the story of the mission and its findings.

The colonel was exasperated. Pounding his fist in his hand, and almost choking on his words, he said, "You mean that you didn't actually go into the village as I ordered you to?"

"No, sir, we watched the village for over twelve hours and saw no signs of occupation."

Weston was deeply agitated.

"You didn't do what I told you to do. That's a direct violation of orders, do you agree?"

"No, sir, I don't agree."

Weston paced back and forth with his hands clenched behind him.

"Well, Captain, whether you agree or not, you haven't finished your job."

He called for the S-4. "The captain has a mission to complete. Get him new guides and a new patrol. He's going back to Visale."

The captain was shocked; so was his superior.

Within an hour, the captain was retracing his steps to a totally unimportant beach village of no conceivable tactical importance.

Five days later he returned to the headquarters, worn out and deathly sick. His report was accepted by Colonel Weston without comment.

In a week the captain was flown out to Noumea for recuperation and then returned to the States.

The colonel had made his point. But at what a cost.

CHAPTER FIVE

Closer Acquaintance

THE SOLDIERS

During the time we had been mucking about in the hills and the valleys, personal hygiene had gone to hell in a handbasket. There was no water—not even a drop—for washing. What water there was needed careful consideration because no one knew when we would get any more.

The one relief from this dirty state of affairs was rainfall. Every afternoon at about 1600, a convectional storm formed over the island and it would rain furiously for fifteen minutes. The same thing would occur sometime after midnight, but the rain was gentler and lasted longer.

At such times we rubbed our heads, faces, and hands to get off as much dirt as possible. This was some help, but our greatest need was a change of clothes, particularly underwear and socks. Alas, whoever had planned this expedition didn't consider such sanitary measures feasible—or even necessary.

I often looked inside my T-shirt and found it was covered with tiny balls of dirt that had rubbed off my chest. In the skin folds of my armpits were black lines of dirt that resisted being rubbed out. And of course we had no soap to wash hands, faces, or socks. (Without water, carrying soap was idiotic anyway.)

It was interesting to see how little we could survive on. In our packs we carried a shelter half (no raincoat); half a mess kit—the part with the handle; a canteen that nested in a canteen cup; a cartridge belt; a helmet; a rifle; and the clothes we were standing in.

Of course, if we had no water for washing we had no water for shaving, so everyone sprouted a beard. It is amazing how nature has diversified beards among humankind. Some men had only some scraggly hairs, some had heavy chin whiskers but no sideburns, while others showed the exact opposite. I was one of several who developed a full, luxurious beard, which had the tendency to attract dirt that settled in the facial pores like black measles.

I always noticed that bearded men were forever fiddling with their chin growth. Stroking, pulling, twisting, and scratching were popular. I subscribed to the latter school. As soon as the sun was up and we began to sweat, the beard would itch from dirt and perspiration. Pimples emerged readily in such an environment, but there was little to do with them.

All of this recital is prologue to the fact that while we were near a river—the Tenamba—I saw fit to take off all my clothes, get the dirt out of all the creases in my body, and shave with a safety razor borrowed from a regimental wireman. Getting the whiskers off was tough work. No soap was yet available, the blade was dull, and I cut myself about five times. It was not a close shave, but it was an improvement.

I also scrubbed my socks, which in spite of vigorous rubbing and slapping on some rocks remained dark gray in color, but they did smell better.

It was apparent that not many of the platoon members were to follow my example of shaving. Benson was not about to give up his dignified appearance of John the Baptist. One or two of the men shaved a little, but retaining Vandykes that reminded me of the painting "Cavalier" by Frans Hals. And Benson gave me the word that night: some of the men were grumbling that I looked like a young punk, not old enough to lead a platoon.

I just put that complaint in my file of other burdens.

*   *   *

On February 13, 1943, we were notified that the regiment was ordered to move to Koli Point to establish a beach defense there. We were to be picked up on February 14 at Doma Cove.

About 1600, Obie told me the regiment was moving east and that my platoon would bring up the rear. I gathered my troops together and, after the usual waiting and milling around, we moved out.

It was almost 2000 hours and getting dark when we moved into a company assembly area at Doma Cove. After the men had settled down, Obie and I walked over to battalion headquarters where most of the officers were gathered. Everyone was in a good mood, including Graber, who looked awful. He had been having bouts of fever, jungle rot, and jaundice, which accounted for my not having seen him for almost three weeks.

We all had a lot of sea stories to exchange and a lot of gripes to ventilate. This kept us busy for hours. It was well past midnight when Obie and I arrived back at the company area. Benson and Begley were still up shooting the bull. Obie and I stretched out on the ground next to our two ponchos and cocked off immediately.

At dawn, I aroused the platoon and encouraged everyone to make coffee since it was not known when we would have another chance to. I always wonder how the miserable-looking, sleepy-eyed creatures that wake up in the early morn ever turn into soldiers in less than thirty minutes. But they do.

At 0800, February 14, the LCTs (landing craft, tank) arrived, each of which took on board a couple of companies—mainly because our strength had been so reduced. It was pleasant bounding around on the sea and watching the coast go by where so much blood had been spilled. It all looked very innocent now, but there was still a gloomy and foreboding appearance to this island—an appearance that in my view was without parallel in the Pacific. By what quirk of fate this ugly, rugged, dark island had become the collision point for the armies and navies of the United States and Japan is hard to fathom.

After about four hours we landed at Koli Point. After a half hour of confusion, we marched some distance east and then inland to an open area where, of all things, our mess tent had been erected and the cooks were preparing a meal. If we'd had any illusions that our taste buds were to be given a gourmet treat, we were disappointed. We had fried Spam, fried dehydrated potatoes, and coffee. At least the coffee was good.

After lunch Obie took all the officers and sergeants to the beach. Each platoon was to establish observation posts (OPs) and select and prepare squad positions, but only the OPs were to be occupied around the clock. I got together with Benson and set up a roster for OP duty. He still looked at me kind of funny since I had shaved the beard off; but he didn't say anything, and I didn't either.

The next day we found that the mission of beach defense also included facilitating the flow of gasoline to the fighters, reconnaissance planes, and bombers at Henderson Field. The planes were doing their best to keep us free from any surprise air or sea attacks by the Nipponese, but in so doing they used up tremendous amounts of gas and lubricants, and that meant that the barrels on the supply ships had to get to shore.

It worked this way. The barrels were loaded into LCTs by lowering netloads of these containers into the bouncing open holds of these ships. An LCT usually grounded fifty yards or more away from the shore; its front ramp was dropped and the barrels were rolled into the sea. It was the job of the shore party—a few navy types and a lot of soldiers—to wade out and coax the barrels to the shore and then roll them inland to where another crew got them up on trucks for their journey to Henderson.

Each day a couple of companies were assigned this duty, which involved eight hours of struggling in the surf, shoving balky barrels when one's toes barely touched the sand bottom, and then muscling them across the beach.

The second time B Company had this duty, something occurred to brighten our day and give new meaning to the word *propaganda*.

After we had started our task of barrel retrieval, we noticed a lot of personnel (marines) down the beach. We noticed, too, that there were cameramen in the party and that preparations were being made to film something for posterity. After about a half hour we noticed about five LCTs moving flat-out to the beach. They then ground to a halt on the sandbar, the ramps came down, and well-equipped, well-shaven combat troops came splashing ashore and dropped into firing positions at the top of the beach.

Evidently this was a successful "take," since the entire party waded out to the LCTs and returned to their mother ship. Thus was recorded the "initial" landing of the U.S. Marines on Guadalcanal.

After a few days of alternately lying around and muscling oil barrels, Obie announced that we had been given a new mission. The 25th Division headquarters was still concerned about groups of Japanese that might still be on the island. In particular, HQ wanted an eye kept on the north-south trails that crossed the island to determine whether any enemy soldiers who might have fled inland during the war would be traveling north to find an escape route. It was thought that such enemy soldiers, if any, would not know that their own organized resistance had ceased and that most of their own troops had been evacuated up "the Slot," past Savo Island.

A north-south trail followed the Metapona River before striking off into the central mountain chain. A few miles up the river was an abandoned settlement called Laycock's Store. This would be a good place to monitor any traffic on the trail, and division wanted a platoon stationed there to block any movement—if there was any. Obie brought the matter up while we were having supper. Then he looked around for a volunteer, but in particular he looked at Bemish.

Mark was quick to get the implication of Obie's look and got mad.

"After busting our fannies for a month, I'm in no mood to volunteer for another tour in the boondocks. If you want me to go, you'll have to tell me."

"That won't be necessary," I said. "I can think of a lot of things that are better than muscling barrels. I don't think there are ten Japs left on this island, and all this beach defense is crap because I don't think the enemy is going to come back here. He has a hundred islands up the Slot where he can sit and wait for us to play the Guadalcanal game all over again."

Obie reached for an EE-8 and called battalion. When he had finished he indicated that the outpost was to be occupied before dark, that trucks would be available to haul us there, and that they would arrive in the company area in ten minutes with a guide.

I spotted Benson and told him to assemble the platoon because we were moving out.

Sure enough a two-and-a-half-ton truck and two jeeps rolled in, and a lieutenant from division indicated he would take us to our destination. Obie came over, clapped me on the back, and thanked me for taking the mission. "As soon as they are through feeding," he said, "I'll send a cook and a stove over so you can have hot meals too."

I thanked him and climbed into the lead jeep, and the convoy moved out.

We drove over to the beach road, and then followed it for about five miles until we came to the Metapona River. Then we followed a bumpy road inland for at least a couple of miles until we came to a clearing about 300 yards in diameter.

The remains of Laycock's Store were two huts, one about twice as large as the other, with the walls missing and only the roofs intact.

The men scrambled out of the vehicles and passed the usual GI comments on the scenic beauties of the South Pacific.

Benson looked the place over and came up with a recommendation: "Let's leave the small shack for the kitchen and bunk the men in the large one."

I nodded assent, and soon everybody was foraging around in the big hut looking for a level piece of ground to sleep on. Fortunately, we now had our barracks bags with us and could put up our mosquito bars. This was necessary because the anopheles mosquitoes were thick in the lowlands and along rivers where occasional stagnant pools bred them by the millions.

Just before dark a truck arrived with our cook, a cabinet stove, pots and pans, and gasoline and water cans. Everybody pitched in to unload the truck while the cook decided where everything should be placed in his kitchen without walls.

We dug foxholes all around the big hut just in case. Benson saw to it that a latrine was dug, marked with toilet paper, and fitted with a shovel. Then everyone was told where it was. Nothing is more agonizing when you gotta go than to stumble around in the dark looking for the hole.

The night was very warm, the temperature seldom varying more than ten degrees between noon and midnight. The sky was clear and the stars were out in force. As I settled down for the night, I mused on the man, Laycock, who came out from Australia to operate a store in a godforsaken place like this on an obscure island in the South Pacific.

THE FIELD

The Solomon Islands were first discovered in 1568 by a Spaniard, one Captain Mendana. Twenty years later he tried to find them again and failed. Dutch and French sailors saw them in subsequent years, but so faulty was their navigation that exact locations were not determined. And it was to be more than 200 years before the charts showed the exact location of the Solomons.

Traders and their slaves visited the islands in the 1830s and provoked such hostility toward whites among the natives that many innocent whites, including missionaries, were slaughtered.

In 1893 the British established a protectorate over some of the islands and plantations were started. Copra, the dried meat of the coconut, was in great demand, particularly for manufacturing soap. And since the coconut palm grows readily in the coastal soils of the islands and native labor was cheap, it didn't take long for enterprising colonials from Australia to get into the copra business. Still, the islands were not attractive to Europeans, and probably no more than five hundred were ever settled on them at any one time.

The natives, dark Melanesians, probably never numbered more than 100,000. These were very primitive folk, speaking scores of local dialects, and, except for those who worked on the plantations gathering and shelling coconuts, they lived in their village, building good, sturdy houses and tending their vegetable gardens as they had for centuries.

The four influences from the outside—Chinese traders, the British government and its constabulary, plantation owners, and missionaries—were all involved with these people, and for close to fifty years there was little or no change in the pattern of life that had been established in the 1890s.

We knew absolutely nothing about the trader Laycock and what sort of life he must have lived and the grinding loneliness he must have experienced on the stark edge of civilization. Benson and I even tried to figure out whether he had given up on his jungle store before the Japanese came. It certainly looked dilapidated enough to warrant a guess that it had been abandoned for some time.

We spent several weeks at Laycock's Store, and only a few events are worth mentioning. First and foremost, we had a visit from the general and a few staff officers. He was cordial as usual, but then got right down to business.

"The tendency for troops just out of combat to let down and get sloppy is something we have to work on," he said. "Starting today, you must begin bearing down and reestablish discipline. I want everybody to shave—every day. Your men must wear the uniform—properly. The sun is too powerful for men to run around without jackets. They can develop skin infections from peeling skin.

"We don't have any information about Japanese remaining on the island, but that shouldn't keep you from sending off patrols every day, in different directions. That will give them something to do and impress them with our mission."

We walked over to the Metapona.

"At least you have fresh water to wash in. But don't let your men drink it without the purifying tablets."

He walked back to his jeep.

"We've got a tough job to hold the division together without any decent recreation or living quarters. I know you'll keep your men on their toes."

I thanked him for his advice, and waved as his entourage headed for the beach.

Almost every night the enemy sent an old Nakajima aircraft down to harass us. It was affectionately called "Washing Machine Charlie." His usual procedure was to fiddle around and cause an air alert around Henderson: the searchlights would be turned on, and their long rays would sweep back and forth looking for Charlie. On occasion, the antiaircraft guns would go off and we could see the flashes in the air, and later hear the "bang" as they flung their shrapnel about the sky fruitlessly.

One night we heard a lot of explosions and could see the sky light up in the direction of Henderson Field. Evidently Charlie had chucked his bomb right into an ammunition dump. The explosions lasted for hours, and we thought of the thousands of hours of sweat that had gone into unloading that ammunition, all for naught.

We were not to be spared, however. The next night the lights went on and the ack-ack banged away, but, strangely, the sound of Charlie's engine seemed to be getting louder.

The sound was definitely increasing—as if he were coming right at us. Then, to our surprise and dismay, we heard the whine of a falling bomb followed by a bright flash and a tremendous explosion. Our reflexes were good, and when we had heard the bomb's whine we hit the ground. Fortunately the bomb landed about 150 yards away and no one was hurt, but some of the bomb fragments hit our two huts and necessitated some repairs.

After checking for casualties we tried to get our radio to work. This was a peculiar device that looked like a broom handle with a box in the middle of it. After a lot of knob twisting and yelling of call signs we finally raised the regimental station; after a number of fade-outs and repetitions, we were sure regiment understood that we had been bombed but with no casualties.

I had told the supply detail that visited us daily to send me some demolitions, and after a day or two a jeep arrived with an engineer sergeant who brought me a box of dynamite, some blasting caps, and detonating cord. He gave me a quick course of instruction, particularly about handling the dynamite.

That afternoon we waded in the Metapona looking for deep holes. A half-stick of dynamite usually resulted in getting a couple of fish, and in an hour we had enough for supper. Our cook was delighted to have something other than Spam to fry, and the men thought the change was great.

Obie came out to visit us quite often, and I kept bugging him about getting a jeep for our use. Sometime during our second week at Laycock's Store we saw two jeeps coming up the trail, one of which was ours. Of course we were delighted, even if it did look a little worse for wear.

That afternoon Benson and I drove to the beach and noticed a tremendous amount of activity: shore parties, LCTs coming and going, trucks hauling supplies. We followed the trucks to their destination and found that the 37th Division was establishing a supply dump. Benson and I discussed this in some detail, particularly with our cook, who particularly wanted flour and baking powder. Just before dark Benson, the cook, and I drove to the supply dump. I had pinned my gold bar on my collar and, as we approached the GI at the entrance to the dump, we slowed down so that he could see I was an officer. Salutes were exchanged. Five minutes later we drove out with six bags of flour, two bags of sugar, and a case of baking powder.

After returning to camp I got on the radio and asked the S-4 what he would trade for three bags of flour and a bag of sugar. He promised some fruit juice and assorted canned goods. True to his word, the next morning a truck arrived and we exchanged goods. Nobody asked any questions, and we didn't give any answers; but we had pancakes every morning for breakfast for a week. After our two weeks in the splendid isolation of Laycock's Store, Bemish and his platoon came out to relieve us. Our return to the company area was without incident. We went back to the task of rolling barrels on odd days.

Now and then there was an air alert, the ships in the channel would up anchor and flee to the west, and everything that would fly would scramble out of Henderson. Sometimes the alerts were false, but often enough flights of enemy planes came over and the sky was filled with dogfights. In these aerial combats planes on both sides were lost, trailing smoke and fire until they crashed into the sea. Judging by the size and shape of the falling planes, many more enemy planes came a cropper from the enemy side.

We enjoyed the dogfights. They were the only diversion on an island without a single theater, post exchange (PX), USO-sponsored relaxation or entertainment, Red Cross unit, or, particularly, one white woman (the only relief from this state occurring when Eleanor Roosevelt stopped over for a few hours on her tour of the South Pacific).

With such a monotonous routine the weeks passed slowly—but

relief was on the way. My platoon was selected for outpost duty down the coast to the east.

We loaded our gear into an LCT and bounced along until we reached the mouth of the Berande River. About 100 yards up the river we debarked from the LCT.

This location had been occupied by another military unit, but which one we didn't find out. It had left behind several squad tents, cots, and a nine-by-nine-foot officers' tent. The outpost had once supported a church group. There was a building only partly standing that we used for our kitchen. There was no other indication that anyone had ever lived there.

Someone had tried to bridge the Berande by lashing empty gas drums together and putting planking on top of them. This rig had evidently been operational for a while, as the ruts in the trails leading to and away from it testified. But now it was broken. Planking was missing, some of the barrels became partly untied, and the whole structure had a large curve in it. We could use it to cross the river on foot, but its use as a jeep bridge was terminated, at least temporarily.

The next day I was visited by an intelligence officer from division who brought along a strange visitor. I was introduced to Sam, a husky, dark brown, fuzzy-haired Solomon Islander, who had been a member of the constabulary and had acted as a guide to the Lt. Col. Evans Carlson and his Raiders.

The officer asked me if I would like to have Sam for a guide. His pay was one shilling (one shilling as Sam would say it, holding up one forefinger), paid daily. I told the officer to bring me some shillings and other trading goods. He gave me enough shillings to last a week, and boarded his LCT to return to base.

Sam proceeded to walk around the camp and meet the soldiers. He spent a lot of time in the kitchen where the cooks gave him plenty of handouts. He had some equipment with him, a pack, some shelter halves, a canteen, and mess gear.

He put up a pup tent next to mine and, when I went to bed, he followed suit. He was usually up before I was, and often brought me the first cup of coffee from the kitchen.

He knew a little, very little English, but a great deal of pidgin. I had studied a manual of pidgin on the long sea trip from Hawaii, and some of it was useful, but the rest of the time we used gestures, facial expressions, and a lot of pointing at things.

I found out that he had learned to operate and maintain an M1 rifle, so I gave him mine. This pleased him no end, and he cleaned it daily and rubbed the stock to a mirror-like finish.

For security we used a walking guard who was relieved every two hours. He never saw any Japanese, but there were some mules (formerly belonging to the marines) running wild that scared the bejeezus out of a number of guards. We also had some cattle that ran around but never came too close to our camp. They had been brought in by the plantation owner to keep the grass down between rows of palm trees.

One evening I noticed a great deal of agitated water at the mouth of the river. A group of us walked over to investigate and determined that the fuss was a school of fish that were feeding on the nutrients that flowed from the interior. We tossed a hand grenade into the boiling water, and after a muffled explosion a few fish floated up to be retrieved by a couple of men.

Ferrigan, who had spent his life on the Pacific coast, identified them as a type of tuna. I asked Sam, "Good to eat?" "Good, good," he said and took charge of getting the catch to the kitchen.

We soon settled into a routine with a few notable events that I shall detail.

NEIGHBORS

There was a native village some distance inland, whose inhabitants came down to see who the new visitors were. The villagers looked skinny and poorly fed; some were suffering from a variety of sores and skin lesions. The women could hardly be classified as South Seas beauties, and there was no problem in restraining the men from making acquaintances with the female population.

The supply boat came out as promised and brought a few cases of canned goods, particularly salmon and tuna for trading goods. Sam took charge of the bartering of native vegetables and fruits for canned goods. We also used the natives for a different purpose: as soon as our TNT blocks had been detonated in the river to catch fish, I would signal the natives to go in and get them. This was because we'd found—to our surprise—that most fish stunned this way sink.

The natives would dive down and come up with a fish in each hand and bring them to a pile on the bank. When all had been gathered, they sorted out good and bad, as Sam explained to me. Sam picked out enough for our supper and then told some of the men to clean them for us. In a minute or less a pile of filets filled the cook's pan, while the natives strung the remaining fish on poles and returned to their village.

It was strange to learn that the natives loved fish but had developed no technique for catching them. At any rate, we found that the sound of an exploding TNT block attracted a few natives (and there were always some nearby, but we couldn't see them) who were willing to do the diving and cleaning in exchange for a share of the catch.

The Berande River marked the eastern boundary of a coconut plantation that extended westward about a mile. In the middle of the plantation stood the wreckage of the plantation owner's house. It was built in the conventional colonial style, elevated on posts about five feet above the ground with a porch that extended the full length of the house. There were four rooms on each side of the house, with an open hallway from front to back in the middle. A small shack in the rear had been used for cooking.

The house had been shattered by the Japanese in their usual style of destroying anything foreign. A few broken chairs remained; all other furniture probably had been used for firewood. Volumes in what had been the owner's library were scattered around what must have been an office, but a few books remained that hadn't been burned, ravaged by chewing animals, or rotted by rain and humidity. I gathered these pitiful remnants of a settled but lonely life and took them back to camp. There were books about coconuts, some books about Australia and New Zealand, and a novel or two I had never heard of.

I was particularly intrigued by the coconut books, from which I learned that there were many species of palms and that they could incur hundreds of diseases from the roots to the topmost fronds. All the diseases were the very dickens to get rid of, and stricken trees required constant and expert care to cure them.

What a remote and harsh climate to be in and squeeze out a living from copra! The Chinese traders who bought some of the crop were noted for their sharp dealing, and I doubt that year's end saw much money left for the niceties of life.

Sam told me of a woman who lived back in the bush who was half-white and half-native and who spoke good English. I thought that she deserved a visit, so Sam, my two scouts, and I decided to go up there. Sam packed half a barracks bag with some of our trading canned goods and a lot of C-rations that no one was eating.

We moved west along the beach and then inland on a narrow trail, finally reaching a small clearing with a small garden, a neat native hut, and a little smoke emerging from a hole in the roof—an indication someone was home.

Sam yelled a few salutations as soon as we entered the clearing, and then he entered the hut to soon emerge with a small, middle-aged woman. She was a bit unkempt, but she had on a dress rather than the native grass skirt. Her color was midway between the native dark brown and Caucasian white.

I approached her, held out my hand, and asked her if she was well. She replied in reasonably good English that she had some trouble with her eyes and that her stomach had been acting up.

I introduced my scouts, and she was evidently delighted with so much attention. She invited us into her hut, which contained a military cot (a gift from the marines), a table, two chairs, an iron pot that held a small fire, some kettles and dishes, and a hand-cranked phonograph with some very old records. Because the chairs were so fragile we sat on the ground, but insisted that she sit in a chair.

We had a long conversation in which everybody participated, particularly my scouts, both Arkansas hillbillies, who could talk the horns off a Brahma bull. Here's a summary of our talks. Her mother was the daughter of an Australian planter on the plantation that was adjacent to the one we were camping on. She had been away from the island only once, when she was ten, and had visited her grandparents in Australia, just outside of Brisbane.

The planter employed a handsome, tall native as his foreman. He had been educated by missionaries and had received some formal education in Fiji. "Missy," the mother of the woman we were visiting, fell in love with the foreman, who formally requested permission to marry her.

In the early 1900s colonials were colonials. The white man was felt to be of a superior race with a God-given mission to help the benighted races become civilized. Obviously father objected somewhat, and mother was shocked. And so the case rested. Missy was desolate, but kept on seeing the foreman and falling more in love than ever.

After two years of standoff, the hard work, intelligence, and sterling character of the foreman overwhelmed all the arguments against his union with Missy. Permission was given, and the Protestant bishop performed the ceremony. Of course there was a little rumbling from other colonials, but the resident commissioner was sympathetic, and that meant a great deal to the family and the newlyweds.

Our hostess, Tania, showed us a very faded picture of a handsome native man in western dress, including coat and tie, and a plain but sweet girl in a white dress with several ribbons.

"My father was called Andrew, and my mother's name was Sally," she said as she fondled the picture, finally placing it in an old Bible.

The mixed couple had had one child, Tania, but were happy with their life. They had their own modest house and often had meals and social visits with the planter and his wife.

During World War I the mother died, and the father was killed in a plantation equipment accident five years later. The orphaned Tania moved in with her grandparents until the planter himself died in 1931. The surviving grandmother sold the plantation and intended to move to Brisbane. Her granddaughter felt that her life was tied up with the island people, and preferred to stay on Guadalcanal, knowing she could make a living working as a housekeeper for the planter who had purchased the plantation.

The grandmother left for Australia but died of residual malaria after six months in 1932. When the Japanese arrived, the planter and his family fled and Tania moved into the mountains to live with the natives.

Her tale had taken over two hours. We gave her the canned goods, to her great delight, and promised to get her some new records, some quinine, and a flashlight.

As we marched back, Bill said: "What a life she's lived."

We all nodded at the strange twists and turns of fate that bring such variety and tragedy to human beings.

In the next weeks I opened a trading service involving the general and his staff, our fish and cattle supply, and trade with the natives.

The G-4 brought out a whole LCT-load of canned goods (largely from supply dumps of evacuated military units). We kept some of this for ourselves in return for half a beef from our cattle herd. The natives brought in fruits and vegetables, some of which wound up in the general's mess. And then there was our fishing business. When the natives haggled with Sam over how many cans of salmon were a fair trade for a bag of yams, I would detonate four or five blocks of TNT and produce enough fish for everyone.

Sam and I took a patrol to a small village about two hours away, from which most of the traders emanated. As we approached the village we could see gardens on both sides of the path. We stopped, and Sam uttered various hoots and howls. After two or three minutes a hoot and a howl were returned from the forest; after another delay we saw a couple of native men approach us and then stop. Sam went to them, and a great deal of pointing and arm waving ensued.

Sam signaled us to come on and he introduced us to the two men. We shook hands and nodded affirmatively: this is evidently a universally understood gesture.

We arrived at the village, which was located in a clearing on an isolated hill. There were about ten huts but no natives. As we stood around, more men came out of the forest, then the women, and finally the children.

The people were in tough shape; malnutrition, disease (particularly malaria), skin eruptions, broken bones that had healed improperly—all of these and more were in evidence.

Through Sam I found out that no Japanese had been seen for a long time. I tried to get a more precise definition of "long time," but this was impossible. Solomon Islanders have no temporal sense that is comprehensible to the Western mind. In a land of no seasons there are no points of reference to locate events in the passage of time. We told them to come to the camp the next day to pick up more canned goods.

*   *   *

I paid a visit to battalion headquarters to give a briefing on our adventures. The battalion surgeon, a tall, bronzed giant of a man with a Roman nose and a big heart, indicated his desire to give some medical services to the natives. I told him to come to our camp as quickly as possible and bring plenty of medicine for tropical diseases. As I expected, he was in our camp the next morning with an aid man, both loaded down with medical bags.

Captain Downer, the surgeon, was a product of New England. He was obviously an outdoorsman as well as a medical man. He constantly urged Sam to pick up his pace, and in less than two hours we were at the village. Sam's hoot-and-holler ritual to gain entrance took less time, and, by the time we arrived, most of the villagers were standing in their doorways.

Sam explained in the native tongue what the doctor was here for. They had seen doctors before, both at the plantations and at Tulagi. Two chairs were brought for patients to sit in, and the parade started. For at least four hours medicine was administered, bandages applied, injections given, salves rubbed on, and some minor surgery on skin problems was performed. He gave some advice on cleaning up some unsanitary conditions around the village, suggestions that would reduce the flies and mosquitoes.

As we walked back to camp, he marveled at the physical resistance of the natives to the onslaught of a host of tropical diseases and bad living conditions. He was particularly vexed that the British had been in the area for forty years but had only marginally dealt with the problems of native health.

Back at camp we had supper, and his boat arrived as we finished. I thanked him and the aid man for his help, and his LCT chugged away to the west.

CHAPTER SIX

In Place

THE PLATOON

It is time to review the status of the platoon since our arrival two months earlier. With one officer and forty men, the platoon had been at full strength when it landed on Guadalcanal. Now, on the Berande River outpost, I had fifteen men left. Though one man had been killed while working as a stretcher bearer in the Matanikau pocket, we had no war-related injuries. However, disease and debilitation had taken their toll: Pops Benson unwillingly bowed out after his general health declined drastically, and Meeks succumbed to a variety of maladies and had to be sent home. An analysis of our losses indicated that the older men, those over twenty-five, were most susceptible to malaria, fevers, skin conditions, and exhaustion.

Dunn was now my platoon sergeant, and a strong, quiet, but dependable corporal by the name of Snow was made squad leader. With only fifteen men, I organized two squads under Ferrigan and Snow and kept the two scouts and one man in my headquarters. And then there was Sam.

Toward the end of March 1943, it was decided that my platoon would be moved farther west to a mission station named Kailo-tu-

Maria. I wasn't able to get a translation, but the Maria referred to the Virgin Mary.

After a couple of days, an LCT arrived and we moved our tents, canned goods, kitchen, and other impedimenta to the new location.

The mission station consisted of a main house, a smaller house, a cooking shack—and a church. The station had belonged to the Marist order and had been occupied by a priest, lay brothers, and some nuns. They had stayed behind when the plantation owners and government officials had evacuated the islands.

Their belief that their religious faith would restrain the Japanese was misplaced. They were massacred by the sons of Nippon, and their bodies lay where they fell until Carlson's Raiders moved through the area. They were buried under the palms fifty yards away from the main house, a vivid and tragic reminder of the enemy's savage hostility to the white man—or woman.

There were four rooms in the main house on one side of the breezeway. Each was still furnished as it had been when its Marist occupants lived there. For some reason, these rooms had not been subjected to the degrading destruction we saw in the Berande plantation house. On the other side of the breezeway was a single large room now occupied by a communications section from division headquarters with a truckload of radios, generators, and other gear.

Dunn decided that the men could stay in the smaller house, and he proceeded to get them bedded down. The cooks were soon established in their shack, and we erected a tent for their quarters next to it.

Of great significance to all of us was the sanitary situation. There was a two-holer behind each house, and for the first time in two and a half months we were spared the muscular agonies of the slit-trench latrine.

Sam and I shared the breezeway and set up our cots and mosquito bars where the winds of the Pacific could flow through and keep the mosquitoes away.

GOLD RIDGE

Soon after our arrival at Kailo-tu-Maria, and about the time we were beginning to enjoy the amenities of living in houses, eating from tables, listening to radio news broadcasts, and having a two-holer, we were visited by an intelligence officer from regiment and his counterpart from battalion.

They exchanged the usual pleasantries and expressed great envy of our situation. But then we got down to business. They unfolded a map of the island (the first map I had seen of Guadalcanal) and indicated a location some miles south of my station in the foothills of the great mountain spine of the island.

They indicated that the Gold Ridge Mining Company of Suva, Fiji, had been operating in that remote location for several years. The company had been somewhat successful in finding gold, and the British government had strongly supported this enterprise, seeing it as a source of wealth and a worthy alternative to the copra industry.

When the Japanese invaded the Solomons, the mining managers and their families had headed for Nouméa and Suva. The Australian coast watchers had used it for a while after the Japanese arrived, but had moved north to other islands after the marines landed.

What division wanted to know was the present state of Gold Ridge. Its location would be a terrific spot for the enemy to send radio messages to Bougainville about shipping and U.S. Navy vessels in Sealark Channel.

There was another aspect to the mission. The army had concocted a new ten-in-one ration: we would be given an issue, and we were to try the ration out on this patrol. We would also be provided with some native scouts who knew the trails to Gold Ridge.

After the intelligence guys had gone, Dunn and I spent some time talking about the patrol. We had a couple of men who were feeling low with fever of some sort, and it was decided to leave them behind. So the patrol was to consist of eight men, including the two scouts, Howie and Bell, Sam, Dunn, and me.

Dunn rounded up his crew and briefed them on the patrol and checked out their gear. We didn't load any rations since the new ten-in-ones were to be used.

The next morning while we were finishing breakfast, the LCT arrived with the rations, two scouts, and some twist tobacco bundles for trading purposes. Sam took care of feeding the two scouts their breakfast, while Dunn and his patrol members examined the rations. Each nine-inch-square box contained a lot of cans and packages to feed several men for a day. The camp was about fifteen miles inland, and the trip there and back could take four or five days, so each man had to carry a very substantial load of rations in his pack.

As usual we took rifles, ammunition, and two canteens, but we wore fatigue hats instead of helmets.

We set off on the trail south within the hour. The scouts—young, eager, and healthy—understood some English. I told them not to go too fast, to pace themselves on me, to stop and signal if they saw anything. They nodded and smiled and fidgeted—and then took off like a couple of gazelles. In five minutes they were out of sight. I decided not to get upset and set my own pace on an obviously well traveled trail. After the usual fifty-minute push we halted for a break. Sam went on up the trail to find the scouts, and about the time we were ready to push off he had corralled them.

We repeated this pattern for the rest of the morning.

About noon we tried the rations. They were too fancy, required too much mixing, and lacked sufficient protein for men using 4,000 to 6,000 calories a day.

About three hours later we came to a sheer cliff that led to a plateau above. There were two native-made ladders in place, and we found them to be in good shape. Sam and the scouts scrambled up the ladders, and we followed more slowly because of the weight of equipment and rations we carried. I was arm-weary when we got to the top, but I immediately saw the whole camp spread out on the plateau. There was a large house similar to the one at the mission station, a number of machinery sheds, and about a half-dozen native huts.

A native wearing a shirt, denim shorts, and shoes was brought to me by Sam.

"My name is Fred," he said. "I am in charge here." I introduced my NCOs, and we shook hands all around.

"Come into the house," he said, heading in that direction.

Dunn sent some men in different directions to look around and followed me to the house.

On the porch I stopped to look north and saw one of the most magnificent panoramas I had ever seen. The entire north shore of the island was visible, and beyond the channel, Savo Island, Florida, and ships at anchor that looked like toy boats. When Dunn clambered up the stairs he was equally impressed.

"Look, there are the hills we were on, and there's Henderson, and over there is Cape Esperance." He looked back and forth. "How innocent it all looks."

We entered the house. There was a dining table and several rockers, a desk, a china cabinet, and several lamps fixed to the walls. It was very plain, very clean, and very tidy. Off the dining room were two bedrooms on either side, each with a bed, quilts and fresh linen, a dresser, and a chair. I went over and touched the bed and tested the pillow. It had been ages since I had even seen a bed.

I returned to the dining room to examine two things I hadn't mentioned before. First there was an icebox, and it was working! It was the kind that operated on gas, and Fred indicated that he had an adequate supply of tanks to last for months.

Next Fred unlocked the door to a storeroom. It was filled with canned goods: meats, fruits, vegetables, jellies, condiments—in other words, a well-stocked mining manager's food locker.

I sat in a rocker. It was deliciously comfortable.

"Fred," I said, "this place looks like you expect your boss man to come back tomorrow."

Fred exhibited a set of perfect white teeth. "Oh yes, yes," he said. "I think he come by and by."

He turned to go out the back door: "I make supper for you. How many?"

"Four," I said, "and that's very nice of you."

Dunn went out to find the two squad leaders.

I went out back. There was a big tank that stored rainwater, a small table, and a washing bowl. I cleaned up as best I could without soap or a towel and returned to the porch. I couldn't get enough of the view.

There was another advantage to this location. Its altitude was high enough to be free of mosquitoes and malaria, so we wouldn't need aerosols or mosquito bars that night.

The meal was delicious: Fred had made a kind of stew with canned meat and native vegetables. In addition we had crackers, jam, and iced tea.

By the time supper was over it was dark, and we adjourned to the porch. Snow and Ferrigan went to see that their men were bedded down in a small adjacent house. The night was clear. The sea was a dark blue, and the offshore islands stood out as black masses. But there were no lights anywhere.

Then, as if especially staged for us, the searchlights around Henderson Field flicked on and their long beams looked like long spears waving in the dark. Then we could see the bright points of light, like fireflies, which indicated the antiaircraft guns were firing. We saw the long trail of tracers from the night fighters that were pursuing Charlie. But we saw no flame, no flash, no burning Nakajima bomber plunging to earth.

"Quite a show," Ferrigan said.

"Fred has turned down the beds," I said, getting up. "I'm taking the front room on this side. You men can argue over who sleeps in the other rooms."

I lost no time getting undressed and climbing into bed, after checking my M1 and leaning it against the wall next to the bed.

There was a nice breeze blowing through the room, and I could hear the NCOs talking on the porch for a long time. I hadn't been so comfortable for months. When I awoke, it was getting light.

I decided to spend a day talking to Fred and the natives and conducting an in-depth inspection of the site. Fred pointed out that a small village was located farther south in the mountains, and I felt that we could send the two scouts up there to find out whether there had been any enemy troops around lately. I assembled Fred, Sam, and the two scouts, and let Fred tell the scouts about the village. This was unnecessary since the scouts knew about the village and also knew its name, Chubu-kiki, and told us that its people had been cannibals on occasion.

As a measure of protection I told the scouts to say, "If you hurt us, the army will come up here and take all of you to Tulagi for punishment." They thought that was a great idea and in a few minutes were on their way into the forest.

Dunn, Sam, and I sat down with Fred and talked about the Japanese. Fred said that he had seen no Japanese at Gold Ridge, even when the coast watchers were there with their radio, which the enemy could have homed in on with their direction finders. However, natives traveling back and forth to the coast reported seeing enemy patrols once or twice, but those never came farther south on the trail than an hour or two's march away.

We were interested in how the equipment for a mining operation could have been transported over the rough trails and up steep cliffs. Fred then painted a glowing picture of how native carriers had suspended pieces of machinery from poles, each supported by two men. And so all of the machinery for a hydraulic mining operation, including all the materials for building the house and sheds, was broken down into two-man loads and hauled through rough terrain and up 100-foot ladders to the site.

"It had," Fred said, "taken a long time and many workers to

move everything from the coast to Gold Ridge." He went on to explain the continual flow of traffic back and forth to Gold Ridge to bring food, fuel, mining supplies, visitors from Suva, officials from the resident commissioner's office, and social visits from planters eager to share the cool breezes, the magnificent view, and the freedom from mosquitoes.

The managers and their wives worked long hours to secure the gold, and to ensure the health and nutrition of the native workers.

"The managers make everyone work hard. Nobody went off to sleep under a tree," Fred said, musing. "Yes, all work hard, but boss is never bad . . ." he searched for a word.

I said, "Not cruel."

"Yes, yes, not cruel." Fred repeated it several times.

That afternoon the scouts returned and reported that the natives at Chubu-kiki had seen no Japanese. I thanked them and gave both a twist of tobacco.

That night Fred again regaled us with a fine meal, served on china from the Burns-Philip trading company, and with a sterling silver place setting and tea service.

As payment for his kindness, we collected all the unused rations and the trading tobacco and gave it to Fred. (If he wanted to share some with the natives we would be pleased; after all, their vegetables had been used for our meals.)

That night we again sat on the porch admiring the beauty and serenity of the scene. Far in the distance a storm was moving across the Solomon Sea. Occasionally, spurts of lightning flickered in the clouds or sent a long, brilliant tentacle down to the sea—but we had no spectacular view of searchlights, ack-ack, tracers, or bomb blasts this night. Charlie had evidently decided to stay home.

As I gazed down on the scene, it occurred to me that the small area I could see was all that we had to show after fifteen or sixteen months of war. The might of the greatest nation on earth was now represented by an airfield, a division or more of tired troops, and a variety of naval vessels that ran for cover whenever the coast watchers reported planes in the Slot. It was a sobering thought. It was even more sobering when I remembered the many strings of islands, big and small, all hot and forested, that lay between this starting point of Pacific operations and Tokyo. At our present rate of progress, it could take a lifetime.

The next day, at first light, we started back down the hill to get as many miles as possible under our belts before the heat became intense. All of the men crowded round to thank Fred for his hospitality and to give him candy or cigarettes.

KAILO-TU-MARIA WITH THE BISHOP

Going home was going downhill. We traveled farther between breaks, took only fifteen minutes for lunch, and arrived at our station at 1500 hours. There everybody took a dip in the ocean to cool off and followed it with a freshwater shower. It was the sheerest pleasure to put on clean and dry underwear and fatigues.

The cooks had prepared a good meal, considering what they had to work with. After supper I sat down to write out my patrol report and included an annex dealing with the ten-in-one ration. I made the case that this was a poor ration for tropical use, with too much variety, too many sweets, and too many different shapes of packages that made the ration difficult to carry. With all their faults, the C- and K-rations were much better for combat troops without access to prepared meals.

The radio operators informed regiment and battalion that we had returned, that no Japanese had been seen at Gold Ridge, ever, and that a written report would be forwarded on the next supply boat.

Again things settled back into a routine, and I had an opportunity to read some of the books that had been the treasure of the Marist father who had been the spiritual leader of this tiny outpost of Christianity.

I inspected the church and found it severely plain. The congregation had wooden benches to sit on and faced a small, undecorated altar. A large crucifix dominated the back walls, with candleholders on each side. There was a small foot-pumped organ that I tried to play and so noticed that some keys were unresponsive. Looking inside the rear of the organ I discovered several abandoned mud-wasp nests. After scraping them out and retying some cords that had rotted away, I restored the full range of sounds to the tiny organ. Some of the reeds had deteriorated so that they only approximated the correct tone, yet a melody or a chord was recognizable and would suffice for future church services. Imagine. An organ on Guadalcanal! It was almost as surprising as finding an operating icebox in the wilderness of Gold Ridge.

That evening the radio operators received a message that Bishop Aubin of the Solomon Islands would visit our camp for a few days. I got ahold of Dunn, Snow, and Ferrigan (all Catholics) and told them who was coming and to get the camp in shape, including the disposal of beer bottles, pinups, and dirty clothes.

Sam and I inspected the rooms in the big house. The radio room was a mess, and I had to lean on the sergeant in charge to clean up his pigsty. The rooms on the west side of the house had not been touched or occupied since the massacre.

Sam knew the bishop, so we both awaited his arrival the next day with our own mixed feelings of pleasure and trepidation.

The next morning, at about 0900, an LCT arrived with Bishop Aubin, who was unaccompanied. A small, thin man with gray hair and a goatee, he wore glasses, a white shirt, and pants and carried a small valise. We greeted each other warmly. Though his native tongue was French, he spoke some English. I spoke a little French. We had no problem in communicating. All of the men were anxious to meet the bishop, who was somewhat of a celebrity in the islands, with the American press having carried several articles about him.

Here, let me give a short history of the bishop, which I uncovered in the course of conversations in the next few days. His name was Jean-Marie Aubin. He was a member of the Society of Mary, usually called the Marist Fathers. He had arrived in the Solomons in 1902, first meeting his superiors at Tulagi. After a period of orientation he was assigned to the island of Guadalcanal, where he was to be alone to carry out his missionary work; there would be little or no support from Tulagi because the Marist order had few resources to expend.

And so, Father Aubin was taken across Sealark Channel in a small boat and landed on Guadalcanal. He was provided with a native boy who knew some of the languages of the natives, but no French.

The bishop said, "I landed on Guadalcanal with three things—my cassock, my breviary, and a spoon. I didn't even have a hat."

His job was mind-boggling. He was to convert the heathen natives to Christianity even though he didn't know their languages. He was to build churches and mission stations and care for the sick. The problem of learning the native languages was, in some ways, not too difficult. Pidgin English spread by the traders for decades could be used as a starter, and the names of things could be learned without too much trouble. But grammar was something else: it was difficult to get pronouns straight, tell time, or listen for slight inflections that changed gender. To make matters worse, a language was usually the private property of a single village; ten miles away another language might be used.

By the 1940s Bishop Aubin had learned almost sixty of these languages or their variations, and had given them a written form, a necessary task before you could teach the natives to read. There was a steady demand for the pamphlets used by nuns and lay brothers in teaching the natives, and a printing press was purchased and located at Visale where the bishop had his headquarters. Here the hundreds of pamphlets in scores of languages were printed and shipped all over the Solomons.

As time went on, more priests, nuns, and lay brothers were sent from France to help with the problem of establishing Christianity in this backwater of the Pacific. How was this effort supported? Every year or so Aubin returned to France to give lectures about the Solomons, an area that intensely interested certain of the French, and compelled them to supply the funds for him to continue and expand his strenuous work in the islands.

I took the bishop on a tour of the station and he was pleased to find that the buildings and the rooms were in such fine shape. When we visited the church he went to the altar and paused to say a prayer. When I told him about the wasps' nests in the organ, he laughed loudly.

But the occasion became more somber when he visited the grave of his massacred friends. He sagged visibly as he stood looking over the tragic scene. His eyes were tear-rimmed as he turned to me.

"So unnecessary, so cruel," he said in a voice that was barely audible.

He leaned on my arm and I guided him to a table in the back of the house.

The cooks had outdone themselves. They had a table for two with dishes and silverware; there was even a set of shakers for salt and pepper. This was the first of many meals I shared with the bishop, and every one of them would be worth remembering.

The bishop's tragedy was that he was back where he'd started. Many of his people throughout the Solomons had fled to all quarters of the compass, some had been slaughtered, and some were probably in the mountains of the large islands but had not been heard from. His native flock had been without spiritual guidance for over nine months. Some of his stations had been destroyed, and the printing press at Visale had fallen victim to the mindless destruction of the Japanese. He was out of money, his organization was in shambles, and the carefully nurtured network of mission stations had been abandoned. Only he remained.

But there was hope: the marines and army organizations had contributed enough money to buy another printing press; there would be help coming from France and the United States. Somehow he would get started again.

The word spread among the natives about our illustrious visitor, and on Sunday they poured in from all directions. Each woman carried a basket in which was a pullover shirt of bright colors that was to be donned before entering the church.

I played the organ for several hymns, with their peculiar harmony based on an organ tone, that the natives sang with gusto. The bishop then conducted a mass, and the natives responded in their tongues in all the right places. They were obviously heartened to have this great and good man among them again.

Our meetings at the little dining table gave me an insight into the life of this exceptional man. He was much concerned about the moral state of society, feeling that the pursuit of happiness had limited and selfish goals, with too little thought given to the needs of millions of illiterate and poverty-stricken people around the world—such as those in the Solomons.

He was most anxious to get medicines for the natives. I passed this word to the headquarters through my resident radio station, and a day or two later the supply boat arrived with at least a half-dozen cases of medicine. Of greatest importance were the 100 pounds of quinine, a medicine so needed by those suffering from malaria. The bishop took a small bottle of tablets for himself, indicating that his personal supply had run out several weeks earlier.

One day he spent quite a while in one of the rooms in the big house. He called me and showed me a small, plain black traveling bag that had obviously belonged to a nun. It contained a black veil, a suit of underwear, and a slip. It also held a small bottle of wine.

The bishop called Dunn, and the three of us drank a cup of the sweet wine as a silent tribute to a martyred woman who had sacrificed everything to serve her church and her order, and had left behind a pitiful handful of personal belongings and a bottle of wine as her legacy to us—a legacy whose material paucity was vastly overshadowed by the enormity of her sacrifice.

One day the bishop indicated that he had to move on to other places. When the LCT arrived we all gathered around to shake hands and wish him well, and he expressed his gratitude for the hospitality and support we had given him. He boarded the LCT and continued to wave to us until he was out of sight. We all felt that we had been in the company of a great and holy man.

A day later the radiomen gave a message indicating that the platoon would be relieved. We packed everything as we had so many times before, and the next day a new platoon arrived. I gave the new officer, who was a replacement from the States, a briefing. I introduced him to Sam who was to stay at Kailo-tu-Maria as a resident advisor. We loaded into the LCT and in an hour we were back at the company base.

BACK AT BASE AND AWAY AGAIN

Obie and I sat down for coffee and for an exchange of events. After the past had been reviewed in sufficient detail, he indicated that I had a pleasant experience ahead of me. Since I had been stuck at outposts since the campaign ended, I was to get a chance to do something different. I was to attend the XX Corps intelligence school, which promised to be a change of pace.

I had a day to lie around the company area, and at lunch I met one of our replacement officers, whose name was Carstairs. He had spent six months lollygagging in different army posts after leaving Fort Benning and was now a first lieutenant, as were all the other arriving junior replacement officers. But all the junior officers who had fought on Guadalcanal were still second lieutenants. Obviously, this bit of army stone-headedness was greeted with great satisfaction by those of us still sporting gold bars.

Furthermore, Carstairs was a weirdo. He was erratic in conversation and often jumped up and walked rapidly away from a meeting. He seemed to be inherently an unstable character, if not a neurotic. How in God's name he had gotten all the way to the Pacific to be assigned to a frontline infantry unit in an infantry division, only the Neanderthals in the replacement system could explain. I was to see this shortsightedness again and again. As officers passed through different commands on their way to war, the strong, athletic, bright guys were siphoned off by intervening headquarters. But the small, timid, or weakly types were bound to wind up in the infantry. So much for the personnel system.

The XX Corps intelligence school was located on the beach west of our current location. There were about twenty-five students from different elements of the division. We had a large hospital tent for a classroom, a pretty good kitchen, some pyramidal tents for the students, and a couple of three-holers for latrines. It was a nice, relaxed place with good food and no pressure, and a lot of time to shower and tell sea stories.

The school was designed to train men for long-range reconnaissance. This kind of intelligence gathering goes beyond that on a conventional battlefield, where you can infiltrate the enemy lines, question prisoners and refugees, and get some idea of what the enemy is up to. But when the enemy is spread out on a core of islands, the conventional methods don't work. Aerial surveillance was not then a highly developed technology. The only course of action was to transport a patrol to an island, let it gather information, and then pick it up and return it to headquarters.

Several such patrols had already been tried. They were never heard from again. One patrol had returned from Ganutu, however, and its members were part of the instruction team. A captain from the regiment, whose name was Hiller, had been a coleader on the mission. As a result of his successful mission he fancied himself something of a local hero. He carried his chin quite high and affected a highly relaxed attitude leavened too much by a heightened sense of his own importance. As one of the old boys, he was living proof that when you wanted something done you asked the hometown gang to do it.

I decided I could put up with Hiller's attitude if he had something of worth to share. And share he would—on the beach, in class, at mess, in the latrine—anywhere and everywhere an audience of at least one materialized.

There were some other interesting aspects to the course, which I shall detail to indicate the state of the art in June 1943.

The general idea was to transport, by navy submarine, a patrol up the Slot to a designated island. On arrival off the coast of a designated island, a rubber boat would be inflated and the patrol would paddle to the beach. Once ashore, the rubber boat would be concealed and the patrol would proceed on its mission.

What was the mission? Determine the size and location of enemy troops; chart beach conditions; determine artillery and anti-aircraft positions.

None of this sounds very complicated. The trick is to avoid being sighted and/or captured by the enemy. As I noted before, only one of several such clandestine expeditions had returned. The odds, I thought, were pretty slim for success.

To fill our minds with the necessary information we had lectures by British officers, U.S. officers, an Aussie coast watcher, and, of course, Hiller. We spent many hours wading in the surf while a navy officer with a bullhorn gave us the fine points of determining underwater conditions and beach slopes. We cut up our boats pretty good on coral and were chased by assorted toothy fish looking for lunch.

We were in the fifth day of this exercise when I received word to report to my unit. I packed my bag and returned to base. Obie met me and provided the news: things were not going well with the New Georgia invasion. The regiment was to proceed ASAP to reinforce the 37th Division—just as I was beginning to enjoy peace.

CHAPTER SEVEN

New Georgia

From February to July 1943 we lost a lot of officers and men to malaria and a host of other tropical diseases.

Graber was sent back to the States, and the new regimental commander showed his complete inability to judge leadership by promoting the regimental supply officer as our battalion commander. Lieutenant Colonel Karansky was a stocky, dark, overweight character who wore a black beard in the fashion of Mephistopheles. He had a nervous tic, which caused him to blink continuously and earned him the unflattering nickname "Blinky." His major qualifications for promotion were that he was one of the good old boys and that he had engaged in a lot of eyewash and wrote snappy reports for Colonel Weston's consideration.

In the company we were down to two officers (Obie and me) and about forty men. Bemish had been transferred to regiment, and Carstairs was sent to battalion. We had a lot of discussions about why our regiment was the first to be sent back into *active* combat. There was some blather about the division mission, but among the junior officers there was little doubt that Colonel Weston was anxious to establish a reputation. As a West Pointer, he had seen a shower of stars descend on the regimental commanders and division staff members, and now he was to have his turn to create a record and perhaps find a star in his own future. How this overweening ambition would translate into combat leadership we shall see.

THE SETTING

New Georgia is a group of islands—only one of which is called New Georgia. In this group were several large islands: Vangunu, Rendova, Vella Lavella, and a perfect volcanic cove sticking out of the sea, Kolombangana.

There were Japanese on most of the islands, but the prime reason for the capture of New Georgia was an airfield constructed by the enemy. You will recall this was the reason for the campaign on Guadalcanal. Just as Henderson Field had become a household word, so Munda Field would soon take its place in the annals of war.

The distance from Henderson to Munda was 170 miles. An operational airfield in New Georgia enabled enemy planes to interdict sea traffic and attack Guadalcanal and its airfields and supply bases. And the capture of Munda would put us 170 miles closer to Tokyo: not much, but every little bit would help.

Once again we gathered all our gear and prepared for a move. The division had given most of our new equipment to the divisions moving north. Now that we were going to the same place, we found ourselves in the same fix we encountered on Guadalcanal when a change in plans moved us into the Solomons: our new equipment was on the docks at Brisbane. (History has a habit of repeating itself.) We loaded into an LST for the journey to New Georgia. The trip was uneventful except for one enjoyable circumstance—we had some fresh food for the first time since January. The U.S. Navy believed in keeping its ships supplied with the best food; refrigerator ships never could be found to furnish the same diet to the army.

It took about a day and a half to reach New Georgia, which looked like all the other islands in the Solomons. The LST dropped its ramp, and Obie led us up a trail for several hundred yards, and then we moved into a small clearing where we were to remain for a while. Most of the men were first sent back to the beach to help with the unloading; they were back in the area about dark, and we settled down for the night.

Just after dawn we assembled and moved east to what was to be a line of departure. It appeared that we were to be sandwiched between two regiments of the 37th Division. After we had established our position, dug foxholes, and sited our machine guns, I had a chance to talk to Obie and some officers from battalion—and found out then why we were so unusually placed on the battlefield. And what was revealed was one of the amazing and tragic sagas of military disintegration.

THE ARMIES

It may be well to preface this story with some observations on the Japanese soldier.

Before a U.S. soldier met the Japanese on the battlefield he had a stereotype in mind, largely formed from articles in newspapers, pictures in *Life*, and newsreels. The stereotype shows a small, stocky, expressionless Oriental with an ill-fitting uniform trudging along behind an officer with a fierce expression, a well-tailored uniform, and a samurai sword. The stereotype includes the capture of Singapore, the surrender of Bataan, and the cruelty of the Death March on Luzon.

The Japanese trooper was supposed to be fearless, scornful of U.S. soldiers, invisible, a superb sniper, and willing to fight to the death rather than give up a position. Of course some of this was sheer nonsense, but unfortunately it took U.S. generals and colonels a long time to figure out how to counter such a creature.

The Japanese were very adept at strong, interlocking defensive positions. To order our soldiers to attack such positions with infantry and rifles was to get a lot of Americans killed. Of course no one wants to be deemed a coward, so during the course of the Pacific War thousands of GIs and marines demonstrated their courageous response to foolish orders by attacking fortified positions and earning a white cross in a Pacific graveyard.

The Japanese had won the psychological warfare before the action started. Their night attacks, their total disregard for their own lives, their yells and "banzais," and their patience in waiting for hours under a bush to kill one American had to be overcome—and on Guadalcanal we did it. The Japanese soldier was a master of camouflage, but there is a negative psychology to hiding in a hole. The enemy who attacks at night could be mowed down in windrows if we organized our positions and interlocked our fields of fire as we were taught to at Fort Benning.

The U.S. soldier did not want to die to prove his bravery. I believe this point is accepted by most military leaders and almost unanimously by the American people. The U.S. combat division develops the most awesome combination of firepower in the world; it is quick, accurate, and devastating. But faulty (almost negligent) logistics often limited artillery to a few rounds per gun per day. On many days, therefore, commanders anxious for glory and promotion ordered attacks that ensured the maiming or death of members of their command. Technology had given the U.S. Army the best weapons in the world. To have substituted an unprotected soldier carrying a rifle for an artillery preparation was a criminal act.

The great pressure on the infantry to capture a hill or redoubt, and thus show the generals a nice advance of the front line on a battle map, was not matched by pressure to get the artillery into position, perform registrations, and get the fainthearted observers up to the front line. It was not uncommon to find the cannoneers of an entire battalion cowering in their foxholes while one sniper took potshots at them. Of course, during the cowering period no missions were fired to support the infantry.

The infantry, as the cutting edge of battle, expects casualties. But unneeded casualties were incurred because of mettlesome, impatient commanders who again and again ordered men to attack positions that had received little or no softening up from the firepower available, or if not available, pressed an attack anyway lest a lack of action damage their image as "aggressive" commanders.

The X regiment, whose place we were taking, had been the center unit of three on line and tasked with the mission of taking Munda Field. It is difficult to find an initial thread to unravel the story of the regiment's collapse. But some assumptions can be made:

- The troops were completely convinced of the Japanese stereotype.

- They had been given no orientation training to break down the stereotype, e.g., the successes of the GIs and marines who fought the enemy to a standstill on the Canal.

- They held weak positions, poor foxholes, and poor weapons emplacements, and had little systematic artillery support.

- Their leadership, particularly among field-grade officers, was poor or nonexistent.

One of the devices used by the Japanese was a limited, short-range nighttime attack against all positions to test their reactions. The three regiments were all subjected to the hoot-and-holler, profanity-shouting, banzai treatment. X reacted in the worst way.

The Japanese decided to keep up sniper, knee-mortar, and machine-gun attacks during the day. This was followed by concentrated doses of the nighttime treatment.

The effect on the X troops was disastrous: they failed to return fire, and some panicked and crouched in their holes. A few company officers did heroic work trying to hold their positions intact and apply return fire. Unfortunately some positions were weakened and men ran screaming into the dark, throwing away their weapons, sometimes being shot by other soldiers who knew the rule of never getting out of your hole at night. The gaps in the line were quickly discovered by the enemy, who slaughtered anyone still crouching in his hole and moved against the flanks of other units now exposed.

The next night all stops were pulled out: mortar fire, infantry attacks, lights, yells and screams, profanity, bayonet stabbings—it was a piece of cake.

First singly, then in groups, the U.S. soldiers exhibited the classic case of panic of World War II. As they plunged to the rear, some now in the depths of neurosis, others just being cowardly, the fabric of morale, discipline, and control evaporated.

By morning, in an unmanageable mass, men were huddling in groups along the trails to the rear and pursued savagely by the enemy that caught up with many of them and—to use an archaic phrase—put them to the sword. The efforts of higher headquarters to understand and rescue the regiment were puerile; no one of higher rank made an appearance to stem the rout.

The remaining problem was to repair the damage.

Ships were brought in. Evacuation orders for each unit were prepared for it, with interminable lists of "psychoneurosis" as the diagnosis for medical evacuation.

The number of the regiment disappeared from the army troop list. The entire incident was expunged from military records. It appears in *no* official history. The regiment had—to use Soviet parlance—become a "nonregiment." Don't try to verify this story; officially this never happened to nobody.

And we were to replace X regiment. We were to plug the hole where Japanese cunning and American lack of training and leadership resulted in one of the dark pages of our military history.

THE RESPONSE

On the morning of July 25, 1943, two battalions pushed off to reach the line of departure. Our battalion made about 800 yards, then was halted because the 3d Battalion ran into trouble in the left zone. Obie told us to spread out and dig in, but this was a lot tougher job than on the Canal. New Georgia was a coral island that had been lifted from the sea by some ancient convulsion exposing the coral to the open air. Over the years a thin mantle of vegetation had covered most of the coral, but as soon as an entrenching shovel penetrated that cover hard coral was struck. It took a long time to use a pick and shovel to create a six-inch-deep depression. And it was very hard to rest in since it was impossible to eliminate all the sharp humps that stabbed the back and the legs.

I noticed, in particular, that we had an open flank. The 148th Infantry Regiment was supposed to be there, but nobody knew where it was. Obie and I talked about this and decided to pull our right flank around into a hook to avoid being outflanked by the enemy. We didn't have too much flexibility in our dispositions because we had only eleven foxholes to cover our sector.

The following morning, July 26, we moved ahead a few hundred yards and occupied a hill. The 3d Battalion also launched an attack with tanks. The accompanying mortar and machine-gun attack destroyed about fifty enemy positions, and our troops advanced about 200 yards. Then the Japanese knocked out two of the tanks, while the other four wallowed around in the brush and debris and, failing to make any progress up the hill, withdrew to the rear. The enemy then opened up from its remaining positions on a ridge to the west and inflicted casualties on the infantry. Seeing that its position was untenable, the battalion withdrew. At the end of the day it was back where it had started, and so were the Japanese.

It is worth noting that on July 27 we had no artillery support: another example of the incredible bungling by the 37th Division staff. Two conditions were used as an excuse by the combat amateurs of the 37th to withhold artillery fire. First, the artillery battalions were on another island, and were so located that the axis of fire was parallel to the front. Second, there were no maps of the interior of New Georgia. Yet any artilleryman worth his salt could use sound or flash ranging to adjust the fires on known points and thus build up a firing chart. That this was not done forced us to attack enemy positions with minimal firepower. It was a strategy of ignorance or timidity.

An attack was called for by our 1st Battalion on July 27, but the company on our left ran into stiff opposition and lost a number of officers and men. Obie signaled us to move ahead in our sector into what was a veritable wall of small trees, vines, and undergrowth. We soon came under fire, and one of my squad leaders, Snow, was killed. We pulled him out and wrapped him in a shelter half. Snow was a big, chunky man with a pleasant disposition; his men admired him and his easy way of dispelling tension by making a joke. Two of his men wept openly, and I had trouble holding the tears back. What a cost for a stupid move into impenetrable jungle.

The next day, July 28, two companies of the battalion tried to break through the position that had rebuffed them the previous day. Again no artillery was available, nor were any registrations attempted to build a framework of fires to assist the infantry. As might be expected, rifle and machine-gun fire had little effect on fortified positions built of logs and coral. After several hours of crawling around and getting men killed or wounded, the two companies were withdrawn to where they had started.

In the afternoon, we detected some movement on our flank and some enemy opened fire and began moving toward us. We opened up with our machine gun and BAR (we had only one of each), and the enemy opened up from a number of positions to our front and flank.

In the middle of this firefight I heard some yelling off to my right. I crawled along a natural ditch to the flank and found that

Obie had been shot through the head. He was irretrievably dead. So we pulled him out and covered him up. I then had difficulty in getting the men to keep firing, because many were unnerved by Obie's death. After about three-quarters of an hour the Japanese withdrew, and from the noise they made they were pulling out their dead. I sent out two men to see what was going on. After crawling about 100 yards into the wall of vegetation, they found only a lot of expended ammo brass and blood here and there. At about 1700 a stretcher detail came and took Obie to the rear. I was the last officer of my company.

We tried to strengthen our position for the night by doing some more pick-and-shovel work on our holes. I found to my surprise that the metallic "clink" my shovel produced was caused by an unexploded white-phosphorous mortar shell. I had noticed a slight tang of chemical in the air for the previous twenty-four hours, but the jungle had so many rotten and/or astringent odors that one more would hardly excite any notice.

I wasted no time in evacuating that position and moved over to share a hole with one of my scouts. I decided that the best way to get everybody's mind off the tragedies of the morning was to spend time on housekeeping. I sent two men for water and rations, and had the machine gun moved and dug in at a location where our flank could be better protected. Incidentally, the 148th Regiment had not yet reached our right flank.

It was incomprehensible that a full-strength regiment could be milling around in an area of less than a mile square for three days without finding our flank. As a result of this game of hide-and-seek, the 37th Division commander (from the safety of his dugout) refused to authorize the use of artillery for fear that this regiment, which he couldn't locate either, would get hurt. Meanwhile the two regiments on the line were getting hurt—seriously.

I continued the busywork by enforcing shaving, inspecting rifles, having a new latrine dug, and having the holes policed up, particularly getting rid of C-ration cans and K-ration boxes.

The ridges south of us were still under attack by the 2d and 3d battalions. A battalion of the 145th Regiment moved laterally to reinforce this effort but failed, and Horseshoe Ridge remained in enemy hands. Again, no artillery—the division staff didn't know where the 148th was.

On July 29 there was little action on any front during the night, to our great relief.

Colonel Weston decided, on July 30, to withdraw the 2d and 3d battalions to enable the artillery to pepper the ridges occupied by the enemy forces that had savagely defended their position against small-arms fire. The withdrawal was to take place at 0600 on July 31, but the division commander canceled the withdrawal at 2000 hours on July 30. Reason? The position of the 148th was uncertain, and at this point the regiment had been lost for five days.

In the afternoon of July 30 enemy soldiers attacked our area and, after a half hour of trading rifle and machine-gun fire, they withdrew. Later on they came in again from different directions, but with their usual shouting and vigor. Again we spread a tablecloth of lead about six inches above the ground, and again after a short time the Japanese withdrew. One of our men received a slight facial wound when flying coral hit him. His buddy cleaned him up and tied a bandage around his head and cheek.

Just after dawn on July 31 the enemy came in again. The same scenario was followed: we kept low in our holes and sprayed the area with rifle and machine-gun fire. This attack lasted about twenty minutes, again with no casualties. About two hours later the enemy came back, and again only about twenty minutes of action ensued. But as a result of these two engagements we were almost out of machine-gun ammunition.

I sent two men back to the dump to get more machine-gun ammo belts. In about twenty minutes I saw them coming up the hill into the position carrying between them a case of the ammunition. They were walking upright, and I told them to get down. They crawled about twenty-five yards pushing the case in front of them, but then they encountered the exposed roots of several trees that made pushing the case impossible. They decided to run for it, the machine-gun position being about twenty yards away. They stood up facing each other with the case between them, one man facing backward and the other forward. A shot was fired from not more than ten feet away, and I saw the bullet pop out of the lead man's belly and the following man's back. Both collapsed, yelling in agony. Everybody was hollering for the medics while two men dragged the two wounded down the hill to comparative safety.

We called back and forth from hole to hole to locate the sniper in our position. A hole just across the trail and about ten feet away did not respond.

Bell took out a hand grenade, removed the pin, let the handle fly off, counted to three, and lobbed it into the unresponsive hole. There was a tremendous explosion with coral flying around like shrapnel. Bell crawled over to the hole, stuck his rifle in it, and fired four shots. He turned to me and signaled an OK. I slid down the hill to where the medics were putting compresses on my two men to stanch the flow of blood. Within a minute they were carried out on litters, still groaning and imploring God to help them. The medic sergeant looked at me, shook his head sadly, and took off down the trail. Both men died within the hour from massive internal damage and bleeding.

This last tragic loss had stretched my patience to the limit. On August 1, I tramped over to the battalion headquarters where Koransky and A Company troops were sitting cheek by jowl drinking coffee.

Koransky blinked a greeting and asked, "What's up, kiddo?"

"The trouble is we're getting the crap beat out of us on that flank. We've lost Obie and two men. Three others have been injured. One man was evacuated with fever. We've had four attacks in three days, and nobody knows where the damn 148th is that is supposed to be covering our flank."

Blinky adopted a sour look. "What do you want me to do about it?"

I looked around at the troops lounging around in every shady spot for a hundred yards around.

"I think you should send a platoon to cover that flank before we all get wiped out!"

"I can't do that," he said blinking rapidly, a sure sign that he was irritated.

"Why not?" I barked. "I see a lot of people sitting around on their ass."

"I don't have to explain anything to you," he growled.

"Well, if somebody would come over and take a look, they'd find out what the problem is."

"Lieutenant, just go on back to your position and do your job, and I'll do mine."

I left in a hurry; if I had spoken my piece I would have been court-martialed.

I walked around visiting the men, pulling in some of the men to make a tighter line. The questions were the same everywhere. When will we get some reinforcements? When are we going to get moving?

I had no answers. I couldn't tell them that the battalion commander resented having his coffee and conversation interrupted by an irate lieutenant.

Fortunately, we had no action during the night of August 1. I say "fortunately" because we received no help from Koransky.

The next morning we heard a lot of thrashing around on our flank, and we all dived for our holes. In a minute or two we saw at least a platoon of U.S. soldiers. They were moving very rapidly and aggressively to the front with a lot of shouting.

We stood up so they could see us, and I shouted, "Where the hell have you guys been?"

One of their men pointed to the rear. "Back there, over that ridge," he yelled.

The platoon disappeared from sight but we could hear the shouting and thrashing for some time. In a little while some more soldiers approached; they were going slower, and my contact with their officer revealed that they were going to secure this area. They moved ahead for about twenty yards and then began to dig in.

At 1030 hours on August 2, 1943, the 148th Regiment had finally found our flank.

We spent the rest of the morning eating and sleeping. That afternoon, at about 1700, a Lieutenant Woodman from A Company came over to assume command. He was one of the good old boys, tall, bespectacled, and with a miserably small mustache. He indicated that we were to move out immediately and advance as far as we could.

We gathered the men together, spread out into a line, contacted A Company on our left, and started out. About 150 yards en route we came to a clearing with a classic Japanese bunker in the middle of it. While two men covered the structure's open parts, Howie and I circled around to the back, where there were a few steps leading down to a doorway. Howie pulled the pin on a grenade, let the handle fly, counted to three, and tossed it in. There was a tremendous bang, but no other sounds.

We didn't bother to look in, and Woodman signaled for us to move forward. We found a lot of little trails, all of which probably had been used in the attacks on our position. The farther we went, the more open the terrain became. Still we were very careful; we weren't about to walk into a classic Japanese ambush that involved their abandoning a position and then waiting for you to charge about enthusiastically until they hit you from all sides.

To our great relief we kept on going almost until dark. We had advanced about 900 yards without an enemy contact, when the word came to hold up—and again there we were.

After eight days of hard combat, we had finally reached the line of departure that had been selected by the 38th Division, which was ignorant of what lay in the approach to the line.

During the night there was no action in our sector. Evidently the Japanese were moving back. Whether they would make a stand somewhere, or whether they would be evacuated as they had been at Cape Esperance on Guadalcanal, was a question.

As soon as it was light we were ordered to continue the advance. The area directly in front of us was fairly open, and it appeared we were on a ridge that encircled the open terrain on the east and south.

There was some sporadic firing from the area of the 2d Battalion, which was operating in a wooded spot on the southern ridge. We were halted for some reason and stood around wondering why we weren't moving.

In the midst of this musing we heard two loud explosions—one from the open area and the other from the trees overhead. We had been fired on by an artillery piece that couldn't have been more than a hundred yards away. The battalion ordered us to take the area under fire with machine guns, and a mortar section was emplaced to drop shells into the area.

On August 3, we continued to receive fire from the enemy antiaircraft guns (which is what they were) for about a half hour. By that time we had raked the area with bullets and mortar shells, and it was deemed proper to attack and mop up that area. We spread out into a long line and gingerly descended from the ridge into the open area, where after some milling around we found five gun positions and two enemy dead. If there had been more enemy troops in this position they had moved westward toward the beach. We halted at this position for the night because the 2d Battalion was still shooting it out with the enemy on the hill mass south of our position.

Once again it occurred to me that we were sitting around waiting for everything to be just right before we moved out to capture the airfield. Nobody had ever heard of keeping up pressure on the enemy while he was running away, and if any force existed to our front we were giving it plenty of time to dig in and raise hell with us when we resumed the advance.

The 2d Battalion had cleaned up the enemy resistance on August 4, and in the middle of the afternoon the advance resumed. While crossing the remaining open area, I was directed by Woodman to reconnoiter the woods on the far side. I went out alone, while Woodman hid behind a tree. When I had determined that no one was in the woods I signaled Woodman, who bravely led the company across the open space.

At about 1500 we heard enemy fire in the 2d Battalion area. The battalion had reached the beach, but the enemy was in control of the beach area and directed fire at its G Company, which backed a hundred yards or so. A Company also received some fire, so it was decided to emplace our battalion as an extension of the 2d Battalion line about 150 yards from the beach. The mortars were brought up and sporadically shelled the beach area well into the night. Some enemy soldiers tried to infiltrate through our lines but were scared off or killed.

After midnight everything was quiet.

We had stopped about 500 yards north of the Munda airfield.

The objective had been taken largely as a result of the actions of our regiment. There had been no artillery, no help from our flank regiment, and no exploitation of enemy weaknesses. There was little for the 37th Division to be proud of in this campaign.

On August 5, as might have been expected now that the fighting for Munda was over, the 161st Regiment reverted to control of the 25th Division. We would be relieved of beach defense by the 148th and 145th regiments.

On August 6, we marched out of the area to a bivouac and rest area and set up tents and kitchens.

*   *   *

Our rest was short-lived. The division ordered the regiment to proceed north and assist in clearing the island of Japanese. Our target was the coast from Sunday Inlet to Enogai Harbor. The regiment was to join up with a marine force that had been nosing around near Enogai without any perceivable results. The move was to begin on August 7. The 2d and 3d battalions were to lead the operation, with the 1st bringing up the rear and the supplies.

There was one trail to the north: it was narrow, with mud a foot deep, and no level patches in its entire length. It required scratching and clawing to go up the grade, and slipping and sliding coming down. The first task was to get to Mount Bao. Each day we scrambled back to a supply dump to pick up rations and ammo for the forward units, and then scrambled forward with our loads.

It was hard, cruel, exhausting work in rain, oppressive heat, and mud. The farther the lead battalions proceeded, the tougher our job became. As is usual in war, we never knew what was going on up ahead. Occasionally we heard some mortar fire, but in the heavy tropical forest it was impossible to tell what direction the sound was coming from.

This ordeal continued for better than two weeks, when a battalion staff officer told me to occupy Mount Bao and make sure the enemy was not using the north-south trail. I had about ten men and a little food and water. We dug in on the hill—not a mountain— and did nothing. After a couple of days we received some supplies, but when these ran low I restricted our ration to one can of C-ration per day for two men. A Japanese food dump nearby furnished some rice, but everything else in the dump was suspect: it was either going bad—or already had.

We tried to learn how to live off the jungle, but it didn't work. We tried roots, bark, and leaves, all of which were inedible.

Finally an aircraft flew overhead, and we waved our undershirts to attract its attention. We must have been spotted because we heard it coming back and saw a parachute with a canister attached coming down.

As might be expected, it got hung up in the branches of the tall trees. One of the men tried valiantly to get to it but failed because the tree trunk was too large. After a certain amount of gaping into the air we decided to shoot it down. After each of us had shot up more ammo than we had expended since we'd arrived in the Solomons, we decided to use a machine gun. We fed belt after belt into the gun and finally the shroud lines parted and the plastic canister came down with a thud.

We rushed to it and eagerly unstrapped the top of the canister. It was loaded with machine-gun belts!

The next day one of the men I sent on short patrols around the position stumbled, fell down a small hill, and broke his leg. It was three or four miles back to camp, we had no communications, and he couldn't walk out—he had to be carried out by litter. We created a stretcher out of long branches and shelter halves. I sent six men— four to carry the litter, two to provide relief—and they disappeared down the trail.

Late the next afternoon they returned with rations, which were gratefully received. Captain Woodman and the company were resting comfortably in the camp, and so sent their best. The man with the broken leg was in a hospital in Nouméa by that time.

After two more days of doing nothing and seeing nothing, a messenger told us to return to camp, but first we had two tasks. A large pile of rifles and machine guns left behind by the two leading battalions had to be destroyed. We dismantled weapons, threw the parts into the jungle, busted stocks, and bent anything that would bend.

The other task was ridiculous. In fact it would have been funny if it hadn't indicated a tragic lack of good sense by the regimental staff. About ten parachutes had come down on Mount Bao, and the troops who'd occupied the position had used them to line their foxholes. Most of the 'chutes were torn from the descent through the trees or full of bullet holes, and the lines had been cut off. In summary, they were useless, sodden, dirty bundles of cloth.

But the S-4, in his infinite wisdom, suggested to the regimental commander that the parachutes were expensive and could be used again. Weston, with equal wisdom, and total disregard for the hardships involved, agreed. It took us better than seven hours of back-breaking work to deliver those useless 'chutes to the supply dump.

When the nine men left to me and I came out of the forest onto the camp road, we were a sight to behold. Three men had no shoes; those had rotted off. Two men had no jackets. One man had no pants. We all had beards and were incredibly dirty.

We felt like Robinson Crusoe, and looked it. As we passed an engineer camp a bunch of men ran out to see us, and then an officer came out and asked us to come eat. We accepted with a shout of gratitude and sat down to our first hot meal in a month. After thanking one and all for the magnificent repast, we picked up our bundled chutes and looked for the company. After a certain amount of frogging around we spotted the company sign.

Woodman had spotted us and came out to welcome us back. He was shocked at our appearance and was angered by the stupid order to return the chutes. We assigned some men to deliver them to the S-4 personally.

The company kitchen was nearby and the cook came out to ask us what we would like to eat. We settled on hotcakes. The cook returned to the kitchen and called us about fifteen minutes later: we ate pancakes until 0200 in the morning and drank gallons of hot coffee. Then we went to sleep wherever we happened to be. The sun was bright before we woke up.

For the next few days there was little to do except eat and rest. The army supply chain had finally caught up with us after eight months in combat. We were given underwear, boots, socks, and new fatigues. It was wonderful wearing clothes that didn't stink or fall apart and boots that had thick soles.

At night we were visited with the same aerial harassment we

had encountered on the Canal. An enemy plane would fly over; the searchlights would go on; the antiaircraft guns would fire; a bomb would be dropped—far off target. And we would hide in our covered holes while the shell fragments from the ack-ack whined and hissed into our position.

Our stay in the rest camp was short. Before a week had passed, my platoon (ten men) was assigned to outpost duty on Sunday Inlet. We were loaded into an LCT and motored to the north side of New Georgia Island. Here we were landed, the platoon formerly in residence was relieved, and we took time to look over our new mission. Sunday Inlet was about fifty yards wide and narrowed down to a stream in about 200 yards. We were to secure both sides of the inlet and guard against the Japanese. No one said whether we should expect an attack, or intercept the enemy trying to escape from New Georgia.

A rubber boat with paddles was available, so I took four men and a machine gun to the east side of the inlet along with rations, water cans, and an SP phone. The former occupants had laid a wire around the inlet to provide communications from one side to the other.

The land on both sides of the inlet consisted of sharp coral outcrops with water in between the humps. This was a mangrove swamp with trees growing out of the water and the heavy miasma of standing salt water. Since it would have been impossible to sleep on the coral, someone had provided covered hammocks that were hung here and there, wherever two trees were close together. The hammocks had a rubberized roof to shed the rain and mosquito netting for sides. You zipped up the netting once you had managed to struggle into the hammock.

It was impossible to stow a rifle or helmet inside the netting, so you were practically defenseless once the zipper had been zipped. It was also difficult to determine how tight the ropes that held the hammock should be. If they were too loose you would bend in the middle and it was impossible to sleep in any position except on your back. If the ropes were too tight the hammock tended to tip over and you'd find yourself lying in the rubberized roof, which was not designed for such weight and usually split and deposited its human cargo on the sharp coral below.

During the campaign to get to the north side of the island a wire had been laid from the base camp—so I had a telephone connection with the rear echelon. It was comforting to know I could let battalion headquarters know if we needed help, but experience had taught me that no one there would pay any attention.

We set up a schedule of guards, one on each side of the inlet: two hours on, and then switch. At the guard post on the ocean edge, from which the other side of the inlet could be seen, the guard had the SP phone to talk to the other side. The wired phone connected to the rear was located in the same position, and we had to muffle the bell because if someone were to call us in the middle of the night, prolonged ringing would be heard for miles in the quiet jungle.

As expected, toward nightfall it would rain. I found out that the hammock's rubberized roof protected you only from rain coming straight down. In the Solomons the rain came from all directions, and before long you were thoroughly dampened and stayed that way for the rest of the night.

The next morning we explored the stream that fed Sunday Inlet and found that if we went far enough upstream, past the point to which the tide carried sea water, we could get acceptable drinking water that was only a little brackish. It was just fine for washing and making coffee. When we filled our five-gallon cans, we put in ten or twelve purifying tablets to guard against waterborne diseases. (We had learned on the Canal that streams, no matter how clear, were filled with germs and parasites that could and did kill white men.)

Although we were somewhat relaxed in getting out of direct combat, I was not to have too long to enjoy the situation.

One morning four of us took the rubber boat to visit the men on the other side of the inlet. The position for those propelling the boat was to sit astride the inflated sides with one leg inside and the other outside. As we were paddling across the inlet my paddle struck something sharply. I thought perhaps it was a coral head that I hadn't noticed before, but when I examined the paddle I found a few splinters and a large white tooth stuck in the wood.

Barracuda. Perhaps he had been speeding to my leg when the paddle intercepted him. At any rate I was overjoyed that he chose the paddle, and we propelled the boat with both feet inside from that time forward.

That night, long after dark, the SP phone hissed. I answered.

"There's a canoe going by the position with several guys in it. It's too dark to tell who they are."

"Which way are they going?" I asked.

"They're heading in your direction about fifty yards out."

"OK, keep your eyes peeled for any more canoes."

I hung the phone on the hook I had fastened to a tree, and looked out at the water. It was pitch-black, with no light or illumination of any kind. I saw nothing; I heard nothing.

The next morning, in a routine phone call to battalion I reported the canoe incident. About three hours later an LCT came in and brought supplies and Harley Sample.

He started right in: "The colonel wants to know about the canoe."

"There isn't anything to tell. They saw the canoe on the other side of the inlet. I looked for it since they said it was headed this way, but couldn't see a thing. It was pitch-black."

"Why didn't those guys fire on it?"

"We couldn't see that they were Japs. Could have been natives trying to move away from the troops along this shore."

Sample was obviously determined to find an issue. When he was irate he looked dumber than usual.

"You should have fired on them!"

"Suppose they had been natives?"

"That's not for you to worry about."

"The hell it ain't. This is my outpost, and we're not going to fire at canoes in the dark, particularly when they weren't trying to land here."

The argument escalated in intensity and rhetoric. I finally told Sample to go back to battalion and leave us alone.

He did. But that was not the end of the problem. Since I was not one of the Washington boys, my case was to be handled "objectively." The next morning the LCT was back with a lieutenant from A Company who was to relieve me.

At battalion headquarters, Koransky was sitting in a tent behind a table. He said, "I don't take it lightly when somebody is insubordinate to one of my staff officers."

"Colonel, we had an argument about the best way to handle a situation, and all he was after was for me to say I was wrong. And I wasn't."

"Well, Lieutenant, I'm not here to argue with you but to tell you. You can either take a formal reprimand to be put in your file or stand a court-martial for insubordination. Think about it."

I saluted, glared at the ugly Sample who was hovering nearby, and left the tent.

Outside the tent I met Lieutenant Woods, one of my Benning buddies, a former lawyer, and the battalion S-1. We talked after getting a cup of coffee from the mess tent. "I know how you feel," Woods sympathized, "but a court-martial is not the way."

"Why not?" I countered. "Sample was stupid in the most glorious fashion. That's second-guessing where I come from, and the commander on the spot should have his decisions backed up."

"I know, I know," Woods said calmly, "and I'll defend you if you want it. But the good old boys won't let you win, and that will look worse in your file than a reprimand."

I thought about it while sipping my coffee.

"OK, Woody. I'll take your advice. I don't like it, but I respect your judgment, and I know Koransky and Sample don't know how to spell 'justice.' "

Woods took me to a tent and I made up a bunk next to his.

The next day I acknowledged receipt of the reprimand, and I spent the following days doing nothing around the camp. Woodman kept his distance, just as I would have expected from a good old boy.

In a few weeks we were back on Guadalcanal. The war in the Solomons was over for the 25th and for me.

CHAPTER EIGHT

Summing Up

August 11, 1984. The writing of a narrative is a linear process, event after event, strung together like beads on a string. This leaves little or no time for occasional pauses to look around and see how far we have come, to evaluate the circumstances we found ourselves in, to judge whether the actions taken were the best or less than the best.

It is time to take a lateral look and to develop some composites about the two campaigns. During a battle you see only a short distance. As time goes on you gather more and more information about what was going on all around you. Often it doesn't make you feel any better, but at least you understand it.

Sending the 25th Division to Guadalcanal was an afterthought. We weren't supposed to go there when we left Hawaii. But a troop ship with another division had gone aground in the tangle of islands off to the east, and we were put in as substitutes. Our equipment, uniforms, and weapons were on the docks at Brisbane, Australia. We had not planned for the Canal, nor had we trained or organized for it. We had to improvise our operations. There were few people—the general included—who did have enough skill and creativity to handle the tasks that faced us. A lot of people did not have such flexibility, skill, or courage—and they deserve some mention at this point.

FIELD-GRADE LEADERSHIP

The field-grade officers of the regiment suffered from a number of disabilities. Most of them were too old for active field command in either the infantry or in the rigorous requirements of jungle warfare. They were in poor physical condition, which had not been improved by the free and easy life on Oahu. Worst of all, they were incompetent. They lacked the professional background to adjust to the new and unusual type of warfare the Japanese engaged in. They had in most cases obtained their rank not by the exhibitions of leadership, combat skills, and soldierly qualities, but by working their way up the seniority chain of good old boys. Faced with the realities of combat, they put on their usual act of bluff and bravado, which collapsed in the savage rain forest.

The battalion and regimental commanders are particularly charged with putting an attack together. The concept of the operation, the use of firepower, and the disposition and actions of troops are their responsibilities. If nobody handles this task the companies fight as separate little armies. And so we did during the two Solomon Islands campaigns.

The commander of an infantry battalion is the highest ranking officer to make his presence felt at the front of the battle line. His personal, on-the-spot leadership is needed to direct the flow of battle, to seek out the soft spots, to reinforce success. Our commanders exercised control from command posts safely in the rear.

The field-grade officers were objects of derision, even among the company officers that had come from the same state National Guard unit. But what was to be done? Little, if anything. Politically, the Regular Army people would have kicked open hornet nests if they had replaced the Guard officers before the fighting started. Then, too, this was not a time when useful evaluation instruments existed to test for field-grade proficiency. Instead, such Guard officers were allowed to flounder and let their troops wander into death and injury without adequate direction or support or specific ideas about what was to be accomplished.

Fortunately disease, exhaustion, and poor physical condition eliminated these sham warriors. Unfortunately they were replaced, in most cases, by the second level of field-grade officers from battalion and regimental staffs—generally those officers who had stayed well back from the carnage on the front.

TACTICS

Before landing on Guadalcanal, we had heard of the bravery of the marines in storming Japanese positions. We were impressed, too, with the courage of individual marines who took out bunkers and pillboxes while exposed to heavy enemy fire. It was pointed out that marine defense dispositions had devastated attacking Japanese formations. Fortifications, machine-gun nests, and planned mortar fires were all effective.

However, there were some significant differences in the way the army divisions fought the Japanese. The first difference was in the use of massed firepower: the use of heavy bombardments before an attack and movement by infantry on a broad front was typical of army offensive operations. Artillery and air power were used throughout a battle, while fire direction was generally centrally controlled at the division level. Battlefield fire control by a division commander was often within a few hundred yards of the attacking echelons; communication by walkie-talkie and sound-powered phone was continuous. All of this resulted in a carefully coordinated attack pattern with the emphasis on firepower and maneuver.

Marines were trained to be aggressive in attack. Army soldiers were cautious, interested in survival. They expected a lot of ammunition to be fired in their support; after all, manpower in the Pacific was in short supply but ammunition was not. When these principles were violated by ignorant or timid senior commanders, we took a beating.

Patrolling to discover enemy dispositions, massed firepower, and maneuver to the flanks was the procedure that most frequently proved successful. Such an approach to offensive operations was frequently criticized by fire-eating marine commanders as being too slow, even timid. Perhaps it was, but a comparison of casualty rates between marine and army units during the Pacific War indicate who was right.

THE COLONEL

In no form of human endeavor does a man at the top have as complete control as a military commander. His influence is pervasive and not subject to comment or critique; his will is done; and whether he is a genius or an idiot matters not. He holds the issues of life and death in his hands.

So it is time to examine our experience and opinion of Colonel Weston. He was tall, thin, homely, pockmarked, ascetic, and ambitious. He was courageous, unfeeling, and not prone to accepting advice or suggestion, shaking his head to reject any idea before it was completely expressed. He selected men who would be totally amenable to his direction. He had favorites, openly admired, and those he disliked (for a variety of reasons). I was of the latter category.

He was a New Englander who mirrored the taciturn, rigid ways of his forebears. He was Regular Army, West Point, and filled with ambition to attain every West Pointer's dream—a general's star. But progress had been slow. The war, of course, for the Regular Army was the golden opportunity for glory, promotions, stars, and a place in the history books. All this was seen as possible, but only through his personal efforts and will. It never occurred to Weston that the command charged with doing his bidding would ever do anything but that, regardless of the cost. A mistake by anyone in his command was unforgivable because it reflected on him.

He would have been at home on the Somme, sending battalions and regiments to their doom without any nagging sense that he might be wrong, that it was all an unconscionable and cata-strophic waste. And now, because of this glorious, most opportune war, he was one step away from joining the immortals, the generals.

THE TWO LIEUTENANTS

Two lieutenants had been assigned to the regiment from the States. They were kept in the regimental headquarters until Weston had decided on the correct mission for their fresh young talents.

Colonel Weston had a bad back (never noted in his physical ex-aminations). In camp and garrison he slept on a plywood board that gave his vertebrae adequate support. But since his arrival in New Georgia, he had experienced many sleepless nights in foxholes at the front or on his poncho in the regimental CP.

Weston summoned the junior officers and apprised them of their mission.

"Back at the regimental rear on Guadalcanal, they have a ply-wood board that I usually sleep on. I have difficulty in getting even a little rest without it. The adjutant will give you an order authoriz-ing your transportation by available means to Guadalcanal. I figure the trip to get the board and bring it back here will take about three days. Do you have any questions?"

The two lieutenants looked at each other and decided they didn't have any questions. None that they wanted to ask Weston.

The adjutant was amused when he handed them some written orders.

"Real interesting job you got yourselves. All I got to say is—if you don't come back with the board, don't come back." He was tickled with that remark and guffawed loudly.

They left his tent with the orders. They had received the mes-sage for Garcia.

They went to the beach where landing ships were unloading day and night. After talking to a group of officers they found one that would take them aboard. There were no available quarters, but they could find shelter on the main deck under the canvas used to protect supplies. Also they were invited to the officers' mess for chow, which as usual on navy vessels was excellent.

It was almost dark when the LST backed out of the landing area and threaded its way through the islands to the open sea. The air was warm, the breeze was gentle, and the sky clear—or at least it was until the Klaxons began to sound and shouts of "air raid" went up. The LCT was headed back to the shelter of the islands, lights were doused, and a blackout reigned. The three other ships in the vicinity were lost to view in the darkness.

In less than five minutes after the alert the unmistakable throb of Japanese warplane engines was heard. The noise became steadily louder, and finally the whistle of a falling bomb was heard. The bomb fell short of the LST but exploded with a terrific roar on contact with the water, with bomb fragments hissing into the ship and clattering on the decking. And then the planes were gone.

As some ack-ack arced skyward from a distant destroyer, ship's officers started scurrying around to assess any damage. One of the windows on the bridge had been shattered, but search belowdecks showed no penetrations to the hull.

The commander, satisfied that there was no serious damage to his ship or crew, set out again on his prescribed course. Needless to say there was little sleep had that night. Our two young travelers discussed the events and allowed as how they were getting off to an exciting start.

With dawn's light they passed Savo Island and an hour later landed on Guadalcanal. Without transportation, map, or any earthly idea of where they were, they passed several hours interrogating army, marine, air, navy personnel, and Seabees. By mere chance, after walking several miles down the coast road, they met an army officer in a jeep who kindly offered them a ride to their destination. He dropped them off at a collection of tents and a sign saying "Division Rear Echelon." They entered one of the tents where a number of enlisted men were busy playing poker.

One of them, seeing that they were officers, came over to offer some assistance. After explaining that they were looking for the regimental supply dump, they were escorted for about a half mile through a coconut plantation where they found a sign indicating that they were in the right place. Here were rows of piled equipment covered with tarpaulins: each hump had a sign indicating which unit's bags and footlockers lay beneath the layers of canvas. Their escort looked around.

"I don't know where the guys are that are in charge here. There's nothing to do here. They may be down at the beach or over at Henderson watching the planes."

Charlie (one of the lieutenants) said: "Thanks a lot for your trouble. But we have one more question. Where do we get something to eat?"

The escort grinned. "Don't worry about that. We have a kitchen at division rear. All the rear-echelon people eat there. Breakfast at eight. Dinner at four. And all the C-rations you want for lunch or snacks."

They thanked the escort, and he went back through the palms to his poker game. Charlie and Jeff decided to explore their surroundings.

Several pyramid tents had cots, barrack bags, tables made of crates, and some folding chairs. One of the tents had a couple of field desks and a footlocker belonging to Capt. Henry Smith. There were two chairs outside the captain's tent, so they sat down and wondered what to do next.

Charlie said, "It's almost 1600. Why don't we stroll back to the division and have dinner?"

Jeff nodded, and they headed to the beach. Again they saw the group of tents and they determined to find the commander of this little community. Instead the commander, Maj. Fred Miller, found them.

"Sorry I wasn't here before but I had to check in some supplies down on the beach. As usual the shipping orders and the cargo markings didn't match. We had a helluva time straightening that mess out. But, what can I do to help you two?"

Charlie explained their mission, while Major Miller broke into a big smile. "So Weston wants his board—and sends two officers to get it." The smile was replaced with a laughing fit.

"Come on, let's go eat; you must be hungry."

As might be expected they found the regimental team, including Captain Smith, in the mess tent. (Nobody missed a kitchen-cooked meal in the rear echelon.) Smith took charge of the two visitors and seated them at his table. During the meal they explained their mission. Smith didn't smile. He was aware of Weston's foibles; in fact, one of his suggestions to the colonel had resulted in a position on that officer's "list" and banishment to the regimental rear.

After dinner Smith took them for a jeep tour of the nearby installations and battlefields. The lieutenants were impressed. These were places that they had read about and seen in newsreels, but standing on such ground gave them a sense of immediate history. When they arrived back at the regimental rear, Smith had two cots and blankets brought into his tent. He lit his Coleman lamp, passed out cigars, and poured some hefty drinks from a bottle of bourbon. There was a lot of talk about the Guadalcanal campaign, and because Charlie and Jeff knew little about the New Georgia campaign, little conversation was devoted to it. It was decided that on the following day they would have breakfast, get a crew to round up the board, and find a ship that was heading north to Leana Beach.

The following day there was unadulterated chaos. Pile after pile of equipment was examined while the sun got hotter and tempers shorter. The board should have been in the headquarters pile. After four hours it was located in the Company F area. No one knew why it was there, but the rear had been reduced to shambles to find it.

With a sigh of relief Smith loaded the lieutenants and the board into his jeep. After a few inquiries on the beach he found an LST going to Leana. He shook hands with Charlie and Jeff and left. It started to rain hard and the wind was blowing hard. It would be a dark and stormy night, as the mystery stories always began.

As the LST passed Savo Island the seas were running high. The ship, being rather small, was tossed around like a cork. Belowdecks, the crew worked feverishly to keep the cargo from breaking loose and scattering all over the hold. The lieutenants helped the crew with their dangerous task—all the while keeping an eye on their precious board, which they had lashed to the wall in the hold.

Toward dawn the LST closed Leana Beach. The wind had subsided, but the rain continued unabated. The two lieutenants and their board struggled down the ramp and into the mud of New Georgia. They started out on the main trail to the front, slipping and sliding in the mud, and eternally trying to get a better grip on the monstrous, cumbersome, bulky board. Hardly a yard would be gained when a corner of the board hit a branch or became tangled in a low-hanging vine, again escaping the hold of its carriers.

After several hours of such struggle they were exhausted, and when they saw some men lying down on the trail, they rested the board against a tree and walked up to the men on the ground. One of them saw the duo and yelled, "Get down, dammit! We're being ambushed!"

The lieutenants dropped immediately—and none too soon—as bullets whipped over their heads, cracking into trees and snapping branches.

There was a long silence following this fusillade. Only the torrents of rain splashing through the heavy foliage broke the silence. After what seemed an eternity the men on the trail got up and cautiously began moving forward. The lieutenants hesitated a few minutes before rising, and when they did the group ahead was out of sight.

Once again, they manhandled the board forward until they arrived at a small camp occupied by a supply echelon. They walked into a tent and the officer in charge (OIC) offered them a cup of coffee. After their second cup they asked for the best way to get to Colonel Weston's headquarters. The OIC stepped outside and called a sergeant, who came in, heard the problem, and offered to be a guide.

The OIC said, "It will take you better than an hour to get there. The trail is a mess but safe. The ambushes all take place nearer the beach."

He shook hands with them and wished them good luck.

They walked out to the trail and picked up the board. The guide had a look of amazement when he saw their burden; but like a good soldier he said nothing and headed down the trail. The trail was an endless string of muddy humps—slippery to climb and easy to slide down and lose one's footing. Every ten minutes of such travel called for a break. Their fingers ached from each frantic attempt to reclaim a hold on the board.

At long last they arrived at Weston's camp. The adjutant rushed out to greet them and direct them to the colonel.

Weston was sitting under a canvas shelter talking to his operations officer. He saw the lieutenants and gestured for them to wait. The adjutant saw the gesture and told the lieutenants to stand fast while he hurried back to his tent to get out of the rain.

The colonel and his S-3 were having a long, serious conversation with numerous forceful gestures by Weston. Finally the S-3 left, and Weston signaled for the lieutenants to approach. For the last time they hoisted the board and moved it into the shelter.

Weston was delighted.

"I want to thank both of you for a job well done. It will certainly help me in getting some decent rest. And now get down to your quarters and get into some dry clothes."

They saluted properly, about-faced, and headed for some food and dry clothing. They had thought Weston would have been interested in their odyssey.

But he didn't ask.

FOOD

A few observations about food are in order. For twelve months we ate meals out of cans. The C-ration offered a choice of three meals: hash, meat and beans, or stew. Each of these was paired with salt, a can of biscuits, and powdered coffee. The K-ration was issued in a Cracker Jack–like box and had a can of cheese and a pack of crackers, along with powdered coffee. The ten-in-one ration (which we never saw in combat) contained a variety of cans and more biscuits (its powdered milk was so rich that it made some of us sick).

This diet took its toll on our teeth, generating for me more cavities than in all my previous years, and made all of us susceptible to infection and disease.

We had fresh meat once—turkey for the 1943 Thanksgiving Day meal.

It was a constant irritation for us that the navy ships, combat or supply, had meat and eggs for their crews. Obviously no one in the navy felt there was sufficient space to carry fresh food for the army. But then, no one in the navy saw a good diet for soldiers as a priority concern. Nothing else during the war better illustrated the separation of the services.

THE TWO WARS

In island campaigning there were two wars. One involved the infantry on the front line, and it was deadly, debilitating, and offering constant tension and fear, as well as mixing in mud, blood, and despair. Everybody else in a division was "behind the lines."

Even though an enemy soldier would occasionally sneak into a rear area and spread terror, such episodes were the exception rather than the rule. The troops in the rear had plenty of water (a luxury), they could get a night's sleep, they could change underwear every other day, they could listen to the radio, and they used lights at night.

Ninety percent of the casualties (death, wounds, disease) were borne by the infantry. Since replacements were slow in coming, infantry companies were the size of platoons after Guadalcanal and the size of squads after New Georgia. In contrast the reduction in strength for support troops was minimal.

When we speak of war, in its fullest sense, we speak of the fighting men—the infantry. Only the medics shared—often in heroic fashion—the stringencies of the front line.

MOVING ON

Our departure from Guadalcanal was uneventful. Once again we bounced across the channel waters in LCTs to the waiting troop transports, and once aboard we quickly stowed our gear and hurried back up on deck. No one wanted to miss the departure from this dismal island. At last the anchors were taken in and we began slowly moving to the south.

If any emotion was dominant, it was relief. At last we were safe from all the terrors that the Solomons had generated to bedevil us for almost a year.

Standing at the rail we could see the full extent of the Canal: its occasional plantations, the hills of the north end where so many desperate engagements had taken place, Cape Esperance where it all had ended, Mount Popomanisiu brooding over the light and shadow of the limitless forests that clothed the land.

By what insidious combination of events had this dark, brooding spot on the sea—one of the most primitive places on earth—become the place for a confrontation between the military forces of the United States and Japan? The war that took place on the land, on the sea, and in the air was among the most violent in our history. And it was a war we had to win. A defeat at the hands of Nippon was unthinkable, and this accounted for the desperation with which the conflict was conducted by both sides.

As we moved south, I caught a temporary glimpse of the church at Kailo-tu-Maria where I had spent so many pleasant hours with Bishop Aubin. While my obligations to Guadalcanal were paid, I remembered that the bishop was still there striving to put his shattered mission system back together again.

All of us stood at the rail looking backward, silent, waiting for the island to disappear over the horizon. It was almost dark when the mountaintops finally sank beneath the horizon, and without any comment we turned away from the rail and left the Canal in our wake.

I walked forward to the prow of the ship. The wind was warm and gentle. The other ships in the convoy were spread out over the ocean like huge beetles. On the flanks of the convoy destroyers were riding shotgun.

I knew that we were heading generally south; in that direction lay New Zealand. It would take a few days to get there. During that time, all of us would luxuriate in eating hot meals, sleeping uninterruptedly, and watching the sea. Every hour put more miles between our ships and the Solomon Islands. And that was happiness enough!

PART
2

In every trip there is a leaving from—and a getting to.

CHAPTER NINE

New Zealand

When we had left Hawaii back in December 1942, we had no idea where we were going. Being aboard ship was refreshing and relaxing and a significant change from the daily routine of accelerated training for combat.

After the layover in Fiji and the briefing on our new mission, the atmosphere changed radically. There was less card playing, less kidding around, and more bull sessions on the Japanese and the kind of war they were fighting on Guadalcanal.

When we had started up the Solomon Islands chain and observed the rugged forest-covered islands, the *getting to* began. The closer we got, the grimmer became the aspect of this primitive island that fate had chosen as a battlefield for Japan and the United States.

But now we were again undergoing a *leaving from*.

Only the infantry in jungle warfare experiences the neverending stress and fear of the presence of the enemy. For the best part of a year we had lived with the daily and hourly strain of being vulnerable. There is no way to describe the galling sense of continuous vulnerability; it has no counterpart in civilian life.

And now—at long last—we were aboard ship, and each hour put more distance between us and the islands that had caused so much death, pain, and despair.

It was as if a great load had been lifted from our hearts and minds. Now it was possible to sleep, really sleep, instead of dozing off and waking in fits and starts. We were eating meals, hot meals, from a table, three times a day. And between meals there were platters of meat, cheese, butter, lettuce, and tomatoes for sandwiches. And milk—what a rare item—that we drank by the quart and went back for more. The sandwich bar was open and patronized all night long.

Our favorite recreation was to sit on deck, in the sunshine, in the warm but stiff sea breezes, and do nothing. The ocean seemed to possess an endless attraction for all of us: the appearance of a bird or a flying fish was a matter of comment, and cloud formations and rain squalls were given minute attention.

There was an inner barricade being built against what we had left. Nobody—I mean nobody—spoke of war, the Solomon Islands, the enemy. There was a conspiracy of silence about the traumatic experience we had just left behind us—and we wanted it to remain there.

Sometime on the trip we were informed of our destination, New Zealand. As with the Solomons we had little specific information about these islands. We pooled our ignorance and determined that New Zealand was part of the British system of commonwealths, that the people were white and spoke English, that they had a modern industrial society, and that they were fighting on our side in the war. But we were uncertain about its actual location.

Other than that we were going to New Zealand, we had little information on what we were going to do there, how long we would stay, where we would stay, or what kind of activities we might engage in. The sailors on our ship indicated that the port of Wellington had been used by the marines for rest and recreation (R&R) and that they spoke of it in glowing terms. Of course there was endless palaver about meeting girls, and having dates, and going to dances, and like that.

All in all we felt that New Zealand was just the ticket to get our minds off the war. Only one thing could be better, which was to go home.

So we peered out to sea and waited for the first indication of the land about which we knew little but from which we expected so much.

It was November 15, 1943, and for hours we had seen clouds clustered over a point in the distance—New Zealand. Little by little those hilly, green, and cultivated islands rose out of the sea, calling as the savage surface of the Solomons could not. The closer our ship wallowed, the more magnificent did this outpost of civilization in the great South Pacific become.

We espied houses, farms, villages, and an occasional sprinkling of smokestacks that meant the existence of some kind of industry. At about 1500 hours we could see in the distance the opening to Hauraki Gulf and, best of all, on its western side the first indications of a city, our destination, Auckland.

An hour later we sailed into the harbor proper, passing ferryboats crowded with girls. Our ship tilted sharply to starboard as every soldier who had not seen a white woman for over a year waved, yelled, and jumped up and down at the sight of so many perfectly scrumptious females.

There was a great deal of shipping in the harbor, a lot of whistles tooting, and much waving at the small boats that scurried around the ship. We arrived at our designated position, dropped anchor, and stopped engines.

We stood on deck feasting our eyes on the signs of civilization: buildings, lights, railroads, and buses. We hurried through the evening meal in order to resume our stations at the rail. Even at midnight few had retired. Most of us were content to watch the lights in the houses on the hills flicker out as the New Zealanders snuggled in for the night.

Finally, convinced that nothing of importance would happen after the wee hours, we shuffled back to our bunks and spent a night of short naps punctuated by sitting up and peering out a porthole to make sure it hadn't all been a dream.

The next morning, November 16, the troop commander gave us the orders for the day. We would be docking before noon, and we would carry off what we carried on: barracks bag, pack, and rifle. The docking was handled efficiently; the New Zealanders had had plenty of experience. We were marched to a railroad siding where we loaded each of the small passenger cars to capacity and beyond. After what appeared to be a long wait, actually less than a half hour, we rattled through the city and headed south through the North Island countryside.

Towns are only a few miles apart in New Zealand, each with an unpronounceable name. The countryside was more like New England than the Midwest. The fields were green with crops, some cattle, and the omnipresent sheep.

The train stopped at Pukekohe, a town with a single main street and a few stores and pubs and a hotel. We marched out of town to what had been a popular racetrack about a mile away, where many rows of "hutments" had been erected in the early days of the war as part of a training facility of the New Zealand army.

There was a large clubhouse, part of which was commandeered by battalion headquarters and the officers' mess. Regimental HQ had preempted part of the Pukekohe hotel, while lesser brass and the personnel section were located a few minutes down the street.

It should be noted that a battalion, after a year in the Solomons, didn't need a lot of room. My company, which at full strength required five officers and 195 men, now had two officers (Doc and me) and eleven men. It took four hutments to house our entire company with plenty of space for stretching out.

The mess halls were made operational the next day as our equipment arrived from the ship. We began a routine of eating three heavy meals a day and all we could eat in between.

The obsession of the troops was to get a pass for six, twelve, twenty-four hours, two days . . . whatever. The New Zealanders were free with advice about interesting places to visit, and the soldiers who visited Auckland returned with information packets that soon became dog-eared from use.

The pass system was very liberal, with as much as 50 percent of a company being granted leave at one time. Of course as soon as the legal 50 percent had exited on trucks and buses, another percent sauntered off into the countryside.

The item of greatest interest was not sights or scenery, but people—girls obviously—men, women, families, children.

In nearby Pukekohe, families—almost all of which had someone in the service—welcomed our soldiers into their homes. And the few men one saw in town were too young, too old, or unable to pass a military physical.

It is always a surprise to Americans to hear English spoken with an accent and with a sprinkling of words that are unknown. We quickly mastered "mate," "cobber," and "bloody." A lot of other words escaped us until we made a definite effort to understand them. Furthermore, there was a definite New Zealander "look" in both the men and the women. The British Isles' ancestors of the New Zealanders gave them rugged constitutions, ruddy complexions, and a habit of looking you straight in the eye. Neither men nor women were dressed very attractively, a result of wartime scarcity, high taxes, and a sense of frugality that would not tolerate fashion.

My own visits to Auckland were pleasant interludes in a reestablished routine of paperwork, processing replacements, and a modicum of training. Auckland seemed an old city, with a lot of narrow streets and narrow buildings that were not very high. Skyscrapers were absent. The important thing was to find a hill and get lost in admiring the harbor, the ships coming and going, and the play of sunlight on the water.

This was a city in a nation at war—a nation with limited resources, a very modest economy, and the need for great sacrifices of men and money. The result was a shabbiness in the buildings and their furnishings that seemed strangely subdued to soldiers accustomed to the glitter of American cities. However, after months in the primitive islands to the north Auckland looked just right. Here were paved streets, electric lights, and buses rattling down the streets, with men and women hustling about and children shouting to each other.

There were also bars where warm beer was served and restaurants where we learned that there were different kinds of "tea." I was especially taken with the "high tea" usually served late in the afternoon. One received a pagoda of small sandwiches, tarts, cookies, and biscuits, and a large pot of tea. Anyone who could polish off a high tea offering won the admiration of the waitresses, and was the subject of much comment and head shaking by those worthy women.

The regiment established a leave policy for the time before and after Christmas. During a four-week period, one week's leave would be granted to personnel—but not for more than 25 percent of the battalion at one time. I had met a fine family in town, and one of its members, Arthur Beatson, had suggested that we go to Nelson for Christmas.

In talking to the battalion adjutant about this trip, he indicated that hardly anyone had applied for leave. I was amazed at this and asked why no one wanted to travel. He guessed that since nothing would be going on during the holiday period, the smart alecks thought they would lie around for two weeks and then ask for leave when the training cycle was about to begin, thus having the best of both worlds.

In the event, my leave was granted and Arthur and I planned our trip, which was to begin in two days. It turned out to be the best Christmas season I spent in the Pacific. We took a slow but steady train to Wellington, New Zealand's largest city. No time was lost looking around the capital city, and we quickly boarded a ferry to take us to South Island. On board we soon found out what everyone already knew, the ferry had a marked list to starboard that one soon became accustomed to.

The water between the islands was quite rough, and I was told that Cook Strait was usually in a state of turmoil. As we neared South Island we moved into a fjord with its precipitous rocky walls. We were also honored by the presence of Pelorus Jack, a huge dolphin that had assumed the mission of escorting ships into and out of Nelson's harbor.

When the ferry docked Arthur spotted his relatives waiting on shore, and we quickly debarked to meet them. His brother with his wife and two children were most cordial, and, after shaking hands all around, we crowded into his brother Fred's car and were transported over a few bumpy streets to their home.

Fred's place was a modest establishment in a neighborhood of other modest homes. The rooms were small but cheerful, and the unfailing good nature and hospitality of our hosts never flagged.

A fine dinner was ready, and we sat down with hearty appetites to enjoy things we saw little of in the dark islands: fresh meat, vegetables, fresh bread, fruits, and, particularly, milk. The talk, of course, was about the war. They were anxious to know what the prognosis was—a matter I had no information on. Most of the able-bodied men of New Zealand were in the army, largely in Europe, and the people at home were deeply concerned about future developments.

It occurred to me a number of times that I was thousands of miles from home, on an island nation in the South Pacific, but there was so little difference in the language and customs of the people that I felt completely at home. Of course they wanted to know all about the "States," and I spent a lot of time convincing them that except for the fact that we had more of everything, they would feel right at home should they decide to visit us in the future. They were particularly pleased when I pointed out that another member of the British Commonwealth shared a common border with us that spanned the North American continent, and that there wasn't a fort or soldier on either side of the boundary in its entire length.

Our few happy days in Nelson soon ended, and we retraced our steps to Pukekohe, where nothing had changed in our absence. Our troops were in full-scale R&R with overnight passes available in abundance. The headquarters had little to offer about our next steps except that a training program would begin after the new year, and the pass policy would provide only a few opportunities for vacationers. This was most disappointing to many of the operators who'd pictured themselves lolling around during the holidays, and then using their pass privileges to avoid the rigors of the coming training program. As my battalion commander expressed it, "You are the only smart one around here. You had a chance to travel and enjoy the holiday season. None of the rest of these turkeys are going to get anything but overnight passes—and damned few of those."

We celebrated New Year's Eve in raucous fashion at the officers' club, but our thoughts were focused on a quick end to the war and the long voyage home.

RECRUITS!

Shortly after the first of the year a shipload of recruits arrived. They were greeted with enthusiasm because our units had been so whittled away by death, injury, and disease.

As usual, the recruits were a mixed bag; some appeared to be in good shape, others not. Little by little we got them all sorted out and assigned to squads, sections, and platoons. One bright spot for me was a young Texan assigned to my platoon as a sergeant: he had some college education and had been a training sergeant in the States. He was tall, broad-shouldered, good-humored, and capable. Furthermore, he looked like a soldier and was a good model for the rest of the recruits.

The training program started rather slowly because of the lack of NCOs with experience. Some had arrived in the replacement pool, but they were slow to accept responsibility for the strangers they were in command of.

Of eleven men who had come out of the islands, five were promoted to NCO rank, two were transferred to higher headquarters, and four were given jobs in the company headquarters.

Our concern was that combat experience was very thin, and we would need a lot of time to bring what was essentially a new unit to combat readiness.

As the training proceeded, it was apparent that the troops were not developing any intensity in their operational training: everybody was waiting for the day to end and for a trip to town. It was obvious that New Zealand offered too many distractions to the field units for a rigorous training program to work. This was true for the division staff, as well. So in early February 1944 we embarked again, leaving New Zealand and its pleasures. New Caledonia was to be our next port of call.

SIGNIFICANT ASIDE

It is appropriate here to call attention to a process that was used by higher headquarters in the allocation of replacements. "Skimming" best describes it.

Replacements were usually allocated in bulk to a division replacement center. Here the men were interviewed, with their records examined and units assigned. In theory this sounds like an equitable way to go, but in practice the center personnel identified some of the replacements as best retained at the division level. This usually meant tall, well-built, college-educated men with useful civilian skills.

As the remainder of the pool went down the chain of command, more and more of the best and brightest were skimmed off. And of course the rifle companies were at the bottom of the ladder: it was exceptional for a rifle company to get any troops with outstanding qualities. Instead there were too many of the short, fat, and relatively uneducated—many from rural areas. The concept that the best soldiers were needed at the "cutting edge" was not honored in replacement policies.

My platoon sergeant was the only exception I ever saw.

CHAPTER TEN

New Caledonia

On February 24, 1944, we sailed into Nouméa harbor after an uneventful trip. The city was spread out on hills overlooking the harbor, and the most imposing sight was the series of high smokestacks that marked the location of nickel smelters. Nickel was an important strategic metal for the United States and its allies. There were many freighters in the harbor, some of which carried supplies for the civil and military populations, but most were there to load cargoes of nickel for the industries of the West. There was little else of importance in New Caledonia.

New Caledonia is northeast of Australia and south of the Solomon Islands. The islands of New Caledonia (Nouvelle Calédonie) were governed by France, and for a long time the territory was a penal colony. In 1940, a mild revolution was staged by the Free French who took over the control of the islands and reestablished the alliance with the United States and other Western powers.

The population was about equally divided between French colonials and the native Melanesians. The latter never had adapted well to white governance but had taken no steps in recent memory to cause trouble.

The island of New Caledonia was rich in minerals that French mining companies had exploited for years, with particular emphasis on nickel and chromium. Most of the white population engaged in farming or plantation crops, producing copra and growing coffee and cotton.

The capital city of Nouméa is where we disembarked. Here we were loaded into trucks and went on a long, hot, dusty ride up poor roads to a town named La Foa.

Here in a large field dotted with eucalyptus trees we were to create a camp. We slept on the ground and ate C-rations until our tents were erected, the latrines dug, and the mess tent made operational.

After about a week we had settled in and established a routine that reduced the necessity of having to think. The training program to whip our replacements into shape got started: there was a lot of marching, patrolling, combat formations, and weapons training. The basic purpose of all this was to turn a collection of twelve men into a team. It was only when they could work together almost by instinct that they'd be called a squad.

There was a certain amount of reorganization, and I was delighted to be transferred to the battalion reconnaissance platoon. Our mission would be to conduct long-range penetration patrols into enemy territory. I was assigned two squads of men, about equally divided between veterans and replacements. Since there was little or no doctrine for such a unit, I was allowed to create my own training program. This gave a chance to apply some of the things I had learned about Carlson's Raiders. My number one boy on Guadalcanal, Sam, who had been a guide for Carlson, taught me many of the ideas I would try out in the coming months.

The regimental commander placed great emphasis on discipline and hewing to the line. Bugles were heard, formations were frequent, and inspections of individuals and quarters, plus constant supervision by regimental and battalion staffs, were the order of the day.

We were back on canned and dehydrated foods. The fresh fruit, vegetables, eggs, and milk of New Zealand were a fond memory. Occasionally someone received a box from the States, which was opened in the presence of considerable company. Cookies were quickly passed out, and it was rare if the recipient managed to keep a handful for himself.

Naturally the replacements fresh from home were appalled by the food, accommodations, and discipline, not to mention the awesome barrenness of La Foa, with no PX or R&R, and the nearest backward colonial city a four-hour ride to the south. One could spend hours listening to them recall their experiences in the army camps, the visits to big cities, the wonderful bars in nearby towns.

One thing that caused some discussion was the liquor ration. Each officer got one bottle a month, and each squad got a case of Coca-Cola. When these rations were issued a squad leader appeared, as if by magic, with a case of Coke and then returned to his men with my bottle. I figured that I got the best of that deal.

We were eventually told that we were in theater reserve, which meant that every time a major operation was implemented we had to be ready for a reinforcement role in case everything didn't go according to plan.

The intensive training program was designed to end at the time of the next Pacific operation. If we were not deployed, we would start over again. As we shall see, this occurred a number of times. When we were finally committed we were probably the most overtrained division in the Pacific.

I decided that long-range patrols across the island were the best preparation for our future mission. Each Monday morning we loaded up with four days' worth of rations and headed east across the island. About two miles out I opened a map, had the men gather around, and pointed out the route and the objective on the eastern shore. After the leaders had a chance to study the map, I folded it and put it back in my pack. One of the squads was designated to take the lead, and this was changed every day to give each squad the experience of breaking trail.

The terrain was very mountainous with many streams and rivers running from the central spine. Our path lay up this steep valley until we reached the divide, after which it was all downhill. I marched at the rear of the patrol and left the decision making to the leaders.

In March I was given a new officer, Lieutenant Wilson, to help with the training. He was a tall, good-looking young man and was delighted with his assignment.

At the end of each patrol we wound up at the tiny village of Nakety. Fortunately they had a small café to which we resorted for food and drink, French style. In this pleasant atmosphere we would wait for the slowpokes and look for the truck that was to pick us up late on Thursday afternoon. And so it went for many weeks.

EVENTS ON THE TRAIL

After we had made a variety of trips across the island using different routes and different objectives on the east coast, I decided to let the men carry out the mission on their own. One Monday, after we had covered about two miles, I veered off the track and set a separate course for the mountains. Since I didn't take any long breaks I arrived at a high grassy plateau just before dark. I built a small fire and after cooking up a can of meat and beans I settled down to await developments.

I expected that sometime just after dark they would stumble onto my camp—but they didn't. I finally decided that they had taken a course farther north and that we wouldn't bump into each other.

During the night I heard some strange noises and twigs snapping and arose to find about a half-dozen cattle slowly munching their way along the ridge. I stirred up the fire and let out a few hollers, but they were unafraid of such shenanigans and continued past my camp without turning to look at me as they went by.

At dawn I packed up my gear and headed east. I had to traverse a steep valley and even steeper slopes of a high ridge—probably the highest in the vicinity. There was a lot of growth near the top, and it took a lot of scratching and clawing before I got through it. As usual, there was a cattle trail on the top of the ridge, and I welcomed an open path. After about an hour I noticed clearings and gardens that indicated I was near the village of Qui Pain. In a few minutes I had been spotted and a few men and children came out to meet me.

I found myself in a native village, the first time I'd had such an encounter since the upland villages on Guadalcanal. The natives were Melanesians, the same race as those we found in the Solomons. However, they were more advanced than those primitives in the islands to the north. They built the same kind of housing that the colonials used in the plantations: a frame of logs covered with clay was the basic style. The roofs extended over an earthen floor and most of the family business was carried on there—cooking, mending, talking, sewing.

A middle-aged man who appeared to be a leader took me in tow and spoke some French to me; I called upon what I could remember of my high school French. Together we created a creaky, linguistic structure to communicate with each other. I was taken to his house, where we sat down on the porch. He told me the names of his wife, children, and relations. The wife brought out a coffeepot and two cups. My host indicated that this was *café calédonien*. It was black, hot, and delicious, somewhat different from Maxwell House but tasty and satisfying.

Late in the day we shared a meal of vegetables, beef, and fruit, and in payment I gave them some of my canned rations.

From our stilted conversation I gathered that some of the villagers occasionally worked for the plantation owners, and a few had seen service in the mines, but by and large they raised their crops and cattle and were almost self-sufficient. They seldom saw anyone from the government unless there was trouble, which was very seldom.

There had been a certain amount of excitement when the Free French had assumed control. Government patrols had gone through the highlands, visiting all the villages and telling the people to stay calm. The change of government may have caused some running around and broken windows in Nouméa, but up here in the wooded highlands, it had caused nary a ripple.

After dark a small fire was built. More *café calédonien* was prepared and consumed, and a lot of conversation went on all around me. Once in a while I intervened with some sage remark, which was greeted with laughter and smiles. Here, as in the Solomons, the natives have a delicious sense of humor, and they show an innate kindness to each other, particularly to their children.

Almost by common consent we all hunkered down for a night's sleep. I was given a special position near the fire while everybody else crowded in on all sides. At least three people were nestled against me. It was great for keeping warm in the cool, mountaintop nights, but it meant sleeping in one position since if anyone moved around there would be ripple effects all the way out to the edges of the congregation.

At dawn everyone was up and around, the fire was stirred up, and the coffeepot was steaming. I was provided with a dishpan to wash in, and after a dish of eggs and biscuit I prepared to go. My host was most effusive in his good-byes, and I nodded to everyone else.

Again I trudged on down the trail to Nakety; I paused every few yards as long as I was in sight of the village. At each stop I waved, and everyone waved back. Finally the friendly village was obscured to my sight, but the memories lingered on. I pressed on eastward with few stops. In late afternoon I reached a hill that overlooked a number of farms, with the village of Nakety in the distance. I was tempted to go down and visit the café, but our rules provided that we stay in the field for three nights before moving into the objective.

I passed an uneventful night, but I enjoyed the clear star-studded sky and the view of the ocean beyond the east coast.

The next morning, I tramped into Nakety and was greeted by several of the French villagers who were accustomed to seeing our patrols on Thursdays. About noontime I spotted the squads moving slowly down the coast road. When they saw me they quickened their pace, and when they arrived, I led the way into the café where we had our traditional meal.

After lunch we sat down under some trees to discuss the patrol. I was surprised to find that they had arrived in Qui Pain about two hours after I had departed. My host provided everyone with *café calédonien* and biscuits. In exchange the men left a large pile of C- and K-rations, which the natives were delighted to receive.

At about 1400 hours a six-by-six truck arrived to pick us up. We returned to camp by taking a narrow, winding cross-island road. In many places the road clung to the steep side of the numerous mountains that we skirted on the route westward; most of the road provided space only for one vehicle. I asked the driver what we would do if we met another truck. He just shook his head, and indicated that he spent most of his time looking for the infrequent turnouts, just in case.

We made at least two dozen such trips, sometimes skipping a week when other training was prescribed. On our last patrol we stopped at an abandoned hut on a trail we had never crossed before. It was hard to figure what the hut was used for, but there were a few small clearings nearby that might have been gardens in the past.

We were sitting around shooting the bull after supper when we heard someone coming up the trail. It proved to be a French farmer on a horse, with his daughter sitting behind him. He wore a shapeless felt hat and a long dark coat, and looked for all the world like a Kentucky hillbilly. His face was weather-beaten and needed a shave. My men however had eyes only for the girl, who had a pretty face, long dark hair, and beautiful white legs, most of which were visible as she sat astride the horse.

We exchanged greetings in French, and our visitor continued on up the trail without stopping. He seemed not a whit surprised that we were sitting in an abandoned hut. We watched them intently as they scaled the crest, which was shrouded in fog. After they disappeared, there was only one subject for discussion: What was a good-looking girl like that doing up in these mountains?

The next day, when we followed the same trail over the crest, there were many eyes looking for a house or farm, or even a horse, that would give us a clue to where our visitors had journeyed. We found nothing to answer our questions. Six months later some of my men were still wondering.

As with all else, my turn for a forty-eight-hour pass to the rest camp finally arrived. This R&R station was called Camp Stevens (and who that was, I haven't the faintest idea), and there was a large rambling structure on a hill just outside Nouméa. The establishment was run by the Red Cross, with five women and three men as operating personnel.

I was registered, given a tiny room (all to myself), a single towel, and a bar of soap. The dining hall had a number of tables, each seating four. You could sit where you wanted, and this gave an opportunity to meet other guests. I found that people were there from all parts of the division, and we traded horror stories about camps, the training programs, and the poor food.

A lot of time was spent sitting and looking at the landscape. There was a phonograph and a collection of classical records, which I played through in the time available. The meals were well prepared, and it was most satisfying to eat from plates with shiny silverware and on white tablecloths.

The rest center personnel were interested in keeping us busy with games, short trips to the Nouméa area, and, best of all, conversation about the States, which they had left only three months earlier.

In the late afternoon of the second day the jeep arrived to take a few of us back to our units. The road was bumpy, dusty, and devoid of any interesting scenery.

My buddies were all anxious to hear about the camp and particularly about the hostesses. So I gave them a long story, going into great detail about minor items, and then it was off to bed.

PARADES

A division sitting in isolation on a Pacific island is fair game for visits from higher headquarters. So it was natural that in the course of time we should have to parade for the galaxy of stars that came our way.

When it was announced that either Admiral Halsey or General Harmon was to favor us with his presence, we were dutifully marched to the parade ground, Qua Tom airfield, a few miles from our camp, for rehearsal.

A division parade is a complicated piece of business. It usually takes several days to mark off the field with small flags indicating where each adjutant would stand, he being the marker for the right flank and front rank of an organization.

There is a reporting procedure where each commander reports to the commander of troops that everybody is "present and accounted for." Then there is trooping the line by the visiting dignitary, and finally the march past the reviewing stand.

Of course no one in the division had been in a parade since leaving Hawaii, and it was obvious we would be rusty. This of course irritated Colonel Weston, who called several special rehearsals of the regiment to whip it into shape. In the course of doing so, he demonstrated his innate ability to act like a horse's ass, and lose even the little respect the men had for his questionable leadership.

At our first rehearsal, he assumed his position about twenty yards in front of the ranks. He then called for "commanders, center." When they got into a rank in front of him, he chewed them out for walking instead of running into position. Then he ordered them to double-time back to their positions, after which he repeated his command and the battalion commanders dutifully scurried out to their positions. It is fortunate that he could not hear the profanity and derision that welled up from the junior officers and NCOs.

Somewhat later after a march past, he again was in a froth.

"You men don't know how to march anymore!" he yelled. "Heads up, chest out, swing your arms, don't drag your feet!"

Then he proceeded to demonstrate by strutting back and forth, kicking his toes forward to raise a cloud of dust. This exhibition by a flawed product of harsh New England winters, West Point, slow promotion, and a hawk-like face, would have been funny if it hadn't been so ludicrous. Of course these shenanigans were never visible to his superiors who saw him only as a conscientious, aggressive, and somewhat ascetic leader. But the reality did not prevail, and in a few months he would trade his eagle for a star.

Eventually we did parade for Halsey and Harmon, and I thought we did a credible job. If Weston thought so, he never said: it was not his style to say that anything was good enough.

One other in the long list of Weston anecdotes is worth bringing up.

The regiment had spent a long week in the field on various exercises, including an attack problem involving a fortified area. We moved into the attack position while artillery and mortars pounded the objective. We attacked with our machine guns chattering away on the flanks and riflemen pouring fire into the embrasures of the fortification. Then the flamethrowers cut loose and the umpires stopped the problem. The attack was successful. We were then ordered to return to camp, but no one was to ride back except truck drivers. The battalion mortar section loaded its heavy tubes and baseplates into a three-quarter-ton truck and marched with the rest of us.

The troops were observed by Colonel Weston as they closed into camp, and when he noticed that the mortars were not being carried he sent for Gillette, the battalion CO. While we all went to the officers' tent area we were quickly called together by Larson, the S-3, to meet at the colonel's tent.

Gillette was livid. After reflecting negatively on Weston's ancestry, he told us that he had been ordered to have the mortar section send its weapons back to the exercise area and carry them back.

Gillette said that he felt that the officers should do this job, and we agreed. We jumped into a truck and followed the mortar three-quarter-ton to the exercise area about three miles away. There we unloaded the different tubes, tripods, and baseplates; attached the harnesses; and loaded them on our backs as we marched off.

We sang "The Battle Hymn of the Republic" and the artillery song. On the last half mile into the camp it looked as if the entire regiment had turned out to line the road and cheer us on. Bottles of beer and spirits were handed to us trudging heroes as loud cheers rang out during our triumphal entry into the battalion area.

We turned the equipment over to the mortar section.

Nothing else we ever did so impressed the men.

Weston didn't see it. He made it a point not to see such things.

ROTATION—REORGANIZATION

The army decided to establish a rotation program for several reasons, among them the following:

- A majority of troops in the Pacific theater were killed, injured, or victims of disease, and were sent back to the States.

- Troops in the Pacific had seen action twelve to twenty-four months before the troops in Europe.

A system was devised that gave points for months overseas, points for medals awarded, and so on. Under this plan the men with the maximum exposure to combat were rotated back to the States. A few men from the battalion qualified for the minimum-point score and went home. (Colonel Weston was given leave to meet his family in the States. No other officer was given such leave.)

As a result of the losses and gains a number of changes were made in the battalion officer corps. We received a new battalion commander, Ralph Gillette, a National Guard officer, one of the old boys from the regiment. He brought Ron Larson, another old boy, as his S-3. The unlamented Harley Sample went to regiment as S-3, which was a typical example of Weston's picking staff officers who were generally held in low esteem by the troops. A couple of junior officers joined us from the States, and they were a refreshing addition to the headquarters.

Overall the changes were all to the good, and we were all able to communicate again, something that was woefully lacking during the Koransky-Sample regime.

On a higher level, our excellent division commander was sent to Eisenhower's command, where he established an outstanding record as a fighting general.

One of his aide-de-camps (ADCs) became division commander, while the other ADC had been given a division after Guadalcanal.

ORIENTATION

In the early days of 1944, the higher headquarters decided that Pacific troops should be given the necessary information to counter the grumbling and criticism so prevalent among the enlisted men (EM).

(I remember when sitting in a foxhole on Guadalcanal in the rain. The sergeant I shared the hole with shook his head and asked me: "What in the hell are we doing, way out here fighting on this godforsaken island? Why don't we let the Japs keep this stinking rock?" I didn't have an answer.)

Now, in 1944, Colonel Weston put together a committee of officers and EM to develop and present a program of orientation. Mark Bemish, who finally got a staff job (S-2) at regiment after a long period of buzzing around the headquarters, was to head up the committee. I was selected as one of the members—a surprise to me, since I was not one of Weston's favorite people.

Mark was good at preparing maps and illustrations. He and some talented G-1s did an admirable job in preparing huge training aids. I set to work preparing a list of topics that we would cover each Saturday morning for three hours with the entire regiment present.

I talked to a lot of officers and EM to find out what they wanted to know. I was flabbergasted at the range of concerns I uncovered: things like the nature of war, the nature of the enemy, and the goals of the Allies in this conflict were not unusual.

There was one question that I'd asked myself and that I couldn't answer: "Why wasn't this program started when we first got into the army? Why wait until so many questions surface that it is embarrassing?"

We talked about U.S. and European history; China and Japan; Germany and Italy; military strategy; duty, honor, and country; patriotism; current events; the role of the different services in the Pacific; battle tactics of the enemy; and postwar goals. These presentations were sometimes good, sometimes not. Some were well received, others were greeted with skepticism or boredom.

It is well to remember that the veterans of two campaigns in the Solomons had seen war at its most savage, and in the worst environment in the world. After all the effort since August 1942 we were still thousands of miles from Japan, and if future progress was as slow as that of the past, it could take a decade to bring the war to a conclusion. For these men, it was hard to develop motivation and commitment to a cause they only understood in a very fragmentary way.

Whether we made any headway in our purpose is hard to evaluate. I came away from a thirty-three-week effort at orientation with one abiding conviction. The military should orient its people from their first day in the service, so that when faced with the rigors of battle they could reach into their innermost being and find the wellsprings of dedication and conviction that would enable them to carry on.

I was afraid in 1944 that we had not done a good job, that we had depended on only conventional training to instill a sense of commitment to our country and its goals. This had not worked, and now belatedly we were trying to engage in a patchwork of talks, lectures, and explanations to stem the tide of cynicism, and sometimes despair, that our men evidenced as they contemplated the seemingly endless task of defeating the men from Nippon.

The months followed each other, while the routine of patrols, occasional field exercises, and Saturday orientations continued. In the fall, there was word that we were finally assigned a mission after almost nine months in theater reserve. In preparation for this mission we were to engage in some amphibious training, and in due time we were transported to a beach area south of our camp where we set up our pup tents and waited.

PRESQU'ÎLE DE VITAL

In a day or two, three nondescript amphibious ships arrived and anchored about a half mile from shore. In the orientation given by their personnel we found that they were British ships, they had participated in a few landings in the past year, and they would be with us for two weeks to give each battalion team an opportunity to practice landings.

Then followed a lot of rigmarole about what boat team we were in, the part of the beach we were to land on, the objective we were to capture. The next day we were ferried out to one of the ships in landing craft and climbed the landing net to the deck, then were shown to our quarters. I shared a small, cramped room with two double-deck bunks. There was one light in the room, with a small washbowl in need of a vigorous scrubbing.

We noticed a decided difference between U.S. and British ships. With all of their faults, and in spite of all the converted banana boats, the U.S. Navy ships were clean. The British, on the other hand, put little store in scrubbing and sweeping decks or swabbing out latrines.

The crew, however, was experienced, cordial, and disciplined.

This was demonstrated when a half hour before evening mess we went to the officers' room where a tub of grog was ready for us. The tub was an impressive wooden structure with wide, well-polished brass fittings and a plaque to honor the king.

These proceedings were very "jolly" and ended when the steward called us to the table. We were seated roughly according to rank and then were served a plate with several boiled potatoes, a slice of beef, and some green beans. We then discovered the second big difference between our navies: the Royal Navy food was absolutely tasteless. Salt and pepper didn't help. None of our crew said anything, but I could see by the grim set of jaws that a can of good old-fashioned C-rations would have been most preferable.

I asked for coffee, got it, and knew immediately that I had made a mistake. It tasted like bilgewater. In the future I drank tea in self-defense.

The steward asked me whether I wanted anything else; I opined that a dessert would be nice. He hustled away and returned with a rectangle of cheese, but immediately sensed from my expression that something was wrong. I repeated my request for dessert—a piece of pie, ice cream, something similar. The steward's face brightened, "What you want, sir, is a sweet." I nodded and immediately received a small dish of grayish-white substance. The steward enlightened me: "It's duff, sir, duff."

After the first mouthful I asked the British officer next to me how it was made. "Mix equal parts of flour and water, boil until thick, cool, and serve," he said in a clipped English accent. I struggled through the remainder of the duff and waited patiently for the captain to rise and terminate the mess.

Back in our cramped cabin, we dug out a K-ration and shared crackers and cheese.

Tomorrow would be a hard day. The single bulb was extinguished, and we rocked gently in the swells rolling in from the Pacific.

The landing exercises taught us nothing new. They were more beneficial to the planning staff and ships' personnel, who polished up their timing and logistics skills. There were the usual critiques in which we were damned with faint praise, while staff members carried out their usual mission of finding something to criticize in all parts of the exercise.

We returned to camp and found we were alerted—again—this time to take part in a projected Mindanao campaign. The battalion staffs were organized to prepare a plan for the invasion. My particular assignment was to make a study of the city of Davao on the south shore of Mindanao island. The material I was supplied was quite interesting and remarkably complete. (I had forgotten that the army had been in the Philippines for years and had prepared extensive plans for its defense.)

We had quite a few meetings, but these proved to be unnecessary because our objective had been changed to Luzon. In the middle of November, training came to a halt as plans and preparations for the Luzon campaign took priority.

There was a lot of frantic scurrying around, building boxes, checking equipment, and dividing all our possessions into the various echelons that would determine their landing priority. As I packed my footlocker, I hoped that it would not again be dropped into the sea as it had been at Guadalcanal and necessitate a diving expedition to recover it.

We moved everything by truck and rail to the Nouméa docks and began the slow process of combat loading. In due time all was loaded, and at 1100 hours on 17 December, 1944, we sailed out of Nouméa harbor.

Adieu, Nouvelle Calédonie.

CHAPTER ELEVEN

On to the Philippines

The trip to Guadalcanal took four days of uneventful sailing. Whereas the trip from the Canal had been one of relief and relaxation, this trip to the island brought back old tensions and foreboding.

When the island came into view, it filled me with the same feeling of darkness and uncertainty I'd had when I first saw it months before. Of course this impression was largely dispelled when, after the amphibious landing at Tetere, we borrowed a jeep and toured the coastline from the Matanikau to the Berande. Guadalcanal was now an enormous supply base for future operations; Henderson Field had been modernized, and large planes came and went as at any busy U.S. airport.

After a day we boarded ships and sailed across Sealark Channel to Purvis Bay on Florida Island. Here we took on provisions and fuel for the trip to the Philippines. When the convoy had completed its reloading we sailed on December 26, 1944, and headed up the Slot.

As we passed Savo and headed into the Solomon Sea our convoy stretched away to our front and back, a massive collection of destroyers, cruisers, and troopships. Patrol planes from Henderson and Munda passed overhead. On the second day out we passed between New Guinea and New Britain. Off to the west we could see the towering peaks of the Owen Stanley Range where the Australians and Americans had slogged up and down mountain trails to confront the enemy at Buna.

On the third day we arrived at Manus Island, with its magnificent harbor, in the Admiralty Islands. We had a chance to visit the fine navy officers' club—a true oasis. This would be our last stop before we again entered combat.

We stayed at Manus Island from December 29, 1944, to January 2, 1945. We celebrated the new year as we sailed north, but it was a muted holiday because we knew that another campaign awaited us in the Philippines.

At least we were able to open the sealed containers that held the maps we were to use in the coming campaign. There were many rolls of maps, and we quickly laid them out on the deck. The maps covered central Luzon and we noticed that Lingayen Gulf appeared to be the gateway from which operations could strike to the east, south, and north. (It took quite a while to gather the maps into sets to be distributed to unit and battalion commanders.)

In one container we found the operation orders that were to guide our actions after landing. We were right in assuming that Lingayen Gulf would be the landing ground. The army and navy plans were voluminous and indicated that a massive effort was to be mounted to defeat the Japanese forces known to be in great strength on the island.

After a few days we noticed a huge island off to the west; we knew it was Mindanao. Our maps also indicated that we were floating over the Philippine Trench, the greatest rift in any ocean bottom, and one of the ship's officers told us the sea was seven miles deep at that point. Some of us spent some time looking over the rail and trying to imagine how far down seven miles would be.

Near nightfall we turned west and kept a small island to our port side. This was Surigao Island, and we were in the strait with Leyte just visible to the north. Only two months earlier, the U.S. Navy had won a classic battle with the enemy in these same waters. We were glad that Barney Oldendorf had been the victor.

The trip to the South China Sea and the move northward seemed interminable. There was little or no information on how the war was going, and it was difficult to see why security had to be so tight on a troopship from which no one could escape.

We spent a lot of time on deck, looking at the vast array of troopships, destroyers, cruisers, and an occasional battleship or carrier. Sometimes, far off to the east, we could spot the close-knit cloud formations that always hung over mountains and highlands. That was Luzon, but we had no idea what specific location lay below those clouds.

Finally, in the early dawn of January 11, 1945, we were steaming west and south into Lingayen Gulf. There were ships everywhere, probably the greatest aggregation of sea power up to that point in the war. As we neared land, we could see that the towns and villages lining the shore had been subject to devastating sea and air bombardment. Only the Lingayen high school building still had a few walls and a chimney intact; but it had been used as a point of reference for so many fire missions that it seemed as though a strong wind could easily topple the remaining skeleton.

U.S. troops had been ashore since January 9, so there was no need for the preparations that usually accompany an amphibious landing. Our ship moved slowly to its prescribed location and the anchor was dropped. The public address system crackled with orders, and in due time we climbed down the landing nets into the waiting LCTs and were ferried to the beach.

We were surprised to be greeted by hundreds of Filipino men, women, and children. It occurred to us that if all these civilians had survived the storm of fire that had raked the coastal area, the enemy would also have survived. Fortunately, there was only sporadic and harassing fire directed at the initial landings. But all this meant that the enemy was waiting for us somewhere else. We would find out in due course.

After a certain amount of milling around and waiting we moved out into the countryside. There were fields, small settlements, and villages everywhere. This was no uncivilized land: here were good, hard-based roads, occasional school buildings, irrigation ditches, bridges, and people. The inhabitants had fled to the interior during the days of bombardment, but were filtering back to their homes with the few possessions they'd carried off and now were happy to return.

We would stop for a while, then get up and march off again. This was kept up for three days and nights, during which time we had little or no information on what was happening or what we were supposed to do. Finally we stopped for good, and everyone sat down and fell asleep.

Hearing a lot of clatter I awoke to find that a kitchen truck had arrived. I alerted my sergeants—which took some doing—and went off to find the commander.

He was sitting on a case of C-rations, alone. He looked as weary as I felt. He motioned for me to sit next to him. He showed me a 1:25,000 scale map with some X's on three towns lying to the east, Pozarubio, Binalonan, and Urdaneta. "That's where the division is going," he said.

"Is the enemy in these locations?" I asked.

"That's the information we get from Div. Intelligence. We expect this to be a full-scale operation," he said.

"When do we start out?"

"Tomorrow. Meanwhile, have your men eat, rest, and wash up. Most of them look terrible."

I agreed and returned to the platoon. I gave Lieutenant Wilson and the sergeants the poop. They were too tired to ask questions, and after I visited the mess trucks for a few edibles and hot coffee, I joined them in the land of Nod.

On January 17, 1945, we moved out at 0700. This was open country with rice paddies, grassy fields, and little cover or concealment. There were a few wooded areas of bamboo and palms with other tropical trees along roads, streambeds, and around *barrios*, or villages. These would be the places from which the Japanese would launch their attacks.

Now was the dry season, and troops put out on the flanks had no difficulty in traversing the dried paddies.

A Company was left in Pao, eight miles west of Binalonan, to secure our march while the rest of the regiment proceeded. As might be expected, the enemy noticed the isolated unit at Pao and attacked; there was a wild melee of firing and fighting, and the enemy lost almost that entire command of eighty-eight men. But word of the fighting made it necessary to hold up the leading elements until the strength of the attack and its results were known.

At 1620 the battalion attacked across an open area toward Binalonan. Evidently the enemy was surprised and offered weak resistance when our troops entered the town. Here the Japanese used what was to become a familiar tactic in Luzon: firing from underneath *nipa* huts where they had dug foxholes. It was slow work flushing them out with rifle fire and grenades. Into the middle of this encounter a lone enemy tank wandered down the road toward our position. It was turned into a funeral pyre by bazooka and rifle-grenade fire.

We moved into the town proper, which consisted of a town square surrounded by buildings. I took the platoon into one building and made an estimate of the situation. There was firing across the square and some mortar fire and an occasional artillery round landing in the town. A number of fires had started, and it was evident they would be burning for a long time.

At dusk we heard a commotion on the back street next to the building we occupied. One of my scouts yelled, "Jap tanks!" and, sure enough, about five came rumbling toward us.

It was our good fortune that the regimental cannon company was deployed at the end of the street, and it opened up with point-blank fire, blowing up the two lead tanks. The street was too narrow for the remaining tanks to turn around, so they proceeded to use their small cannon and machine guns to pepper those of us crouching in the buildings. The bazookas and rifle grenades hammered the remaining tanks, and the crews trying to escape their battered vehicles were caught in a hail of rifle and BAR fire. All the tanks were now disabled and burning. When they started to explode, we left the building and moved onto the square where foxholes had been dug in the past. The infantrymen accompanying the tanks were driven off or slaughtered.

After dark there appeared to be no more enemy activity, but burning buildings, tanks, and vehicles lit up the landscape. We could see no movement anywhere. This was in keeping with our battle-tested practice of digging in after dark and staying there. Anything that moved was considered the enemy and was immediately taken under fire.

I was therefore shocked when at about 2000 hours my sound-powered phone indicated a call coming in. It was Sample.

"Colonel Weston wants a patrol out to the east of the town toward San Felipe to see if the Jap armor and infantry have withdrawn."

"We are parked in the middle of the square. We don't have any idea where our troops have their perimeter off to the east. If a patrol goes wandering over there they'll be shot."

"Sorry," Sample said, "the old man was emphatic about getting your patrol out."

I hung up. Then I called Sergeant Ferguson, the first squad leader, and explained what was needed.

He was flabbergasted. "If we go over toward the edge of town, we'll be mowed down."

We talked some more, and then I decided to make one more appeal to sanity. As I suspected, Sample said no. I asked whether they had phone connections with the eastern perimeter to warn our troops there that a patrol was coming through.

He said no.

I told Ferguson, "Take your men down that street behind us. Do a lot of talking. Make a lot of noise so our guys will know you're coming through. When you leave the perimeter, go down the road for a hundred yards and lay low until daylight. Then proceed carefully for one mile, and then return quickly and report what, if anything, you saw or heard."

Ferguson shook his head and gathered up his squad. I could see them moving along the street in the firelight until they disappeared from view.

I prayed I wouldn't hear any gunfire. I didn't. Hour after hour, the men and I sat alert, waiting to hear any sounds from the east.

This was a totally unnecessary patrol. But it could have been handled by the eastern perimeter and a few listening posts along the road. It was another example of the incredible determination of Weston to make whatever sacrifices necessary to ensure his quest for a star.

The next morning, at about 0530, Ferguson returned. He had seen nothing. He had heard nothing.

I phoned regimental HQ. "Tell Sample that the patrol has found no evidence of enemy activity on the road to San Felipe," I told the operator.

The call was never acknowledged, but I didn't expect it to be.

SAN MANUEL

This was the most violent, concentrated, and sustained battle the regiment had ever engaged in. The enemy command had selected its terrain carefully, prepared positions for tanks, artillery, antitank guns, machine guns, and troops. The Japanese were determined to make a stand in this *población*, the largest town we had yet encountered both in size and in the number of buildings it contained.

The Japanese 2d Armored Division held the town, and it intended to repulse all attackers with heavy losses and inflict the first substantial defeat on the U.S. forces since their landings at Lingayen. This was the battle the Japanese wanted, at the right place, at the right time.

On January 18, at 1300 hours, our battalion was relieved by the 2d Battalion and we entered a bivouac area, to rest, to assess our losses, and to reorganize as necessary.

Wilson and I gathered the men in a small clump of trees and traded anecdotes about the activity in Binalonan. Everyone had been scared out of his wits by the tank battle just outside the building we'd occupied. One of the men had dashed out and dropped two grenades into a tank just outside our door when he saw the occupants raising the hatch cover. After the explosions no one had exited the hatch.

Ferguson was still upset about the patrol he had taken out on the San Felipe road. He indicated that they had passed a lot of foxholes occupied by troops from other companies. They took a terrible hazing from these guys, including remarks about the sanity of any dumbbell who would stumble around the front line in the dark.

Ferguson didn't feel safe until he moved his patrol well down the road and away from our positions. The enemy he could cope with. The GIs from the 1st Battalion were another story.

That night, after a hot meal, I met with Gillette and Larson.

As usual we had a map spread out on the tailgate of the mess truck. We saw that the road to the east passed through San Felipe some miles out. Beyond that, to the north, was a high ridge that overlooked the town of San Manuel.

I was to take the patrol out after first light, pass around San Felipe, and get up on the ridge to see whether the enemy had any positions there and to observe San Manuel for signs of enemy activity. Wilson and I briefed the squads on the next day's assignment and then we all hunkered down to a good night's rest.

On January 19 we moved out at 0700 and moved north of the road while staying parallel with it. There was a lot of air activity, most of it in the direction of San Manuel. Artillery firing off to the south indicated that some fighting was going on in the area of the adjacent regiment.

We moved slowly across fields and streambeds, and paused frequently to observe before crossing to our next phase line. Wilson marched with Ferguson and his squad on the left flank. I stayed with Austin and his men on the right. At about 1000 we slid past San Felipe. We could see no activity in the *barrio* from our position about 600 yards to the north. But ahead we could see our objective, a long ridge generally trending north and south and ending at the San Manuel road.

I pulled the two squads closer together as we approached the ridge. The ridge was wooded, but not enough to prevent observation for at least a hundred yards. It took us about two hours to reach the summit, where we stopped, spread out in a protective formation, and rested. After polishing off a can of C-rations I called Wilson, Ferguson, and Austin together for a powwow.

So far the patrol had been uneventful, but our instincts told us we were in enemy country. We decided to keep our base at the present location and to send a squad south along the ridge to check on the observation into San Manuel. The other squad would proceed north to look for signs of enemy activity in the Arboredo River valley that we were looking into at the base of the ridge. Each patrol was given two hours for reconnaissance unless it saw signs of the enemy, in which case it was to return immediately to base.

About ten minutes after the patrols left, one of Ferguson's men from the north patrol returned with the news that they had sighted some enemy soldiers in the valley below. I sent a man to the south to tell the other squad to return to base while Wilson and I headed north.

About 300 yards from the base we met Ferguson, who motioned us to come to his observation point. Below in the valley was a small *nipa* hut with two soldiers aimlessly walking about. After a few minutes one of them entered the hut, and after another five minutes two men emerged.

This was the first time in the war that I had seen *live* enemy soldiers. In the Solomons I had only seen them dead. But here they were, wandering around in their sloppy uniforms and totally unaware that we were watching them. It was not clear to us what they were doing there. We guessed that they were manning an outpost of some sort, but in their position they had limited visibility and we couldn't see any trail that they might be blocking.

We watched for about a half hour, and decided after observing their comings and goings that there were no more than five men in the shack. None of them carried arms, and we suspected that as infantry they had rifles and that these were inside.

We figured nothing would be gained by firing at them. The distance was over 200 yards, and we would alert their entire outpost system that we were in the area. I was sure that the battalion did not want this ridge to be occupied when it would be useful to our future operations.

We returned to base and found Austin and his men waiting. I explained what we had seen, and Austin told us that the tree cover on the ridge was too thick to provide any observation southeast to San Manuel. So we decided to return to camp and report our findings. Gillette was surprised that the ridge had not been occupied, since aerial reconnaissance had shown heavy troop and arms emplacements in and around San Manuel.

He told us that Company A was moving out to establish a river block on the Arboredo just north of the road into San Manuel to protect our flank, and the battalion was going to move its base comp to a point midway between San Felipe and San Manuel. The move would begin just before sunset.

Late in the afternoon of January 19, the artillery began to roar and flights of dive-bombers flew over our position toward San Manuel. The attack lasted almost a half hour with artillery, aerial bombs, and strafing doing their best to make life miserable for the enemy. We could see great clouds of black smoke rising into the air where fuel dumps and vehicles had been hit and were burning. At 1800 the battalion moved out with A Company in the lead. It was dark when Larson told me where the battalion CP would be located. I deployed the two squads for perimeter security and then found a dry ditch for my own quarters. Wilson and I talked for a long time about the day's events and what the operation against San Manuel would bring.

The night was clear. The stars shone brightly, but the sounds of war—the harassing artillery fire, the occasional chatter of a machine gun a long way off—were proof that we and the enemy were getting ready for something big.

For the next few days following January 19, higher headquarters seemed unable to make up its mind how and when it wanted to deal with San Manuel. Intelligence had already indicated that the town was a strongpoint with weapons of all types, including tanks in position covering all avenues of approach.

It was obvious that the enemy had conducted sufficient reconnaissance to know the disposition of our two regiments that the division had committed—and that San Manuel was their target. It was equally obvious that the more time the enemy forces had to recover from the air and artillery attacks of January 19, the tougher those forces would be to deal with.

Yet the battalion advanced only one company into the area I had reconnoitered, establishing a few positions and then crossing the Arboredo to the ridge parallel to the river. And the enemy launched a few small-scale attacks against these positions, obviously to test the strength and dispositions of the A Company units.

The battalion moved along the road and established a CP about 800 yards east of the edge of town. Here we waited while patrols went north and south, but not toward San Manuel. It was finally decided that the attack would be launched 0715, on January 24, thus giving five days of grace to the enemy.

THE BATTLE OF SAN MANUEL

On January 24 we were aroused at 0400 and had a hot breakfast of pancakes, bacon, oatmeal, Spam, bread and jelly, and coffee— "just before the battle, Mother." At 0445 Gillette, Larson, and my platoon moved forward to reconnoiter positions from which we were to attack at 0715. It was very quiet, and we were very quiet. At 0515 we could see the town in the morning mist.

The battalion was to attack the southwest corner of San Manuel, moving generally from west to east. Our left boundary would be on the main road, while our right would be on a creek that meandered along the south edge of San Manuel. Our zone was approximately 400-plus yards wide, but a Filipino cemetery, about 150 yards square with an entrance on the main road, sat directly on the line of advance, which meant that our troops had to pass through it during the attack.

The battalion had been marching toward us, and at 0615 it was halted while the company COs came forward to get their orders.

Gillette decided to attack with two rifle companies and to keep one in reserve. There would be an artillery preparation for fifteen minutes at 0700, after which the attack would begin.

My platoon was to keep an eye on the open right flank, with special attention to the stream and heavy tree growth and underbrush that provided a natural avenue of approach into the battalion position.

Off to the north the 2d Battalion, designated as the main attack unit, was making similar preparations. It was to concentrate its efforts on the northwest corner of the town and drive to the southeast. The concept was a pincer movement to squeeze the enemy forces in the west part of town and drive them to the east.

At 0700 the artillery preparation began. The concentrations were heavier than anything we had seen in the Solomons. Different calibers were firing—from 105mm guns, just a few miles back, to 155mm "Long Toms," a long way back. At 0715, the forward elements moved out very slowly from their positions about 800 yards west of San Manuel. (Up to this time no return fire had been received from the enemy. This was normal Japanese procedure. When the infantry came abreast of the cemetery, a few shots were received from the line that bordered the first north-south street.)

At this point we were prepared to throw a Sunday punch. A group of five tanks had been placed in support of the battalion, and Gillette had assigned them the task of making a break through the enemy defenses.

They came rumbling up with hatches open, tank commanders standing erect like statues, not deigning to look sideways at the less fortunate foot soldiers to the side, who had to scamper left and right to get out of the way. It was obvious that this was not to be a coordinated tank-infantry attack, since the tanks moved briskly ahead while the attacking infantry were left some distance behind.

The tanks moved into the tree line on the edge of town, and then all hell broke loose. From the sound, our tanks were firing, enemy tanks were firing, and antitank guns, mortars, and machine guns were firing. In less than five minutes, our tanks returned, very rapidly. A mortar shell had gone through the hatch of one of them and killed part of the crew. The other tanks were buttoned up and showed single-minded devotion in getting the hell out of there. They disappeared from our view as they moved west.

Gillette didn't know where they went, and neither did regiment. Later that day they were discovered many miles from the perils of battle, nursing their wounds. So much for the first and only tank attack I was to see in the Pacific War.

Our frontline elements now received heavy fire whenever they moved. Our mortars tried to help out, but did little good. The attack slowed to a crawl and finally stopped. There were several hundred yards of open fields between us and the enemy; we had incurred some casualties and had great difficulty getting them out because the appearance of medics triggered more enemy fire.

By 1100 everything was quiet again. We stayed put: no one saw any sense in crossing open fields swept by fire. It was obvious that the air attacks, the artillery preparations, and the abortive tank assault had had little effect on the enemy's defensive capability. The four days we had wasted letting them dig in deeper and preparing more positions was costing us dearly.

Weston of course was disappointed. San Manuel was to be another feather in his cap, and a bogged-down attack wasn't going to look good on the commanding general's situation map. Typically, Weston ordered more of the same: another artillery preparation and a continued attack at 1400. We sat in the intolerable heat looking at our watches. The artillery came in on schedule, Wilson and I watched the front line move about fifty yards forward, and then all hell broke loose. Again.

A few squads here and there made a little forward progress before being pinned down again. If we hadn't figured it out before, the enemy was in San Manuel in great strength with weapons of all types and calibers. He was dug in and down, and bombs and shells had had little effect. We knew that from the Solomons.

For the rest of the afternoon we traded rifle, machine-gun, and mortar fire. Our men were in the open. The enemy was largely in covered foxholes, and he had only to wait for us to make a move. When dark finally came the word was passed for us to move back. Gillette and Larson were in a despondent mood. We had lost some good men and didn't have a damn thing to show for it.

At least a hot meal was brought up to our fallback position. Again I put a perimeter around the CP. Wilson, Ferguson, Austin, and I talked for a long time. (I had a disturbing thought several times that night. Supposing Weston, eager as always to show himself as the aggressive commander, wanted to send out a patrol to see whether the enemy was in San Manuel!)

While the 1st Battalion was getting nowhere with its operation against San Manuel, the 2d Battalion, which was mounting its attack in the northwest corner, also had its problems.

This operation—the main attack—had made some progress for about two blocks into the town, but then was sent reeling back by a strong counterattack using tanks, infantry, and weapons of all kinds. The battalion regrouped generally along its line of departure and hunkered down, while all available artillery was called on to destroy and disrupt the enemy defenses. The conflagrations, explosions, and heavy smoke emanating from the town indicated that the shelling was having some effect.

It might be well at this point to describe the layout of San Manuel. It was made up of a grid of streets that formed blocks irregular in size and shape. There were six north–south streets and seven running east to west. A large square with a public building occupied a central position on the western edge of town. The Arboredo River formed the eastern boundary, with only the main road having a bridge to cross the river to the east.

The enemy had turned the town into a fortress. There were weapons emplacements, dug-in tank and artillery emplacements, covered foxholes, trenches, and sniper positions. There were many easily defensible buildings, one or two stories in height, throughout the town, which held stores, offices, and markets. There were many conventional residences, huts usually on stilts, beneath which the enemy had concealed both men and weapons in deeply dug-in emplacements.

The men of the 2d Battalion had made a minor penetration into this hornet's nest, but what they did not know was that the Japanese 2d Armored Division had selected this location to make its stand. It was prepared for a major battle, and the preparations showed that the unit was staking a considerable portion of its resources on this effort.

About noon, after hours of harassing artillery fire, the 2d Battalion attacked again and the enemy launched a tank attack. This time, however, our antitank and self-propelled guns were well forward, and their fire was effective and devastating. The infantry quickly followed up this advantage and got a foothold in the northwest corner of San Manuel. However, enemy fire, particularly from machine guns, forced the infantry to dig in under huts and inside the more substantial buildings.

This concluded the operations for that day. The battle would last for four more days.

On the next day, January 25, the battalion was withdrawn from its position on the west side of the town and moved north. We were to go into position on the left of the 2d Battalion, thus extending the northern front farther to the east. While we were not told the reason for this move, it seemed that a single substantial front could exploit any weakness in the enemy defenses as pressure was applied all across the line.

Progress was very slow. Tiny advances were made here and there by small groups, but the enemy resisted savagely, and often a small gain was canceled by a counterattack. We applied all our different patterns of firepower, mortars, artillery, self-propelled cannon, tank guns (the tanks were back), machine-gun fire, grenades, and bazookas. The Japanese replied in kind, which caused us to dig even deeper entrenchments while they did the same. There was probably more massed firepower per square foot used in San Manuel than anywhere else in the Pacific.

On January 27 a coordinated attack was launched, but to no avail. There were a few places where gains of a hundred yards were made, but casualties were heavy and the problem of removing wounded men was extremely dangerous. The enemy knew we would take drastic measures to retrieve our wounded and they found additional targets in the soldiers and medics engaged in this action.

At nightfall many fires burned brightly, and we were in approximately the same position we'd held in the morning.

Our battalion CP was in a dugout beneath a flimsy house. At dark, I deployed the platoon in a perimeter to provide security because we were on the front line, which made a left turn from a street running north to a street running east. Our troops held both sides of the intersection's L shape, while the enemy held the blocks in front of us.

There was no hot meal that night, but a couple of cans of coffee had been dragged in. Gillette and Larson were dead tired, as I was. It had been forty-eight hours since I'd had a catnap, and from the sounds of gunfire on both sides it didn't appear that any of us would get any further rest. I sat with Larson for a long time looking over the parapet into the burning town. We agreed that we didn't know how it was all going to end.

The artillery liaison officer with us indicated that our sporadic harassing fire would be kept up all night, and that he had a lot of defensive fires plotted in case the Japanese tried anything.

The night passed with galling slowness. I looked at my watch about 0530 and thought that it would be daylight in a little while.

There was some hint of activity on the enemy side; I passed the word for everyone to be alert. And then we heard an increase in noise, motors, and gunfire. Again, all hell broke loose for recess. Larson yelled at the artillery liaison man, "Fire our defensive fires—now—heavy!" In about a minute the shells started roaring in, while at the same time the enemy attacked. Infantry could be seen running between buildings while the sound of tanks increased.

The artilleryman yelled at us: "They're going to shoot the corps!" And then the corps heavy artillery rounds arrived.

It is impossible to describe the absolute height of noise produced. This was dangerous to us too. Large pieces of shell fragments blasted through the house over our heads, and some of the closer blasts shook the house to its foundation. We could see enemy soldiers and tanks about a half block away, and everybody in our CP began firing while the artillery fire escalated to an unbearable fury. Great pieces of the house were being shot away, and only the floor above us remained intact.

Tanks were hit and went up in deafening explosions. The direct fire of our cannon company and tanks added to the din. The artillery fires lasted for fifty-five minutes before they were lifted.

In the smoke and haze we could see no more enemy soldiers or tank activity; it was obvious that what was left of the enemy was retreating to the south and east. And our planes were roaring overhead to make their withdrawal across the plain a total disaster.

We got out of the CP. Our house had been shot away, but

troops were popping out of their holes all over the place. Up and down the streets of the L intersection, men and officers were standing around looking at the carnage. We counted ten smashed enemy tanks and countless artillery pieces, antitank guns, and mortars.

San Manuel was ours. (A small bird sat on a ruined tank and chirped.)

The battle for this objective was costly for both sides. The 2d Battalion in particular had heavy casualties, some units losing more than 50 percent of their strength. The elements of the Japanese 2d Armored Division, which we had first encountered in Binalonan, lost tanks, weapons, vehicles, and supplies. We counted 775 bodies and forty-five destroyed tanks.

There was little to be learned from enemy tactics in the San Manuel battle that was not already known. The Japanese penchant for digging in was well-known: tanks, guns, artillery, mortars, and personnel were all positioned in deep holes. In the case of the infantry these holes were often covered with logs and mud, making them relatively impervious to artillery fire. We had seen such emplacements all over the Pacific and were not surprised to see them employed in Luzon.

The enemy had made good use of the terrain in the central plain of Luzon. Because the *barrios* and *poblaciónes* were surrounded by flat rice fields that offered cover only in their shallow ditches, our infantrymen were repeatedly pinned down crossing these paddies and took frequent casualties.

Such a situation called for the use of armor, but little was made available to us. Heavy aerial bombs would have demolished many of the underground emplacements, and delayed-action fuses on heavy artillery would have had a similar effect. Again these munitions were not used in San Manuel, leaving the problem, as usual, to the infantry.

The Japanese fought with tenacity, but their willingness to die in a hole, rather than escape and fight another day, was the fatal flaw that led to their defeat. The banzai attack and fighting to the death in a hole were not courageous but silly.

The U.S. soldier had courage as well as sense. If he couldn't make any progress, he stopped and got out of there. True, there were some commanders, safe in their headquarters or 500 yards behind the line, who criticized these retrograde movements as lacking spirit. These same commanders had, on the other hand, great admiration for those who charged ahead to meet certain death. I always thought that such views were distorted, irresponsible, and silly.

In the Civil War and World War I, we lost whole generations of young men to senseless infantry attacks against fortified positions. You can't fight the next battle with dead heroes. But higher commanders are often obsessed with seeing movement on their battle maps: the three-star general prods the two-star to get a move on. He in turn prods the one-star, who prods the eagle—and so on ad nauseam. How many lives were sacrificed to being in too great a hurry to move, instead of grinding the bastards down, is shown in our battle statistics.

The critical element is time. When the higher brass are impatient, the inevitable result is an improvident push into action with disproportionate death and injury.

Armchair theorists who think that the American soldier is too prone to hunker down and let airplanes, tanks, and guns do the dirty work, seem to regard only the red badge of courage as worthy of praise. But it is not part of our ethos, tradition, or training to have men killed or wounded when time and matériel can avert such needless losses.

Some of our commanders didn't know that.

THE REST OF LUZON

The battle for the central plain was far from over. Enemy forces were desperately trying to delay the advance of the division. Their plan was to withdraw as much of their troop strength as possible to the north, where they could set up defensive positions in the Caraballo Mountains and the long rugged mountain range that stretched from the plain to the northern edge of Luzon.

National Highway 5 wound north between the mountains and finally entered the long Cagayan Valley. The town of San Jose was the key to the enemy plan. The Japanese had to hold us west of that town and allow the bulk of their troops to escape north for the second phase of the Luzon campaign—the mountain war.

On January 30, the 161st Regiment was relieved from the occupation of San Manuel and assembled in Santa Maria, a small town to the south. Here we had a chance to bathe and put on clean underwear and socks.

We used the rest time to reorganize the battalion because officers, NCOs, and EM had incurred large numbers of casualties. At about this time I was promoted to captain and given command of the battalion Headquarters Company. (The company's former commander, Ernie, was sent to Company B, whose CO had been killed when his jeep hit a land mine.) My job now was to support the various staff sections and to provide a CP for the battalion commander.

Wilson took command of the battalion Intelligence and Reconnaissance Platoon, which he deserved. It also was at this time that a new commander took Gillette's place. The new one was a stocky, good-looking soul, younger than Gillette, and the former regimental supply officer. I was hopeful that he wouldn't be as much of a disaster as the previous S-4 who had been foisted on the 1st Battalion. We also received a new XO to replace Larson, and I knew him from the days when he'd had A Company.

Our few days of rest came to a halt when it was decided to send the 1st and 3d battalions across country to Mapangpang in an attempt to cut off the enemy elements that would be retreating from a heavy attack by the 35th Regiment at Lupao.

It was on February 3, after twenty-seven miles of rice paddies, unimproved roads, and trails, that we arrived at Mapangpang, a small nondescript *barrio* the enemy chose not to defend.

On February 4, while the 1st Battalion stayed put, the 3d moved to a position 2,000 yards southwest of San Isidro to await attack orders. On February 6, the 3d Battalion entered San Isidro without an attack and drove lightly resisting enemy troops to the hills. It was indicative of the low morale of the enemy forces that they abandoned weapons, vehicles, and supplies. Outside of town, on a small trail, fourteen tanks were found abandoned by their crews.

On February 7, at a short distance to the south, the 2d Battalion had erected roadblocks on the road leading into San Jose. At 0400 enemy troops and vehicles ran into the roadblocks, and most of the vehicles were destroyed and the soldiers killed or dispersed. These remnants ran into strongpoints of the 6th Division just south of San Jose and were eliminated as an effective force.

By February 10, 1945, the heavy exactions taken of the Japanese troops, and the resulting ragged withdrawal by them to the north, marked the end to the campaign in the central plain. The major portion of the Japanese 2d Armored Division had been destroyed, essentially eliminating it as a fighting force and ensuring that it never again appeared in the order of battle.

The hard part of the war was still ahead of us.

CHAPTER TWELVE

War

THE MOUNTAIN CAMPAIGN

For two months we had to fight from one *barrio* to the next. Each of these that the Japanese had made into a fortified area was surrounded by miles of flat, treeless, and featureless terrain, which was ideal for the defenders.

Now we were back in the mountains, which revived memories of the struggle in similar terrain on Guadalcanal.

Our strategy was simple. One division (the 32d) would push east from the west coast through Baguio to link up with the 25th Division, which would attack north on National Highway 5 with the objective of reaching the Cagayan Valley.

A line drawn from the Lingayen Gulf to Dingalan Bay separates the plain to the south from the mountains to the north.

North of this line the entire western half of Luzon is covered by rugged mountains. The eastern half is covered in the southern quarter by the Caraballo Mountains. And north of these mountains there is a great plain that stretches from Bayombong to the port of Aparri on the north coast of Luzon.

The division plan assigned the mountains west of Highway 5 to the regiment. East of Highway 5 the 27th Regiment would move on a parallel course. The 35th Regiment would make an "end run" from Rizal to Cananglan and thence west to Puttan on the highway.

It was noted at the outset that this would be a tough, grinding campaign. The enemy would defend the valleys—and he would defend the hills. He would dig in and fight to his own annihilation. If and when we broke into the northern plain, his defeat would be total.

We had been in Luzon a little over a month, doing battle across the plains. Now we moved north on the hills and mountains on the west side of Highway 5. The advance was slow: we were searching out pockets of resistance and occasionally finding major defensive positions.

In my capacity as Headquarters Company commander I selected positions for the command post, where we provided communications, supply, ammunition, and mess facilities to the company and attached personnel.

We had a new battalion CO after the San Manuel action, a chunky, handsome former regimental supply officer named Anderson. We also got a new XO, a tall, rangy, craggy-faced Washingtonian named Bartlett. They made a good team and spent many hours supervising the troops. This was an exhausting job because individual companies occupied tactical positions sometimes a mile or more from each other.

Each morning trucks arrived from the *barrios* around San Jose. These trucks were loaded with Filipinos who were to carry food, water, and ammunition to the forward elements. This was a chaotic operation complicated by ignorance, language problems, and sheer cussedness.

Once a carrying party had been formed and loaded up, a military party of six men would guide them forward. (It usually took at least two hours to sort out all of the Filipinos into three parties. Those who could speak English we made bosses, who could tell the others what to do.)

Of course, the enemy soon found out what all the people dressed in white with floppy straw hats were all about, and sometimes laid ambushes for carrying parties.

Now and then the people in a party would be seen galloping along the trail and heading for the highway to get away. Then they'd jog south on the highway, but eventually sit down to smoke a cigarette and talk things over. After this happened once or twice I sent a machine gun team down the road. When the joggers reached the machine-gun position, a belt would be fired into the air, at which time all intentions to flee to San Jose vanished and the carriers would return sheepishly to the base camp to form another party.

In the months that we used carrying parties only six Filipinos were killed. We took the same number of casualties in the soldier teams that accompanied them. To keep things in perspective, in the first week of the mountain operation we lost fifteen killed and sixty-one wounded and accounted for 102 of the enemy. The Filipinos were doing a most essential task—but there was no way we could guarantee them freedom from danger.

Many times the command party members would not return until after dark. The CP tent was blacked out so they could come in, eat a hot meal, brief the staff, and get a good night's sleep. The reports from the front were not encouraging. The Japanese had had weeks to tunnel into the hills and mountainsides and were resisting fanatically. Only a direct approach using grenades and flamethrowers seemed to work against their positions.

On one mountain the Japanese had tunneled into the side and emplaced a howitzer. We copied their program by tunneling through a hill and installing a 90mm antiaircraft gun at the mouth; over an open breech, a gunner with field glasses would look through the barrel that was sighted on the enemy tunnel. When the howitzer was poked out a 90mm shell was sent flying over—and on the second shot we put one into the tunnel, which erupted in a gigantic explosion. No more enemy artillery.

Since the procedures at the base camp were routine, I often accompanied Anderson and Larson, the S-3, to the forward positions. Usually we sought an observation post from which we could watch the operations of the particular company we visited. In most cases, the artillery observer with the forward elements had already located a good point from which to survey the terrain, and we naturally gravitated there.

One of the basic problems with an OP was that too many people would congregate around the damn thing and present a good target for Japanese mortar or artillery.

Before long a battalion CO, an S-3, and an artillery officer would be joined by a company commander and perhaps a platoon leader, along with communications personnel and other assorted notables. As Headquarters Company commander, I made it a point to spread these people out with a warning that I didn't want to see them within 100 yards of the OP, and I particularly wanted them on the back slopes of the ridge we were on. The Japanese knew that such a gathering meant that a senior officer was present and they would do their best to make life miserable for us.

Each night we huddled in the blackout tent to go over the day's activities, make up reports, look at the casualty lists, and prepare for the next day. We were steadily losing men in the rifle companies, and it was distressing to see the names of old friends who had been killed or evacuated through our aid station to the hospital in San Jose.

One day after the command party had departed for the front I felt particularly fatigued. I lay down on one of the bedrolls in the CP tent and tried to shake off the tired feeling with a short nap.

I don't know how long I slept when I heard the whine of an artillery shell and a terrific explosion nearby. I scrambled out of the tent as two more rounds came in and landed just beyond our position. There was a large tree about twenty yards from the tent, and I rushed to get behind it as I heard another round wheeling in. As I hit the ground at the base of the tree, the incoming shell hit the tree branches above me and went off with a deafening bang. Immediately I felt a sharp, stinging pain in my back and I knew I was hit. I wasn't hurt badly, but I was hit.

I remained in position for a few more minutes and then decided the shelling was over. The first aid tent was about 100 yards away, and I walked over to see Benny Jack, our bespectacled, bald-headed surgeon.

He saw me coming, and when I told him I had been hit, he motioned me into the aid tent. I took off my jacket and T-shirt while he examined me. "It's not bad," he said, "just a small shell fragment." But enough for a trip to the hospital. He put a bandage on the wound but left the shell fragment in place.

I picked up my pack in the CP tent, turned the company over to Alex, my XO, and climbed into a jeep for the trip to San Jose.

The hospital surgeon took out the fragment and put it in a bottle and gave it to me; he did a little surgical trimming and applied a dressing. An aid man took me into the ward tent and gave me a cot. The ward tent accommodated about thirty soldiers with less severe wounds. (In my case, the dressings were changed several times a day to ensure drainage and prevent infection.) Those with severe wounds were evacuated to the States.

There was very little to do except wander around outside the ward and observe the flow of military traffic on the nearby roads. The weather was hot and dry, and so there was dust everywhere.

After a day or two I was visited by my XO, who dropped off my mail. He indicated that the battalion was heavily engaged and continuing to suffer fatalities and injuries. Everything else was routine.

HIATUS I

After about a week of sitting around, I asked for permission to move to the regiment's rear echelon in San Jose. I indicated that I was just occupying space that could be used by those in greater need of hospitalization. To my surprise, my request was granted, and a day later Warrant Officer Clark came over with a jeep and picked me up.

The rear echelon was located in an open space in a residential area of San Jose, behind several huts occupied by Filipinos. There were several squad tents that housed the regiment's company clerks and the office of Warrant Officer Clark.

All the paperwork from the companies, battalions, and regimental headquarters was sent to this office. Morning reports, casualty reports, payrolls, and official correspondence all wound up here for typing, recording, and forwarding to higher headquarters. All the effects of deceased military personnel were taken from the supply area and brought to the office for processing.

Clark was a pudgy, good-humored type who had always been in personnel work since the States. He had worked his way up from private first class to warrant officer and was happy to stay right where he was. I didn't blame him one bit. I helped him check payrolls and verify the casualty lists. Almost every day, the casualty section produced two legal-sized sheets citing the dead and wounded of the previous day. We both agreed that the Cagayan Valley was a butcher shop.

After several days in the rear echelon I received another surprise. I had been released from my assignment as Headquarters Company commander of the 1st Battalion and assigned as regimental personnel officer. This made me Clark's boss, which suited him just fine. It also made me responsible for signing all orders and correspondence for the regimental CO.

I put in a call to the regimental forward CP people to see whether there was anything they wanted. Spencer, the regimental XO, got on the line and gave me a variety of tasks. We also decided that each second or third day I would visit the forward CP and bring up papers needing the regimental CO's consideration and pick up mail and reports for the rear.

So the next day the casualty sergeant and I started up the highway for the CP. About five miles up the road a bored GI signaled us to pull over. We were informed that the road had a wide curve ahead that was under enemy observation and that the road was shelled when vehicles were visible.

The sergeant looked pretty grim, and so did I. He revved up the motor and we set sail down the road, hell-bent for destruction. Fortunately the enemy didn't see us, or we went too fast, but we got through it without having any artillery.

A little farther on we spotted another GI. This time we were told that it was snipers: occasionally they took potshots at the convoys that continually traveled the highway. Again we broke the speed laws (if there were any) and we didn't draw any fire.

At last we arrived at the CP, found the XO, and heard that Weston was going to get a star and had already moved to division headquarters. The new CO, Johnson (a West Pointer), had been the regimental G-3; now he would get his Combat Infantryman Badge (CIB) and an eagle. With any luck he, too, had a quick star in his future.

We drove back to San Jose without any incident. We settled in a routine and established a division of labor between Clark and me. After a week or two we were told to examine a large wooden building, a former agricultural school, on the edge of town.

It was a large building, two stories high, with a basement and a veranda on all sides. It looked like a palace after our crowded backyard in town. The next day we packed up, moved, unpacked, and settled in. It was the first time that I'd had a wood floor under my feet in all the combat zones since I'd left the States.

After allocating workspaces, sleeping rooms, and furniture, we settled in. We employed several Filipinos as clerks and interpreters, and they found us several women to clean up the place, wash clothes, and occasionally do some cooking. We were encouraged by the Philippine Compensation Commission (PCC) to employ as many natives as possible to get money into circulation. So, in addition to clerks and household help, we found that we had another way to spend money.

Each night I received a call from regiment indicating how many carriers it wanted for the next day. At 0600 each morning about ten supervisors would appear outside our headquarters. Each was assigned a two-and-a-half-ton truck, with driver, and headed into the nearby *barrios* to pick up workers. Each supervisor was told how many carriers to pick up and which forward CP to deliver them to.

At the end of the day the trucks returned to our location with their carriers. My payroll sergeant and a Filipino clerk sat at a table with bags of Filipino pesos. Each supervisor lined up his men and marched them past the table, where each man was given two pesos. The supervisor then loaded the carriers into his assigned truck and took them home.

About once a week I went to the PCC finance office and picked up the payroll, usually 100,000 pesos. The finance officer would take my signature, and I'd return to the office with the loot, which was put into a sturdy chest with a big lock. (Incidentally, the money was of no use to our troops because it was valueless outside the Philippines.) So our days were busy with paperwork, traveling to the forward CP, and hiring and paying laborers.

It was a pleasant hiatus in what had gone before, from which will be described.

CHAPTER THIRTEEN

Taka

When will their glory fade,
Oh, the wild charge they made.
—ALFRED, LORD TENNYSON

War is the aggregation of the daily struggles of small groups of men.

Before a campaign is successfully closed, the important battles must be won. In each battle some strategic location must be seized and held. Finally the foot soldier must move ahead, whatever the odds, or the battle line falters and ultimately stops.

In the vast Pacific War fabric, Taka was but a single strand, of momentary notice to a few high commanders before it passed into the limbo of territory that we would occupy. But to a small group of men, once upon a time, Taka was a brooding monster dominating all approaches to the Cagayan Valley of northern Luzon.

Taka was what the Japanese called the hill that stood higher than its brothers, all marked by precipitous slopes and deep valleys. It was bald on top but, lower down, covered by a mass of impenetrable tropical forests. In the forests and on the bald top, the Japanese had burrowed in with the desperation of those who feared the sudden, all-embracing rush and roar of the pinpoint artillery barrage. Our huge corps artillery guns had already pounded the naked ridge of Taka until the pitted surface resembled nothing so much as the face of one suffering from the pox. But there was never a sign of the enemy, never a rifle shot, or the tiny crack and thud of a grenade. There was only silence and the brooding presence of Taka and the thousand eyes that manned its approaches day and night, alert to a moving shadow or the crack of a twig to provoke the out-pouring of lead and the hoarse cries of the sweating machine gunners.

A bird could fly to Taka, and a lizard might scale its sheer walls or penetrate its tangled undergrowth. But for a man there was one route, and just one: a narrow, yard-wide ridge that extended to a little group of grassy hills to the south of Taka—the Fingers. Viewed from the air, they resembled the digits of an open hand stretched toward the huge mountain itself, but ever rebuffed by the grim, powerful mass that looked down on all.

And now we were sitting on the Fingers and regarding the natural fortress before us. "We" were fifty: a few soldiers and Fili-pino guerrillas sent to watch and wait while the battalion that had battered itself against the bastion withdrew to lick its wounds, bury its dead, and curse the gods of earth, wind, and rain who had cre-ated Taka.

Brave men had crossed that narrow ridge and worked their way along the weathered and artillery-scarred sides, only to be met by smashing shells and hissing bullets that thudded into the eager bodies of screaming, stumbling men. Three times they were driven back, and at last their commander, seeing the desperate weariness, decimated ranks, and the dreadful imposing presence of Taka, shook his head slowly and crumpled up his mud-stained map and threw it at the mountain. Then he followed the last of his disheartened men as they went down the Fingers to the valley below.

It was getting dark by the time the last of the retreating battal-ion had faded away. The valley separating us from Taka was filled with shadows of dark blue, and far below we could hear the rushing sound of the rapid streams that flowed on three of the prominence's sides.

The NCOs and I gathered for a council of war. Our mission was rather obscure. We certainly couldn't prevent the vastly superior forces of the enemy from overrunning our position on the Fingers, and we had no orders to advance. So, evidently, we were to sit and watch and wait for that nebulous thing, the enemy's reaction.

We took stock of our resources, and when we compared our strength with what we knew was gazing down on us in insolent, silent defiance, our hearts beat a little faster, and our voices were lowered to a whisper lest some of the host across the valley hear our plans. We had a machine gun squad of five men, a reconnaissance section of six men, thirty-six Filipino guerrillas and their two officers, a medic, and me. Only half of the guerrillas had rifles, and about six had helmets; almost all of them wore loose, white cotton clothing that could be seen for miles. Only the two officers spoke English.

When the meeting broke up, the machine gun was emplaced to cover the sole, spine-like approach to Taka. The guerrillas were separated into groups of three and immediately dug foxholes. I spread the remainder of my men to close the circle we had formed around the summit of the middle finger.

The moon rose early in the evening, and the sound of men digging was mingled with the monotonous buzz of countless crickets, the swish of the valley's streams, and the occasional spine-chilling screech of a night bird as it flapped crazily in the forest below.

Gradually the digging ceased, the whispered conversations tailed off, and the part of the evening arrived when the soldier holds his breath and grips his trench knife tighter while he listens. Only with combat troops is there this phenomenon. Men may be laughing, joking, trading views of the day's woe, or just busying themselves making a mud hole into a reasonably accurate semblance of a human habitation. Then it would happen: almost as if by universal consent, without words or consultation, everyone would settle low in his hole, with no voice heard, no movements apparent, and all partaking of the dreadful apprehension and hush of the moment.

After an hour or so of this, the general tension would be relaxed. Your buddy would give you a dig in the ribs, and in low, throaty whispers ask who would sit up for the first two hours. Then you both would settle back, with trench knives back in their sheaths and taut muscles loosened, and the cool night winds would refresh the tired soldiers' bodies.

I elected to stay up for the first two hours of the watch, and to pass the time, crawled over to the holes of the Filipino officers. They had been talking in Tagalog as I approached and evidently were disturbed over something. After exchanging views on the day's events I asked them what they thought of the situation. They expressed regret that I did not have uniforms, rifles, and equipment for their men and said they had been promised these things before they were to do any fighting. This worried me a little because I knew of the sensitivity of the Asian and his habit of walking off to tend to his own affairs if a bargain was not kept. One of the officers, a graduate of the University of Manila, told me about overhearing some of the men discussing returning to their villages. I promised I would do my best to help them, and returned to my foxhole slightly upset.

I awakened my buddy and second in command, SSgt. Austin Bryant. He sat up with the nervous, scared, and quick, jerky motion that combat troops are known for, and I told him of my misgivings.

Companionship is a precious thing. The Creator made men who could listen to your woes and in a few minutes make them vanish through their sane, solid, and fearless advice. By this you could know the intense bond of fellowship, regard, and manly affection that comes so seldom, if at all, in this time of selfish and superficial relationships. But such was our bond.

Bryant was a thin, gawky kid from somewhere in the West. His manner was nervous, his temper volcanic; he had no fear of any man alive or dead, and was generally regarded as the ablest patrol leader in the regiment. He had two prominent buckteeth that stuck out even when his mouth was closed and dark eyes that flashed in his anger and sparkled in his joy. He was not tall, but a man among men; one of those who springs up in time of danger, fights well and victoriously, and then slips back into anonymity—an unseen fiber of our nation's strength.

He mulled over what I had told him, and then counseled me to get into the hole and get some shut-eye because there wasn't a damn thing I could do that night, anyhow. I scrunched down to get some sleep and, before pulling my poncho over my head, saw Bryant's toothy profile outlined against the full moon, a symbol of confident, fearless infantry.

I awoke with a blind, scrambling start. I had heard it, too, but was made doubly aware by Bryant's fist punching my leg. It was the short, barking plop of a Japanese knee mortar. He hugged the sides of the hole as we pictured the arc of the whizzing mortar round hurtling into our position. And about four seconds after I awoke it landed with a deafening report, and the round's fragments sang angrily into the darkness. Two more plops, and seconds later there were two explosions near the machine-gun nest. I stuck my head up and could see everyone was awake and crouching in anticipation. I grabbed the sound-powered phone that connected me with the machine gun and whistled low. I was answered instantly by the squad leader, who told me of the sounds of men talking and branches breaking over on the narrow connecting ridge about seventy-five yards away and slightly below his gun position, so that anyone coming from that direction would have to advance uphill. I told him to refrain from firing unless it was absolutely necessary and to sit tight.

Soon I could hear the voices too. The wild, frantic, boastful voices of the enemy calling back and forth to each other to build up their courage and resolve for the death assault. The voices did not come any closer but rather increased in intensity. Now and then there were concerted yells, and such occasional interpolated English words as *Yankee* and *kill*. From the sound of their thrashing about in the dense brush along the ridge path they were drunk, apparently having been given a glorious send-off of sake and rice cakes by their commander.

The mortar started plopping again, and with an increased tempo of explosions the warriors' screaming and howling went on. One of the rounds landed on the edge of a foxhole and wounded a guerrilla, who let out a short, barking cry and then quieted as his friends comforted him.

Suddenly the plopping stopped and I heard the faint whistle of the SP phone. The machine gun squad leader was whispering in heavy gasps, telling me that about twenty men had emerged from the thick brush below his position, had spread out, and were slowly advancing, yelling and brandishing rifles with fixed bayonets. I fired a parachute flare, which soared high with a trail of yellow sparks and then burst into white, blinding brilliance. This was the signal for pandemonium. All of my front positions opened fire with grenades and rifles on the plainly silhouetted enemy troops, who broke into a run toward us. The howls and wails of the wounded enemy were ghastly. Many rolled down the hill like snowballs after being shot, or collapsed like punctured barrage balloons as the grenades crashed and ripped into them.

The attack lasted less than a minute—and it was all over. The anguished cries of the Japanese wounded were greeted with blasts of rifle fire, and they died where they lay or else crawled to the precipitous edge of the connecting ridge and let themselves fall several hundred feet to a sure death.

While there was still some moonlight left, Bryant and I crawled to each position to check for wounded; one man had been hit in the cheek by a grenade splinter, another had been grazed on the right arm by a rifle bullet. We left the aid man to tend to these two and, after replenishing the grenade supply all around, crawled back to our hole. It had been a cheap but telling victory. My fears, however, were substantial: the enemy knew our strength to a man, and he looked directly down on us. And if he took a fancy, he could send plunging machine-gun fire straight down into our uncovered entrenchments. So we sat and watched the specter of Taka, more foreboding and fearsome than ever as the last rays of moonlight lit its eminence. We waited all night, but when the sun arose from the eastern grayness the enemy had not paid us a second visit.

As soon as it was light enough to distinguish the inert forms of the dead Japanese down the slope, two Filipino scouts crept out of their holes and cautiously advanced on the bodies. When they were satisfied that no booby traps had been attached, they examined the corpses, removing papers, identification tags, insignia, and, more important, rifles and ammunition.

The fog rising from the valley wreathed Taka in gray gloom. Since the night's skirmish not a sound had been heard from the ponderous forests. More than ever, though, we were conscious of the eyes that watched us, of the hidden men who crouched behind the cold metal of their machine guns. The Japanese were closely guarding the narrow strip of land over which they knew we had to force our way if we were to stand on Taka's summit and see the way to the rugged upper reaches of the Cagayan Valley.

The Filipino officers barked sharp orders to their exhausted men, who felt no qualms about sleeping now that the sun was up. As the guerrillas rose from their holes, their white suits stained brown with mud, scratching themselves with animal satisfaction, I wondered by what miracle the high command had expected me to turn these unarmed, untrained, and uninterested simple farm folk into a unit capable of withstanding the military forces that might any moment come down the sides of Taka into our tenuous position.

Staff Sergeant Bryant was busy stirring up a stew of beans, crackers, bouillon cubes, and our last canteen of water. The twigs he had gathered were damp, and the thin spire of smoke from the tiny fire beneath his helmet drifted across the valley and impudently settled among the treetops of Taka. The radioman in the next foxhole, who had been busy wiping the night's accumulation of moisture from his set, finally pieced together his long, whip-like antenna. Having twisted it into place, he began the interminable gibberish used by all radio operators to get in touch with headquarters. After about five minutes of this, he apparently made contact, for he began the laborious task of writing a message in code. There was much confusion inherent in this process, and a good deal of profanity was mixed up with the coded words. At last he gave the legendary "Roger, out," and ten minutes later informed me that an air attack was to be made on Taka at 0700 and that immediately afterward I was to send a patrol across to investigate the results.

I looked at Taka, at the thinning fogs clinging to its summit, and at the muddy, incredibly narrow ridge that jutted toward us like a threatening spear. I handed the scribbled and wrinkled message to Bryant. He choked on a large spoonful of beans when he read: "A patrol to Taka to determine the results of the air strike." He shoved the message back into my hands, and then slowly, beautifully, he called down fire and brimstone on the unsuspecting heads of those responsible for the message.

It was 0630 hours, and we had thirty minutes to wait for the Air Corps to demonstrate its method of helping the foot soldier. Bryant passed the word to the NCOs, and I called one of the Filipino officers and instructed him to ready six of his men for a patrol. I started preparing a battle pack of poncho, shovel, and chocolate bar. As I tightened the last strap I was aware of a dirty but powerful hand clutching my arm. I looked up into Bryant's cold, determined, steel-blue eyes.

"Just what in hell do you think yer doin'?" he asked in the special polite snarl he reserved for his commanding officer. Without waiting for a reply he answered his own question: "Remember that we decided that I'd lead the patrols; an' you'd lead the fights."

There was no answer to that one. For two and a half months that had been the formula. He led the rooting, exploring, exhausting patrols, and I had taken over the planned attacks. O ye gods of war, did ever the yearning heart of a platoon commander, lonely, desperate, and battle-weary lieutenants have such a man, equal in all ways to share the burden? Did other leaders look into the grim, confident faces of their soldier-brothers and draw on the well of strength, resolution, and hard purpose as I had with Bryant? Had other men been able to put aside the triviality of rank and clutch the hand of the deep, true, battle-friend? Lord, Lord, how I hope they had such solace.

Bryant threw my pack back into our hole, and then sat down on the hole's edge and began to clean his rifle with that care and tenderness that only the infantryman exhibits before a battle. The sun was out and bright now, and the last mists had left the heights of Taka.

We heard a low hum to the south: six tiny specks were hurrying in our direction. I looked at my watch. It was 0658. Closer and closer came the specks until we could make out the blue paint and white stars on the bellies of the navy torpedo-bomber planes they had assigned to this mission. They flew directly overhead, about 1,500 feet up, and our Filipinos jumped and waved their arms, yelling wildly. The planes circled, maneuvered into single file, climbed for altitude, and then came roaring down out of the blue morning sky at Taka. They flew directly overhead on their strafing attacks, and when the machine guns opened up the valley was filled with the chaos of clattering ordnance and the rush and roar of the diving planes. The tracers lined their fiery courses into Taka and screamed off in brilliant ricochets. Great patches of dust spouts were kicked up on the bald dome of the mountain, and a slight breeze hung a pall of gunsmoke and brown dust over the forest on the western slope.

Now the planes wheeled back to the south, reassembled, and then spiraled high for altitude. Their wings flashed in the sun as they peeled off and hurtled down. As their shrill whistling came closer and closer, we instinctively dove for our holes as the planes zoomed over our heads. We watched the two 500-pound bombs drop lazily from the first bomber and disappear into the woods near the summit. Instantly we could see the flash, the spreading shock waves like black ribbons, and then the hard, stomach-punching *c-r-r-rump* and crash of the steel and fire.

As each plane thrilled us with its load of din and destruction, we involuntarily cheered and yelled. We leaped out of our holes, pounded each other on the back, swore at Taka, cursed the emperor, grinned like foolish apes, and then jammed our hands deep in our pants pockets as we regarded the smoking, dust-grimed visage of our mortal enemy, Taka. We were excited by this show of strength. We told each other that we were damn well glad those planes were on our side. We made foolish, proud, boastful talk, feeling a compulsion to take advantage of the temporary ascendancy we held over the evil mountain. Then slowly, gradually, talk died out and finally ceased. Men wandered back to their holes and sat musing and looking at the cap of gloom that still shrouded the hideous, pockmarked forehead of that monster to the north.

Bryant slung on his pack, loosened the sling on his rifle, and gave a final once-over to the two grenades hooked to his belt. I came over to him and we stood silently looking at the valley, the narrow ridge, the thick forest and jungle, and the ugly splotched summit of our hideous goal. He turned to me, stuck out a grimy hand to which I gave a hard squeeze, and then, whistling sharply at the six apprehensive guerrillas that were to accompany him, trotted off with his anxious, loping gait. The Filipinos were strung out like beads behind him.

I moved to the machine-gun position where we had a telescope set up for observation. I watched Bryant and his men descend the Fingers and head for a point about 100 yards west of where the connecting ridge began. It was soon evident that Bryant did not think the air raid had driven off the enemy forces for good, and that he somehow intended to climb along the side of the ridge instead of proceeding along its exposed, fire-swept surface.

The patrol disappeared from view, and though I watched the area of this ridge intently, I could not spot their movement. I kept my eyes glued to the eyepiece until they ached and after a half hour I turned the scope over to the machine-gun leader. I walked out to the farthest edge of the Fingers and sat down. The tension was killing. No one spoke; all eyes were staring at Taka, at the immense breast of rock and jungle where an American and six Filipinos were tempting death with guts, sharp wits, and determination.

Now and then the man at the scope would relax, blink wearily, and shake his head to my unspoken question. The sky was clear now, and the sun gave an early hint of its searing intensity to come. Heat waves rose from the valley and danced across the image of Taka like transparent spirits. There was no sound, save the bubbling rush of the valley streams far below and the distant murmur of a far-off reconnaissance plane.

My thoughts wandered back to warm days at home: to idle hours spent fishing in the hot, humid Michigan summer, to the green fields and fatted cattle, to the fresh smell of the earth, and to the cool, tempering breezes that hurried from the Great Lakes to make the day tolerable.

A cry from the man at the scope snapped the reverie. I rushed to his side and looked. There, by some feat of strength, nerve, and cunning were Bryant and the patrol about ten yards short of the summit of Taka. They were lying in a small clearing and would have been invisible except for the glaring white of the Filipinos' clothes.

I grabbed the special eyepiece and screwed it into the scope. It increased vision about 50 percent and enabled me to see Bryant and one of the men were watching something on the mountaintop with all-absorbing attention. Then, one by one, the other men crawled to

Bryant's side while he pointed out the object of interest. After what seemed an eternity, the six white dots that marked the Filipinos on the mountainside straightened out into a line and started moving toward the open area of the dome. A sudden penetrating realization of what was happening flashed into my mind. Bryant was *launching an attack!* Bryant and six men, having infiltrated through God-knows-how-many enemy positions were determined to take possession of the mountaintop! I watched with horror as they emerged from the forest line into the clear. Finally the prolonged silence was broken by the sound of rifle fire. Bryant and the six were in the middle of a Japanese position, and now we could plainly see the enemy soldiers popping their heads up from many camouflaged spider holes around the tiny patrol. As the astonished enemy raised themselves, they were bayoneted or shot full in the face.

While watching this terrifying spectacle, I had been yelling for the rest of my men to grab rifles and ammunition and tear down the slope, cross the ridge, and help Bryant if at all possible to hold the top of Taka.

But slowly, horribly, I could see that the enemy was overcoming his initial surprise and fear, and was fighting back doggedly. Somewhere to the west of the patrol, and out of my sight, a machine gun had opened up, and now the patrol hit the ground while the dust was kicked up around it.

One of the Filipinos was hit and rolled around in the dust, kicking frantically. I watched Bryant throw a grenade in the direction of the machine-gun nest, heard the thud of its detonation, and then saw his tiny lonely figure rise and fade from my sight as he ran toward the west. There was a sharp burst of gunfire and then silence.

The men I'd sent to Bryant's aid had been turned back by heavy fire on the connecting ridge, and stood bleakly, looking at the top of Taka as its foreboding silence returned once again.

It was over. There was no sound in all the vast valley, or on the grim immensity of Taka.

We could count the dead members of the patrol lying on the bare brow of the wretched mound. All were there united in death— all except Bryant.

Four days later, when two battalions and a hurricane of fire had been hurled against Taka and the bastion had finally fallen, we found his body riddled with bullets, facing the enemy even in death. He lay where he had single-handedly carried the line of battle forward.

CHAPTER FOURTEEN

More War

Warrant Officer Clark and I had settled into a busy routine of carrying parties, reports, inventories of deceased effects, and visits to the forward CP.

On one of these visits I encountered a big Texan who had been assigned as a replacement in my platoon in New Zealand. He had received a commission, moved up the ranks because of his combat performance, and was now the acting commander of a battalion. We sat down at a table in the mess tent and nursed cups of coffee. He looked exhausted. In spite of his awesome physical conditioning and presence, he was fatigued to the bone. It showed in his eyes and the dark circles beneath them.

I asked him about the current operation.

He sighed and shook his head. "The men are tired, particularly the old hands from Washington. They're counting rotation points on their fingers and trying to avoid getting killed before they can go home. They are less and less prone to move out during attacks. I find them hiding and malingering all over the place.

"The new men are not in good shape, and haven't been trained for combat. Every day I find men being killed and wounded because they didn't have the foggiest idea of how to survive on the battlefield. I've had to pull men out of foxholes and kick them in the ass to get them going."

There was a long pause while he stared into his cup.

"I don't know how long we can go on like this."

I patted him on the shoulder, wished him good luck, and returned to San Jose.

One late afternoon I received a phone call from my former battalion CP. The message was tragic. The CO, his XO, the artillery officer, and a radio operator had been killed on an OP. Three enlisted men were seriously wounded.

I exploded in anger. "This happened," I yelled at Clark, "because I wasn't there to keep those bastards spread out on the OP."

I told Clark about the number of times I had traveled to the edge of insubordination by telling my superiors to spread out and take better cover. On some occasions, irritated by my fulminations, they moved an inch or two but still presented the enemy with a lucrative artillery target. And now they were dead. Good friends, good officers with whom I had shared a lot of palaver, and talks of home, and the simple pleasures of civilian life. A tragedy that never should have happened; but I hadn't been there to prevent it.

In a few days Clark and I had inventoried the effects of our dead friends, which was all that remained of them. This was always a depressing process, going through footlockers and barracks bags with their few, long-hoarded possessions. There were always the pictures, a book and magazine, extra underwear, socks, a set of suntans, low-quarter shoes, and bundles of letters. (We always examined the latter carefully to ensure that correspondence with some blithe spirit in New Zealand or New Caledonia didn't get sent home to a grieving family.) After the inventory we sealed up the containers, made out the certification, and turned the cargo over to the quartermaster for the long voyage home.

ROTATION AND REPLACEMENT

The men of the regiment had arrived in Oahu on December 24, 1941. When we arrived in Luzon we had already been in the war zone for thirty-seven months. During this time the original group from Washington had steadily dwindled. On Guadalcanal and New Georgia, alone, disease and casualties had taken a heavy toll. Now, with but a few left of the original complement, they were still in combat after forty months. It was not surprising, therefore, to find the Old Guard men becoming very cautious as they neared their date of rotation.

The army had set up a system of accumulated points that could entitle a soldier to go home after so many months in combat, and modified by such things as medals received. A month was one point; a medal, five points.

Almost all members of the old regiment were within a point or two of rotation. They knew it was necessary to avoid a fatal wound—although a slight wound and its accompanying Purple Heart was worth five points. The experience of my friend from Texas was typical: all sorts of ruses and tricks were used to avoid danger, and this put an incredible burden on company and field commanders who still had objectives to take. They were loath to punish malingerers with a court-martial; these men had already fought bravely in three campaigns.

To compound the difficulties, the replacement system was a disaster.

Men put into the replacement pool were subject to being siphoned off by each echelon through which they were processed. Men with useful skills and education were shipped to headquarters units and technical services. Eventually, a good sample of what was left would arrive at my CP for an interview: the small, the timid, the least educated, and the sickly.

As an example, on a trip to corps headquarters in the rear, I saw fine, tall, well-muscled young men playing basketball. I was told they'd been selected from the pool because the corps commander wanted to beat the pants off the army commander's team.

In another case a small, skinny, tired soldier was brought into my office as an infantry replacement, to go to one of the units fighting for their lives in the mountains. He was wearing carpet slippers. I asked him what the trouble was with his feet. He shook his head and took off his socks to reveal feet that were round, like large baloneys with toes sticking out.

"How long have you had this?"

"Ever since I left the States."

"Have you shown your feet to people along the line?"

"Yes, sir, but they said they could do nothing. I was assigned to a combat unit."

I hit the roof.

While he put his socks and slippers back on I ordered a jeep. Ten minutes later I led him into the division surgeon's office. The surgeon looked at his feet with horror. "He just arrived as a replacement," I said. The surgeon said, "He's going back to the States."

And he went.

This poor, crippled soul had been punished by a long, painful trip across the Pacific because venal and incredibly stupid personnel in the replacement chain had neither the wit nor the guts to stop his futile progress to Luzon.

No wonder it took us so long to win!

PHILIPPINE COMPENSATION CLAIMS COMMISSION

As soon as U.S. troops had entered the Philippines, many Filipinos went to work for the various armed services. I used Filipinos as clerks, laundry personnel, supply point helpers, and drivers, and in carrying parties. In addition, various guerrilla units were incorporated into the army, and our engineers used hundreds of laborers in building roads and bridges.

It was to be expected that with a war going on many of the Filipino employees would be killed or injured. Our government felt that the families of those incurring death or injury should be compensated in some way. As a result the Philippine Compensation Claims Commission (PCCC) was established, and in due course I was made an agent of the commission, and directed to seek out families in our area and prepare the necessary forms for the compensation they were entitled to.

So, at least twice a week I took a driver, a Filipino to act as interpreter, several cases of C-rations and other foods, and headed into the hills.

It was not easy to find some of the families. Either their villages had been destroyed and they had moved elsewhere, or their villages were hard to locate on our army maps.

In most cases, we'd arrive at a *barrio* and our interpreter would engage in a long, drawn-out conversation with a villager. Usually we were quickly taken in tow by the mayor or some other *barrio* official, and then we would march to the house of the appropriate family. We'd accumulate a large entourage of curious villagers who'd stand outside while the interpreter, the driver, and I entered the hut. After much pointing and unintelligible conversation, my interpreter would say, "This is Mrs. Rizal." We would exchange handshakes and nod, after which the interpreter would get the information I needed.

I always made out two copies of the simple form, giving one to Mrs. Rizal and keeping the other to send to Manila.

Many of the villages were in very remote areas, and the more remote the village, the more primitive the circumstances of the villagers.

In one village, we entered a rather large house in which the aggrieved wife had all her relatives sitting around the walls. The three of us sat in the middle of this array in intense heat with little or no breeze to ventilate the place. Most of the young women wore nothing above the navel, and this occasioned a great deal of interest on the part of my driver, a young private just out from the States who had not experienced the similar flavor of native life in the Solomon Islands and New Caledonia.

At times some of the young women would bring us cups of water, and my driver then was completely agog at such close-up views of the ample mammary development of the maidens. I had to caution him not to appear much interested. My interpreter, to whom this was old stuff, paid no attention at all.

Many of the compensation cases were quite tragic, with a single family sometimes losing a father and a brother. The grief we observed was genuine and deeply felt, but could not make up for the lost loved ones. Furthermore, my interpreter indicated that most of these women would remain widows, living on the edge of poverty for the rest of their lives.

In the three months that I had operated as a PCCC agent, I developed considerable insight into village organization and the structure of the families, which varied considerably. In all cases we found the Filipino people to be courteous, hospitable, hardworking, stoic, and in love with Americans.

They had been treated brutally by the Japanese, and they were glad that we—and Douglas MacArthur—had returned.

FALLEN WARRIOR

One afternoon in May 1945 we received word from the forward CP that Colonel Weston had been killed by a sniper. In the conversation I had with the regimental XO, as he gave me the details of what had happened, I noticed no tinge of remorse or distress in his voice. I had none either. Weston indeed had some fine characteristics as a combat leader. He also had more of the negative characteristics than any officer I had ever served with.

As a West Pointer he had not performed in any spectacular fashion before Pearl Harbor. The correspondence in his file saw few commendations as well as a scant number of the "reply by endorsement."

He had adopted an aloof manner with peers and subordinates, probably as a stratagem to keep them from finding out that he could not carry on an interesting conversation. He often looked and sounded like an ascetic, I presume because of the harsh country of New England from which he came.

He had earned a certain grudging respect, but his men did not like him—and I think he did not like his men. They were the tools of war to be deployed in appropriate fashion and propelled into battle. His urgency in field operations compelled his men to stumble and lurch into enemy fire with disastrous results. He showed great concern for the wounded, but that did not extend to the unwounded.

He knew that his career depended on aggressive actions by his troops. He pushed hard to secure advances that were meaningless in a long campaign, but showed up as tick marks indicating forward movement on the division commander's map. Keyed up to exploit this one precious opportunity of war, he was under continual strain to say and do the right thing, and always stay ten steps ahead of everyone else. From Schofield Barracks to Luzon he hustled to get responsibility, recognition, and promotion.

A short while before his death he got his star. In his mind, the path upward was now forever open as long as he continued his stubborn, frenetic activity—and the rest would take care of itself. A Japanese sniper interrupted this aggressive process with a single round. It was not the kind of death Weston would have preferred; but then many of the men who obeyed his relentless urgings also got a death they didn't prefer.

At a time when MacArthur was making military history by "hitting them where they ain't," and letting the Japanese forces wither on the vine, the mountain struggle in Luzon involved little or no tactical finesse. We moved straight ahead, and the enemy formations knew we were coming and exacted a heavy toll until they were overwhelmed by manpower and firepower. This was the opposite of what MacArthur had done in the long campaigns through the Pacific islands. Weston was comfortable with this decimation of the regiment. I calculated 135 percent casualties for the five months we were in the line. Some men were wounded twice, almost everyone else at least once.

That was Weston's legacy. *Requiescat in pace.*

NO END IN SIGHT

Much of our work at the PCCC was routine. But up Highway 5 the war continued unabated, with the regiment throwing battalion-sized punches. First a left hook, then a right cross. Fight a battle to get to the top of a ridge, only to find that the Japanese were dug in on the reverse slope, and fighting just as tenaciously as they did on the forward slope.

Each attack cost us casualties. The enemy lost more men than we did, but this was no consolation, for I believe they knew that few if any of them would get off Luzon alive. On the other hand, the rotation system was slowly siphoning the tested veterans out of the thinning ranks and replacing them with bewildered, partly trained, but willing substitutes.

In April the division brass finally had a good idea: it occurred to them that the infantry must be getting tired. After all, the soldiers had marched and fought from Lingayen across the central plain and through the Caraballo Mountains. They had taken substantial losses and had decimated the Japanese defenders.

The brass's idea was the essence of simplicity. Each regiment would send a battalion to the division rest area for two weeks. At the end of that period, the battalion would return and release another unit for a breather in the rear.

We visited the first battalion to be sent on vacation. The battalion's men were able to get their barracks bags and extract a clean uniform, clean underwear, and a dry pair of boots. And there were tents, cots, mess tents, and even a movie screen.

I took a crew along to get our personnel records in shape. It was deeply satisfying to see some of my officer buddies and share sea stories with the men of my former units. I noticed how tired they all looked. I also noticed how many of them were gone, due to death, injury, and rotation.

The slow, grinding fighting continued in the mountains until mid-June of 1945. One battalion was taken by landing craft to

Balir Bay on the east coast of Luzon. Santa Fe had been captured and the 25th and 32d Divisions had effected a junction on Old Spanish Trail, thus accomplishing the 25th's mission.

In these last two months of the war there was little to differentiate one day from another: always the air strikes, artillery concentrations, and slow advances against suicidal enemy troops.

It is hard to equate the conduct of the enemy in these battles with that of the troops we met in the Solomons. Japanese soldiers in the early days were imbued with offensive spirit, many times placing us on the defensive. Now they hid in holes, sniping occasionally, but seldom emerging for soldier-to-soldier combat. They waited like trapped animals to be shot, bayoneted, burned, or blasted to death. There was little honor in such action; to us it was a loss of life without dignity. But then we had long since given up trying to understand *bushido*, loyalty to the divine emperor, and obedience to the arrogant warlords.

At long last, on June 30, the division was relieved from its mission. The regiment was assembled and trucked to Crow Valley, in a camp located south of Lingayen Bay and east of a range of coastal mountains on the west coast of Luzon. We had a broad, flat area in which we could construct a conventional camp with rows of residential, mess, and headquarters tents; latrines; and specified roads for traffic. Even more luxurious, we now had canvas cots and mosquito bars. To complete this plush state we received our footlockers and barracks bags. It was a return to normality—at least to South Pacific normality. And it was most welcome.

For several weeks we did little but eat and sleep. Slowly we got rid of the grime that had ground its way into our skins. Almost everyone began shaving daily, and an improvised barbershop did a land office business.

In spite of the replacements I had processed in the preceding four months, the units were still under strength: as men reached the magic number for rotation we sent them off on their happy return to the States. The long-timers were in shorter and shorter supply. I often dropped in to the battalion tents to chat and usually went away surprised at how few faces were familiar (but less tired, less haunted by fear, less despairing). But it was obvious that the number of casualties of three campaigns, along with the losses due to rotation, was eroding the cohort of soldiers that had left Hawaii so many months earlier.

In an attempt to provide diversions for the men, baseball and volleyball made their appearance. Movies were made available each night in an improvised theater area. The camp was filled with GIs who cheered the movie heroes and heroines, and especially the pretty girls like Betty and Rita.

TIME OUT

I managed to wheedle a three-day pass to Manila, and boarded the truck convoy with other eager travelers. After several hours of bumpy road we entered the city that had been so ravaged by war. We were deposited at a midtown tent facility that had been set up as a rest area. Each of us got a cot, pillow, one blanket, and, marvel of marvels, one sheet. There was a hot-water shower and a well-organized mess hall, although the menu was conventional military fare (Spam had not disappeared).

Like the phoenix rising from the ashes, the Filipino population had returned in full force to the capital city. The streets were cleared of debris, and uncounted shops catered to the buying habits of the GIs who flooded the streets like alien invaders. I joined the throng and wandered through dusty streets, listening to the cries of the Filipino hucksters. I finally came to the Pasig River, where I could see the destruction inflicted during the last days of the savage Japanese defense.

At one time we had held one bank, the enemy the other. There were office buildings on the other side that had been packed with snipers, machine-gun nests, and artillery positions. We brought up heavy artillery and fired point-blank into the enemy positions until many of the buildings sagged or toppled over. To add to the chaos, the retreating enemy mined many buildings with high explosives that they detonated as they withdrew to the south.

U.S. Army engineers had provided bridges across the Pasig at a number of locations, and these were swamped with jitneys, army trucks, and pedestrians. I crossed one of them to inspect the wreckage on the other side. Little was being done to clean up the mess, except for clearing the streets. The destruction was terminal; it occurred to me that the cleanup might take years and then there wouldn't be an army to help.

I recrossed the bridge and looked for a restaurant that had at least a half-star rating. All of them were crowded with GIs, a tribute to a democratic upbringing. I finally took a chance and entered one, and ordered a steak and potatoes. The steak was small and very, very tough; the three potatoes were the size of marbles. One small piece of bread was tasteless, as was the coffee. I was convinced that I had eaten my first (and last) *carabao* (water buffalo) steak. Now even the military mess looked great.

As night began to fall I was reminded that Manila still had no electric power. The generating plants had been destroyed along with about everything else in town. The shops and cafés lit their candles and kerosene lamps; some of the better-off using Coleman lanterns. A little of this light flowed into the streets and made it just possible to keep from bumping into others—a difficult task considering the flow of humanity.

I felt it wise to get back to the rest center without delay. I wasn't sure how safe it was to be cavorting around in a ruined city after dark with little or no light. There were a lot of dark doorways, in many of which Filipino girls with garish makeup held their candles and tried to interest passing GIs in a good time. A lot were interested; most of the GIs had a pocket full of pesos and very few places to spend them.

I finally got back to the center. Since it had an electric genera-
tor, it was lit up like a small-town carnival. In keeping with the idea
that soldiers always like to eat, I found the mess hall prepared for
this contingency. On the serving counter there was an assortment of
breads, cold cuts, cheese, lettuce, tomatoes, cookies, milk, and coffee. I sat down with a few visiting firemen from the regiment and
we compared notes on the attractions, distractions, and souvenirs of
Manila. There was a consensus that taking a jitney ride, no matter
how wild the driver, was the best way to see the highways and by-
ways of the more exotic parts of town.

And so to bed.

On the afternoon the next day I shared a jeep with two other
officers to return to Crow Valley. Leaving Manila was easy. A devastated city with a huge population scrambling to get back to normal, make a buck, and find food was hardly a location for pleasant
memories.

As we drove through the countryside we saw little activity in
the fields, but the *barrios* were crowded with GIs and Filipino hucksters of all types and dimensions. Some "cafés" had opened up and
served a Philippine version of whiskey, which was guaranteed to
paralyze the tongue and gums after two drinks.

The sounds of hilarity emanating from the *barrio* cafés indicated
that a good time was being had by all. Unfortunately most of the
barrios concentrated on providing booze and broads. The authorities
had no desire to foster alcoholism, blindness, or venereal disease,
and in a few days "Off Limits" signs popped up in most of the *barrios*, with MPs standing around just in case you were illiterate and
couldn't read the sign.

The camp was also overrun with Filipinos looking for work
and handouts. Girls were everywhere picking up laundry from the
GIs, the standard price being two pesos and a bar of laundry soap.
It took only a sliver of soap to wash a shirt, some socks, and a set
of underwear, so the girls must have had a tent full of soap to sell
to other natives. (The results of the laundering were marginally sat-

isfactory. Everything was gray—leading many to guess that the washing had been done in a *carabao* wallow.)

A lot of young boys haunted the mess lines waiting for soldiers to give them the leftovers, which were then collected in #10 cans or barracks bags. The boys also took care of the shoe-shining business: they did a good job but they used up to a half can of shoe polish to complete their work.

For diversion a few of us in the personnel section offered to go on patrol in the mountains to the west. We carried weapons, several days of C-rations, and shelter halves. Once in the hills we encountered a group of primitive natives (Aetas) who were looking for crayfish and other denizens of a small mountain stream. They were a family, wearing few or no clothes and miserably thin, yet good-natured and totally unafraid of us.

Each one (except the baby) had two or three empty tin cans, which had obviously been scavenged from the camp garbage dumps. They showed us the handful of tiny crustaceans they had been able to find in the stream, and one woman had a cloth bag holding different kinds of roots and wild vegetables.

As usual we unloaded enough C-rations to keep them in provender for at least a week. When we departed the next morning—after sitting around their campfire until after midnight—there were smiles all around and handshakes for everyone.

The war continued. Iwo Jima and Okinawa were the scene of savage warfare.

STILL NO END

Ahead lay the invasion of Japan. We were told to get ready for Operation Olympic, the first landings in Japan, on the island of Kyushu.

My division was to make the beachhead.

In the next weeks we again launched into a training program. For those of us who had already gone through three such programs on New Caledonia, it was a case of déjà vu. Formations were practiced, tactical exercises were implemented, and live firing exercises with mortar and artillery support were carried out.

Replacements were arriving to bring all units up to strength, and once again I screened each new arrival carefully for his physical record, previous training, and recent assignments. As usual the higher headquarters were skimming off the stronger and smarter personnel. Whether the generals up the line knew what was going on was hard to determine, but it was a despicable practice and a slap in the face to the combat units that were to bear the brunt of battle and receive the lion's share of casualties.

The replacements were a mixed bag. A number of them had been drafted earlier in the year and sent overseas with a minimum of training. Others were victims of personnel reductions in the many training facilities that were being phased out: some of these had two or more years' service; many were married, with children; and most had lived comfortably on post in the States, while others were sent to the meat grinders in Europe and the Pacific.

Some of these men and officers felt nettled that they hadn't been able to finish out the war in the States instead of being shipped out "at the last minute." They got very little sympathy from me or any of the other veterans of three campaigns.

The training continued with grim determination in view of what we knew faced us on the mainland of Nippon.

While the training and preparation went on, there was a lot of conversation in the mess hall and around campfires about what faced us in Japan. We knew that the major portion of the Japanese army had been slowly siphoned off to the home country. Children were being trained as soldiers; fortifications were being dug or erected in every village; and kamikaze pilots were drinking their last cup of tea before going out to protect the homeland.

There was no doubt that it would be a long and bloody campaign. Millions of Japanese would die; more millions would be injured. The losses among U.S. forces would exceed all the casualties incurred in all theaters of operation since December 7, 1941. (At least a million casualties was an estimate that went through the rumor mill.) It was hard to generate any enthusiasm for an attack on the Japanese homeland, but there was a grim determination to bring the war to a close and destroy, to the last man, if necessary, the military apparatus that had brought so much misery to the people of Asia and the Pacific.

One of the few diversions we had while preparing for this dismal future was the camp theater, where there was a movie screen and benches for several thousand viewers. The films were standard Hollywood fare: comedies with pretty girls and funny guys, an occasional war movie (I remember Errol Flynn in Burma), and some westerns. The audiences, on the whole, were young (under twenty-five) and they enjoyed the funny stuff and the grim stuff. Basically it was a tie with home. The films showed what was supposed to be happening in the States; and in fact small-town movie houses were showing the same fare.

But always—like an itch that wouldn't go away—there was the coming war.

CHAPTER FIFTEEN

Peace

AUGUST 6, 1945

This was a night when we were enjoying another of Hollywood's best. The audience as usual was boisterous when its fancies were tickled.

Suddenly the projector was stopped and a few lights went on. A chorus of voices yelled disapproval. After a certain amount of crackling and banging the PA system came on.

A voice said: "This is a message from Supreme Headquarters. Today an air force plane dropped a new type of bomb on the Japanese city of Hiroshima. The bomb is said to have the explosive power of 10,000 tons' TNT."

First there was silence, then pandemonium—an explosion of joy, awe, and confusion.

The lights went out and the film continued, but a large part of the audience was lost. There were little groups everywhere, yelling at each other, gesticulating, pointing, and waving arms.

I hurried over to regimental headquarters where everything was submerged in chaos. The brass had broken out the drinking supplies, and everyone drank and yelled into the morning hours. Later I lay on my cot wondering what it all meant. Wondering too how this would affect the course of the war.

The next day or so there were no official pronouncements.

AUGUST 9, 1945

Once again a movie was being shown. Once again the projector stopped. And then the announcement: "The air force has dropped an atomic bomb on the Japanese city of Nagasaki." A repeat of the riotous August 6.

Things settled down in the next few days. Training went on as usual. We had no newspapers, and army radio carried little or no follow-up information. At headquarters we hashed, rehashed, and re-rehashed what we knew. There were two schools of thought: (1) it wouldn't mean a damn thing, and (2) this was the last straw for the Nips.

All time and activity were overshadowed by one unanswered question.

AUGUST 14, 1945

The movie is playing. The projector stops. The announcement says: "The emperor has instructed the military forces to surrender." There is pandemonium. Everything that happened before happens twice.

At 0400 I lay down on my cot. For the first time since we'd sailed from Pearl Harbor, I felt that an incubus had been lifted from me. I said a prayer of thanks and went to sleep.

But nothing was changed. We got up at the usual time, ate at the usual time, followed the training schedule, assigned all the details, and continued interviewing new arrivals.

There was, however, a difference. Everybody had a stupid, inane grin on his face. People whistled while they worked. The tactical training was carried out with vigor and enthusiasm; even the officers couldn't find anything to gripe about and congratulated the troops for the esprit they showed in battle maneuvers.

Next? We were going to Japan. But until that happened the training was called Blacklist Operation, just in case we had to make a military attack landing on the shore of a defeated nation.

We were told that we were to make our landing on October 2, 1945, if the war had continued. Now it was proposed that we land on . . . October 2, in peace, we hoped.

Time passed. The Japanese surrendered to MacArthur on the USS *Missouri* on September 2 in Tokyo Bay. And it was finally, irrevocably over.

After September 8, training time was cut in half and troops were engaged in boxing and crating equipment, dismantling campsites, and undergoing inspections and orientations.

Engineers had started on August 19 to construct White Beach Two. Lingayen Gulf was the embarkation site. In addition to slots for LSTs, AKAs (cargo ships, attack), and APAs, they built dump areas, bivouac areas, lighting facilities, and a road net.

There was a lot of rushing around to get things ready, and the regiment decided that since I was eligible for rotation (after we landed in Japan of course) I should search for a new personnel officer. That was no problem. I had marked a friend of mine, slight of build, soft-spoken, and sharp as a tack, for the job. When I got him settled in, I was off to a new assignment as a loading officer for one of the Liberty ships.

I moved to a warehouse and was given a lot of paper, charts of the ship's holds, and tables to determine the size, weight, and volume of equipment. My job was to find a way to fit all the trucks, jeeps, boxes, and crates into the various hatches of the ship. I worked with a few of the ship's officers for several days, and, as the equipment arrived, everything seemed to be working famously. We were to leave on September 26, so we worked day and night to get everything done.

On September 24 we had a powwow of ships' officers and loading people. Somebody was looking through the paperwork when a guy piped up and said, "What about the ammunition?" We all looked at him as if he was nuts. "What ammo?" we chorused.

"The ammo in the forward hold," he retorted.

There was nothing in the paperwork we had about ammo, so someone went to the ship and came back with a manifest showing 500 tons of artillery ammunition in the forward hold.

There was a lot of yelling and arm waving, but the first mate, an experienced merchant marine officer, said not to worry. The ship could carry it, and if our loading was now out of balance he could use the ballast tanks to trim the ship.

We all let out a sigh of relief and continued with last-minute details.

On September 26 we left Lingayen with two Liberty ships and seven LSTs. There should have been more, but ships were late in arriving and the rest of the first echelon would have to wait until September 28.

I was glad to leave Luzon. I could look forward to at least a week of rest and conversations with Callaghan, the first mate, who had become a buddy.

Lingayen Gulf was crowded with ships as we left, including some of the combat ships that were to escort us. We weren't sure that everyone in Hirohito's navy had received the word, and we were taking no chances that some submarine commander didn't want to go out in a blaze of glory.

We were out to sea less than a day when we received radio information that a typhoon was forming ahead of us. We were within fifty miles of Okinawa when the storm hit and the convoy turned into the storm to "ride it out." It had been our intention to enter the harbor at Okinawa, but the harbor was closed and the ships in it were being sent out to sea.

Along with the typhoon I encountered another trouble. Feeling very achy and with chills, I went to the sick bay where they gave me a blood test. After almost three years in the Pacific I had contracted malaria. I spent the next week alternately sweating and suffering from chills. Several times a day they gave me a half cup of assorted pills to swallow.

I had never felt worse in my life or more debilitated. I understood then why malaria had been such a scourge where peoples
were subjected to it. I had seen many villages in the Pacific islands
where entire families were prostrate, and where their only hope was
to get a little quinine to assuage the fever that seemed to sap every
ounce of energy.

After a week, the malaria was under control and I was allowed
to go back to the quarters I shared with another officer. Only then
did I notice the violent dipping and yawing of the ship as it plowed
through mountainous seas whipped up by the typhoon. We were
steadily driven back to Luzon, and about the time the winds subsided we were off the east coast of the island. We had traveled 1,200
miles, and were farther from Japan than when we started.

I spent some time on deck with Callaghan, who lent me some
foul-weather gear even though the air temperature was in the eighties.
My blood was still as thin as water.

Once again we headed for Okinawa, and with our luck we ran
into another typhoon. This time it carried us in a different direction,
east and slightly south toward Guam. When we finally escaped
from this storm, we encountered still another typhoon, but this
time we evaded most of the wind and water being churned up. Although the ships of our convoy had been sorely pressed by the violent trio, no ship had been damaged and no injuries were reported.

We did have a few anxious moments when one of our guards
belowdecks reported noises in the forward hold. We went down
there to find that the ropes securing some of the ammunition crates
had become loosened and the crates were sliding back and forth in
the hold as the ship pitched. No time was lost getting a detail to
catch the boxes, stack them along the bulkhead, and tie them with
many ropes. Callaghan and I breathed more easily when everything
was snug again. We both reflected on what would have happened if
some of the artillery rounds had escaped their crate and been detonated by their striking a hard object with their percussion caps.

The rest of the trip was peaceful and on October 9, 1945, thirteen days after we'd left Lingayen, we stood outside Wakayama harbor and prepared to enter. Our initial destination had been Nagoya, some 150 miles to the north, but the minesweeping had been slow, and so we anchored at Wakayama to await orders. We waited eighteen days for something to happen, and the orders finally came to proceed to Nagoya.

When we finally arrived there we saw that only three or four modern buildings were still standing. The rest of the city had been shattered by our incendiary bombs.

Something interesting happened while we were moving to our designated berth at the Nagoya docks. We had cut our speed until we were almost standing still. The ship's captain, an Annapolis man, was on the bridge directing the operation. We felt an almost imperceptible lurch. I looked at Callaghan and he looked at me; a slight grin came over his face, and he bent close to my ear. In a voice that indicated a struggle to keep from laughing he said, "The old man has run the ship aground." (For a captain to run a ship aground is just a notch from treason. For a regular navy officer it could mean walking the plank or being stranded on a desert isle.)

The PA system crackled, and the anxious voice of the captain echoed through the ship: "Lieutenant Callaghan to the bridge. On the double." Callaghan looked at me with that silly grin that now covered his whole face. "See?" he said.

Callaghan sprinted up the ladder to the bridge. After a while we were spinning the props and fishtailing backward, and about a half hour of these naval maneuvers had us free. Another half hour had us safely docked at Nagoya.

Afterward, Callaghan told me that there was no mention of going aground in the captain's log. But the log did indicate that Lieutenant Callaghan had piloted the ship during the docking procedure.

For the moment there was nothing to do but wait. Nobody had any orders for us, so we spent some time looking at the shattered city. We unloaded a jeep and drove through Nagoya at night. Some buildings were standing—they had electric lights: as we walked around them we found that they were totally occupied by ladies of easy virtue.

Nagoya is a city as large as Detroit. It is located on a vast plain at the head of Ise Bay. The bombing raids of early 1944 destroyed most of the homes and shops, which were largely made of wood. Only the buildings made of brick, concrete, and steel still remained; these were sprinkled across the landscape in small isolated clusters. It was hard to imagine where the people had gone—other than those killed or injured. We saw few civilians anywhere except in the vicinity of the surviving buildings. Also, a great concern of ours was how we would be received by a people we had fought with unremitting ferocity since 1941.

As the troops began circulating in the city and the countryside, there was an atmosphere of suspicion and fear shown in the inhabitants' peering cautiously from their windows or standing silently and sullenly in little groups.

After a few days, when it was apparent that our men meant no harm, there was a relaxation of attitude and people would respond to the waving hands and the shouted greetings. As usual, it was children and the soldiers who made true peace first. Candy was always a popular icebreaker, and the kids quickly learned English phrases such as "Hello, Joe," and "You got candy, Joe?"

Amazingly, during my stay in Nagoya I heard of no incident of violence, particularly from the hard-line Japanese military men for whom we knew our presence was an affront and a disgrace. But the people had had enough of war, militarism, and destruction of their homeland. The disappeared homes of Hiroshima and Nagasaki had not been lost on them.

The most powerful influence of all undoubtedly was the emperor's rescript proclaiming that the fighting should cease.

In the next few days I was relieved of my shipboard duties. We had an interesting final lunch with the ship's officers, and we all promised to see each other back in the States. I took a long jeep ride to my new location: the Nagoya Naval Air Base. There a number of large buildings on the base had somehow escaped destruction, and it was into these buildings that the regiment would be assembled, at different times and from different directions.

One building had hundreds of cots, which were quickly occupied by the incoming troops. After settling my gear I traveled to the regimental HQ in a large empty building with a few tables and even fewer chairs. There was a lot of busywork going on, unpacking field desks, untying file cabinets, and setting up different sections. I visited the guys in the personnel group and found that nobody knew what was going to happen next. After exploiting that gold mine of information, I sought the regimental mess and had some coffee and bread. I then returned to my cot; I was still weak and fatigued from the bout with malaria. During the long days on board ship I had suffered an attack of pleurisy, and had survived by bundling up in borrowed foul-weather gear and standing watch with Callaghan.

But I still felt punk, and spent hours in my cot covered by all the blankets I could muster. After my next breakfast I looked up the medical detachment and asked for a checkup. They reviewed my records from the ship's doctor, took a blood sample, listened with their stethoscopes, and gave me several bottles of pills of assorted colors and uses—vitamins, blood pills, atabrine etc.

The entire regiment had been assembled on October 30. On November 1 the regiment was disbanded and converted to the 4th Infantry. The National Guard was out of the war. The disbanding of the regiment was entirely a paper transaction. The regimental colors were returned to the state, but everyone remained in his former assignment. The only difference was the regiment's designation as the 4th. The purpose for which this National Guard regiment was initially sent to Oahu and its subsequent campaigns in Guadalcanal, New Georgia, and the Philippines had been accomplished.

I thought the redesignation was premature. It could have waited until those who made up the bulk of the regiment, and had served for so long, had sailed for the States. Once again it looked like the Regular Army was anxious to reestablish the organizational purity of the division.

We needed a lot of Japanese help for a hundred and one jobs. So each day there were long lines of Japanese applying for work. Those who spoke English were especially valuable. The Criminal Investigation Corps did a little interviewing to screen out "questionable" applicants, but few were turned away. Before long all the facilities at the base had a large complement of Japanese workers—there were no negative incidents with this help, and a cordial relationship seemed established.

The Japanese police were allowed to control the civilian population as they had before the surrender. There were some protests and demonstrations because of the harsh conditions, but these were aimed at the Japanese government and not at the occupation forces.

The biggest plus for us was the presence of Douglas MacArthur in Tokyo. No one, repeat, no one could have established the authority of the occupation as well as he did. Next to the emperor he was the most respected man in Japan, and the job he was beginning would tax his genius to the utmost.

But now it was time to think of home.

It was time to think about points. As described earlier, the military had devised a system of accumulating points to determine who would be sent home and when this would take place. One thing was obvious: everyone who had been in the regiment since Oahu and was now in Japan had more than enough points to go home. Only the replacements received in New Zealand, New Caledonia, and the Philippines would fall short of the magic number.

Obviously the army finally woke up to this fact and ran around trying to interest officers and men in continuing their service in the division. I was offered a promotion to major to continue and to stay in Japan. I asked about bringing my wife over to Japan, but they couldn't even dream up a promise that they intended to disregard. (Besides, I thought I should have been promoted at the same rate as our counterparts in Regular Army regiments.) I declined, with thanks. I didn't see much profit in the "better late than never" syndrome.

So we continued to mill around the naval base, waiting for the masters of logistics to find one of the thousands of ships in the Pacific to take us home. There started a certain amount of out-processing, getting our records in shape, and conducting some interviews to complete the historical records.

At long last someone ferreted out a ship to take several hundred of us back home. We got loaded on and went to our quarters. I shared a room with three other officers. On the trip I spent most of my time sleeping because I still felt washed out from the malaria and pleurisy. It was interesting to sail at night on the Pacific with the lights on; we had never seen a ship's light after we left San Francisco in 1942.

After a few days we docked at Pearl. A lot of the men went ashore, but the city had changed so much that I decided to stay on board and preserve my memories of Honolulu and Kaneohe in the hectic days after the big raid. After a day or two we set sail for the Golden Gate. Again the cruise was uneventful, and our arrival at Angel Island was the first stimulating event after the long crossing.

A few days were needed to process us out and get our railroad travel billets. The time for impatience was in the two and a half days that the train took to get to Chicago.

At last, at last, we entered the railroad station, and in a few minutes I was in the arms of my dear wife.

About the Author

After World War II, FLOYD W. RADIKE returned to his home in Michigan where he was a career educator, teaching in Detroit. In 1949 he rejoined the Michigan National Guard, ultimately rising to the rank of brigadier general. He retired in 1975. *Across the Dark Islands* is the late author's only book.

DATE			